MznLnx

Missing Links Exam Preps

Exam Prep for

Dynamic Earth: An Introduction to Physical Geology

Skinner & Porter & Park, 5th Edition

The MznLnx Exam Prep is your link from the texbook and lecture to your exams.
The MznLnx Exam Preps are unauthorized and comprehensive reviews of your textbooks.

All material provided by MznLnx and Rico Publications (c) 2010
Textbook publishers and textbook authors do not particpate in or contribute to these reviews.

MznLnx

Rico
Publications

Exam Prep for Dynamic Earth: An Introduction to Physical Geology
5th Edition
Skinner & Porter & Park

Publisher: Raymond Houge
Assistant Editor: Michael Rouger
Text and Cover Designer: Lisa Buckner
Marketing Manager: Sara Swagger
Project Manager, Editorial Production: Jerry Emerson
Art Director: Vernon Lowerui

Product Manager: Dave Mason
Editorial Assitant: Rachel Guzmanji
Pedagogy: Debra Long
Cover Image: Jim Reed/Getty Images
Text and Cover Printer: City Printing, Inc.
Compositor: Media Mix, Inc.

(c) 2010 Rico Publications
ALL RIGHTS RESERVED. No part of this work covered by the copyright may be reproduced or used in any form or by an means--graphic, electronic, or mechanical, including photocopying, recording, taping, Web distribution, information storage, and retrieval systems, or in any other manner--without the written permission of the publisher.

Printed in the United States
ISBN:

For more information about our products, contact us at:
Dave.Mason@RicoPublications.com

For permission to use material from this text or product, submit a request online to:
Dave.Mason@RicoPublications.com

Contents

CHAPTER 1
Meet Planet Earth — 1

CHAPTER 2
Global Tectonics: Our Dynamic Planet — 11

CHAPTER 3
Atoms, Elements, Minerals, Rocks — 21

CHAPTER 4
Igneous Rocks: Products of Earth's Internal Fire — 30

CHAPTER 5
Magmas and Volcanoes — 40

CHAPTER 6
Weathering and Soils — 47

CHAPTER 7
Sediments and Sedimentary Rocks: Archives of Earth History — 54

CHAPTER 8
Metamorphism and Metamorphic Rocks: New Rocks from Old — 66

CHAPTER 9
How Rock Bends, Buckles, and Breaks — 74

CHAPTER 10
Earthquakes and Earth's Interior — 81

CHAPTER 11
Geologic Time and the Rock Record — 88

CHAPTER 12
The Changing Face of the Land — 95

CHAPTER 13
Mass Wasting — 99

CHAPTER 14
Streams and Drainage Systems — 104

CHAPTER 15
Groundwater — 111

CHAPTER 16
Glaciers and Glaciation — 118

CHAPTER 17
Atmosphere, Winds and Deserts — 125

CHAPTER 18
The Oceans and Their Margins — 133

CHAPTER 19
Climate and Our Changing Planet — 141

CHAPTER 20
Earth Through Geologic Time — 147

Contents (Cont.)

CHAPTER 21
   Resources of Minerals and Energy   156
ANSWER KEY   162

TO THE STUDENT

COMPREHENSIVE

The *MznLnx* Exam Prep series is designed to help you pass your exams. Editors at MznLnx review your textbooks and then prepare these practice exams to help you master the textbook material. Unlike study guides, workbooks, and practice tests provided by the texbook publisher and textbook authors, *MznLnx* gives you **all** of the material in each chapter in exam form, not just samples, so you can be sure to nail your exam.

MECHANICAL

The MznLnx Exam Prep series creates exams that will help you learn the subject matter as well as test you on your understanding. Each question is designed to help you master the concept. Just working through the exams, you gain an understanding of the subject--its a simple mechanical process that produces success.

INTEGRATED STUDY GUIDE AND REVIEW

MznLnx is not just a set of exams designed to test you, its also a comprehensive review of the subject content. Each exam question is also a review of the concept, making sure that you will get the answer correct without having to go to other sources of material. You learn as you go! Its the easiest way to pass an exam.

HUMOR

Studying can be tedious and dry. MznLnx's instructional design includes moderate humor within the exam questions on occassion, to break the tedium and revitalize the brain

Chapter 1. Meet Planet Earth

1. _____ is the use of the principles of geology to reconstruct and understand the history of the Earth . It focuses on geologic processes that change the Earth's surface and subsurface; and the use of stratigraphy, structural geology and paleontology to tell the sequence of these events. It also focuses on the evolution of plants and animals during different time periods in the geological timescale.
   - a. Suspended load
   - b. Strike-slip faults
   - c. Valley glaciers
   - d. Historical geology

2. _____ is the idea that Earth has been affected in the past by sudden, short-lived, violent events, possibly worldwide in scope.

   The dominant paradigm of modern geology, in contrast, is uniformitarianism (also sometimes described as gradualism), in which slow incremental changes, such as erosion, create the Earth's appearance. This view holds that the present is the key to the past, and that all things continue as they were from the beginning of the world.
   - a. 1509 Istanbul earthquake
   - b. Catastrophism
   - c. 1703 Genroku earthquake
   - d. 1700 Cascadia earthquake

3. _____ is the principle that the same scientific laws and processes are constant throughout space and time. It applies specifically to sciences that require a long timescale such as geology, astronomy, and paleontology. It was first defined by Charles Lyell (1797 - 1875), who incorporated James Hutton's gradualism into the idea of _____.
   - a. AASHTO Soil Classification System
   - b. Uniformitarianism
   - c. AL 333
   - d. AL 129-1

4. In the natural sciences, _____ is a theory which holds that profound change is the cumulative product of slow but continuous processes, often contrasted with catastrophism. The theory was proposed in 1795 by James Hutton, a Scottish geologist, and was later incorporated into Charles Lyell's theory of uniformitarianism.
   - a. Gradualism
   - b. Megamullion
   - c. Haloclasty
   - d. Fluting

5. The _____ is a chronologic schema (or idealized model) relating stratigraphy to time that is used by geologists, paleontologists and other earth scientists to describe the timing and relationships between events that have occurred during the history of the Earth. The table of geologic time spans presented here agrees with the dates and nomenclature proposed by the International Commission on Stratigraphy, and uses the standard color codes of the United States Geological Survey.

   Evidence from radiometric dating indicates that the Earth is about 4.570 billion years old.
   - a. 1700 Cascadia earthquake
   - b. 1509 Istanbul earthquake
   - c. 1703 Genroku earthquake
   - d. Geologic time scale

6. _____ is the removal of solids (sediment, soil, rock and other particles) in the natural environment. It usually occurs due to transport by wind, water, or ice; by down-slope creep of soil and other material under the force of gravity; or by living organisms, such as burrowing animals, in the case of bioerosion.

   _____ is distinguished from weathering, which is the process of chemical or physical breakdown of the minerals in the rocks, although the two processes may occur concurrently.

a. AL 129-1
b. AL 333
c. AASHTO Soil Classification System
d. Erosion

7. _____ is the chemical element with atomic number 77, and is represented by the symbol Ir. A very hard, brittle, silvery-white transition metal of the platinum family, _____ is the second densest element and is the most corrosion-resistant metal, even at temperatures as high as 2000 >°C. Although only certain molten salts and halogens are corrosive to solid _____, finely divided _____ dust is much more reactive and can even be flammable.
   a. AL 129-1
   b. AL 333
   c. AASHTO Soil Classification System
   d. Iridium

8. A _____ is a sand- to boulder-sized particle of debris in the Solar System. The visible path of a _____ that enters Earth's (or another body's) atmosphere is called a meteor, or commonly a 'shooting star' or 'falling star.' If a _____ reaches the ground, it is then called a meteorite. Many meteors are part of a meteor shower.
   a. 1509 Istanbul earthquake
   b. 1703 Genroku earthquake
   c. 1700 Cascadia earthquake
   d. Meteoroid

9. The _____ is a British rock formation of considerable importance to early paleontology. Hutton's angular unconformity at Siccar Point where 345 million year old Devonian _____ overlies 425 million year old Silurian greywacke.

The _____ describes a suite of rocks deposited in a variety of environments during the Devonian period but extending back into the late Silurian period and forward into the earliest part of the Carboniferous period.

   a. AL 333
   b. AL 129-1
   c. AASHTO Soil Classification System
   d. Old Red Sandstone

10. _____ is a sedimentary rock composed mainly of sand-size mineral or rock grains. Most _____ is composed of quartz and/or feldspar because these are the most common minerals in the Earth's crust. Like sand, _____ may be any color, but the most common colors are tan, brown, yellow, red, gray and white.
    a. Shale
    b. Claystone
    c. Superficial deposits
    d. Sandstone

11. _____ is a technique used to date materials, usually based on a comparison between the observed abundance of a naturally occurring radioactive isotope and its decay products, using known decay rates. It is the principal source of information about the absolute age of rocks and other geological features, including the age of the Earth itself, and can be used to date a wide range of natural and man-made materials. Together with stratigraphic principles, _____ methods are used in geochronology to establish the geological time scale.
    a. Stage
    b. Relative dating
    c. Lichenometry
    d. Radiometric dating

12. In geology, an _____ is a body of igneous rock that has crystallized from molten magma below the surface of the Earth. Bodies of magma that solidify underground before they reach the surface of the earth are called plutons the Roman god of the underworld. Correspondingly, rocks of this kind are also referred to as igneous plutonic rocks or igneous intrusive rocks.

Chapter 1. Meet Planet Earth

    a. AL 333
    b. AASHTO Soil Classification System
    c. Intrusion
    d. AL 129-1

13. In chemistry, the _____ of a chemical compound is a simple expression of the relative numbers of each type of atom in it, or the simplest whole number ratio of atoms of each element present in a compound. An _____ makes no reference to isomerism, structure, or absolute number of atoms. The _____ is used as standard for most ionic compounds, such as $CaCl_2$, and for macromolecules, such as SiO_2.
    a. AASHTO Soil Classification System
    b. AL 129-1
    c. AL 333
    d. Empirical formula

14. _____ is one of the three main rock types (the others being sedimentary and metamorphic rock.) _____ is formed by magma (molten rock) being cooled and becoming solid . They may form with or without crystallization, either below the surface as intrusive (plutonic) rocks or on the surface as extrusive (volcanic) rocks. They make up approximately 95% of the upper part of the Earth's crust, but their great abundance is hidden on the Earth's surface by a relatively thin but widespread layer of sedimentary and metamorphic rocks.
    a. Extrusive
    b. Ignimbrite
    c. Igneous differentiation
    d. Igneous rock

15. _____ is the chemical compound with the formula SO_2. It is produced by volcanoes and in various industrial processes. Since coal and petroleum often contain sulfur compounds, their combustion generates _____.
    a. 1700 Cascadia earthquake
    b. 1509 Istanbul earthquake
    c. 1703 Genroku earthquake
    d. Sulfur dioxide

16. A _____ is a physical quantity that describes in which direction and at what rate the temperature changes the most rapidly around a particular location. The _____ is a dimensional quantity expressed in units of degrees (on a particular temperature scale) per unit length. The SI unit is kelvin per meter (K/m.)
    a. 1703 Genroku earthquake
    b. Temperature gradient
    c. 1509 Istanbul earthquake
    d. 1700 Cascadia earthquake

17. _____, is the process of coastal sediments returning to the visible portion of a beach or foreshore following a submersion event. A sustainable beach or foreshore often goes through a cycle of submersion during rough weather then _____ during calmer periods. If a coastline is not in a healthy sustainable condition, then erosion can be more serious and _____ does not fully restore the original volume of the visible beach or foreshore leading to permanent beach or foreshore loss.
    a. AASHTO Soil Classification System
    b. AL 129-1
    c. AL 333
    d. Accretion

18. The _____ of any physical feature such as a hill, stream, roof, railroad, or road refers to the amount of inclination of that surface where zero indicates level (with respect to gravity) and larger numbers indicate higher degrees of 'tilt'. Often slope is calculated as a ratio of 'rise over run' in which run is the horizontal distance and rise is the vertical distance.

Chapter 1. Meet Planet Earth

There are several systems for expressing slope:

1. as an angle of inclination from the horizontal of a right triangle. (This is the angle >α opposite the 'rise' side of the triangle.)
2. as a percentage (also known as the _____), the formula for which is [×]> which could also be expressed as the tangent of the angle of inclination times 100. In the U.S., the _____ is the most commonly used unit for communicating slopes in transportation, surveying, construction, and civil engineering.
3. as a per mille figure, the formula for which is [×]> which could also be expressed as the tangent of the angle of inclination times 1000. This is commonly used in Europe to denote the incline of a railway.
4. as a ratio of one part rise per so many parts run. For example, a slope that has a rise of 5 feet for every 100 feet of run would have a slope ratio of 1 in 20.

Any one of these expressions may be used interchangeably to express the characteristics of a slope. _____ is usually expressed as a percentage, but this may easily be converted to the angle >α from horizontal since that carries the same information.

a. Diamond Head
b. Compaction
c. Heavy metal
d. Grade

19. _____ is a silvery white and ductile member of the boron group of chemical elements. It has the symbol Al; its atomic number is 13. It is not soluble in water under normal circumstances. _____ is the most abundant metal in the Earth's crust, and the third most abundant element therein, after oxygen and silicon. It makes up about 8% by weight of the Earth'e;s solid surface.

a. AL 129-1
b. AL 333
c. AASHTO Soil Classification System
d. Aluminum

20. The _____ of an object is the extra energy which it possesses due to its motion. It is defined as the work needed to accelerate a body of a given mass from rest to its current velocity. Having gained this energy during its acceleration, the body maintains this _____ unless its speed changes.

a. 1703 Genroku earthquake
b. 1700 Cascadia earthquake
c. 1509 Istanbul earthquake
d. Kinetic energy

21. _____ is the most common metalloid. It is a chemical element, which has the symbol Si and atomic number 14. The atomic mass is 28.0855. As the eighth most common element in the universe by mass, _____ very rarely occurs as the pure free element in nature, but is more widely distributed in dusts, planetoids and planets as various forms of _____ dioxide or silicates. On Earth, _____ is the second most abundant element (after oxygen) in the crust, making up 25.7% of the crust by mass.

a. 1700 Cascadia earthquake
b. Silicon
c. 1703 Genroku earthquake
d. 1509 Istanbul earthquake

22. The _____ was a powerful explosion that occurred near the Podkamennaya (Lower Stony) Tunguska River in what is now Krasnoyarsk Krai of Russia, at around 7:14 a.m. on June 30, 1908 (June 17 in the Julian calendar, in use locally at the time.)

Although the cause is the subject of some debate, the explosion was most likely to have been caused by the air burst of a large meteoroid or comet fragment at an altitude of 5-10 kilometres (3-6 miles) above Earth's surface. Different studies have yielded varying estimates for the object's size, with general agreement that it was a few tens of metres across.

a. Tunguska event
b. Amblypoda
c. Andrija Mohorovičić
d. Ambulocetus

23. In geology, _____ refers to heat sources within the planet. _____ is technically an adjective (e.g., _____ energy) but in U.S. English the word has attained frequent use as a noun.

The planet's internal heat was originally generated during its accretion, due to gravitational binding energy, and since then additional heat has continued to be generated by decay heat from the radioactive decay of elements.

a. Grade
b. Cleavage
c. Geothermal
d. Tarn

24. The _____ is the mechanically weak ductily-deforming region of the upper mantle of the Earth. It lies below the lithosphere, at depths between 100 and 200 km (~ 62 and 124 miles) below the surface, but perhaps extending as deep as 400 km (~ 249 miles.)

The _____ is a portion of the upper mantle just below the lithosphere that is involved in plate movements and isostatic adjustments. In spite of its heat, pressures keep it plastic, and it has a relatively low density. Seismic waves pass relatively slowly through the _____, compared to the overlying lithospheric mantle, thus it has been called the low-velocity zone. This was the observation that originally alerted seismologists to its presence and gave some information about its physical properties, as the speed of seismic waves decreases with decreasing rigidity.

a. AL 129-1
b. AL 333
c. AASHTO Soil Classification System
d. Asthenosphere

25. The _____ is the layer of igneous, sedimentary, and metamorphic rocks which form the continents and the areas of shallow seabed close to their shores, known as continental shelves. This layer is sometimes called sial due to more felsic, or granitic, bulk composition, which lies in contrast to the oceanic crust, called sima due to its mafic, or basaltic rock. (Based on the change in velocity of seismic waves, it is believed that at a certain depth sial becomes close in its physical properties to sima.

a. Continental drift
b. Lithosphere
c. Thrust fault
d. Continental crust

26. An _____ is the result of a sudden release of energy in the Earth's crust that creates seismic waves. They are recorded with a seismometer or the related and mostly obsolete Richter magnitude, with a magnitude 3 or lower _____ being mostly imperceptible and magnitude 7 causing serious damage over large areas.

a. AL 333
c. Earthquake
b. AASHTO Soil Classification System
d. AL 129-1

27. The _____ is the rigid outermost shell of a rocky planet.

In the Earth, the _____ includes the crust and the uppermost mantle, which constitute the hard and rigid outer layer of the planet. The _____ is underlain by the asthenosphere, the weaker, hotter, and deeper part of the upper mantle.

a. Subduction
c. Continental crust
b. Mantle convection
d. Lithosphere

28. _____ is molten rock that is found beneath the surface of the Earth, and may also exist on other terrestrial planets. Besides molten rock, _____ may also contain suspended crystals and gas bubbles. _____ often collects in a _____ chamber inside a volcano. _____ is capable of intrusion into adjacent rocks, extrusion onto the surface as lava, and explosive ejection as tephra to form pyroclastic rock.

a. Sedimentary rock
c. Large igneous provinces
b. Magma
d. Groundmass

29. The _____ is the layer of the Earth's atmosphere that is directly above the stratosphere and directly below the thermosphere. The _____ is located about 50 to 85 kilometers above the Earth's surface.

The stratosphere and _____ are referred to as the middle atmosphere.

a. 1509 Istanbul earthquake
c. Pluvial
b. Polar front
d. Mesosphere

30. _____ is the part of Earth's lithosphere that surfaces in the ocean basins. _____ is primarily composed of mafic rocks, or sima. It is thinner than continental crust, or sial, generally less than 10 kilometers thick, however it is denser, having a mean density of about 3.3 grams per cubic centimeter.

a. AL 129-1
c. AASHTO Soil Classification System
b. Oceanic crust
d. AL 333

31. In geology, _____ is the process that takes place at convergent boundaries by which one tectonic plate moves under another tectonic plate, sinking into the Earth's mantle, as the plates converge. A _____ zone is an area on Earth where two tectonic plates move towards one another and _____ occurs. Rates of _____ are typically measured in centimeters per year, with the average rate of convergence being approximately 2 to 8 centimeters per year (about the rate a fingernail grows.)

a. Motagua Fault
c. Mirovia
b. Continental collision
d. Subduction

32. The _____ of the Earth, its innermost hottest part as detected by seismological studies, is a primarily solid sphere about 1,220 km (758 mi) in radius, only about 70% that of the Moon. It is believed to consist of an iron-nickel alloy, and it may have a temperature similar to the Sun's surface.

The existence of an _____ distinct from the liquid outer core was discovered in 1936 by seismologist Inge Lehmann using observations of earthquake-generated seismic waves that partly reflect from its boundary and can be detected by sensitive seismographs on the Earth's surface.

    a. AASHTO Soil Classification System   b. AL 129-1
    c. AL 333   d. Inner core

33. _____ is typically about 50-100 km thick (but beneath the mid-ocean ridges is no thicker than the crust), while continental lithosphere has a range in thickness from about 40 km to perhaps 200 km; the upper ~30 to ~50 km of typical continental lithosphere is crust. The mantle part of the lithosphere consists largely of peridotite. The crust is distinguished from the upper mantle by the change in chemical composition that takes place at the Moho discontinuity.

_____ consists mainly of mafic crust and ultramafic mantle (peridotite) and is denser than continental lithosphere, for which the mantle is associated with crust made of felsic rocks. _____ thickens as it ages and moves away from the mid-ocean ridge.

    a. AASHTO Soil Classification System   b. AL 129-1
    c. AL 333   d. Oceanic lithosphere

34. _____ describes the large scale motions of Earth's lithosphere. The theory encompasses the older concepts of continental drift, developed during the first decades of the 20th century by Alfred Wegener, and seafloor spreading, understood during the 1960s.

The outermost part of the Earth's interior is made up of two layers: the lithosphere and the asthenosphere.

    a. Nappe   b. Mantle convection
    c. Continental crust   d. Plate tectonics

35. _____s is a field of study within geology concerned generally with the structures within the lithosphere of the Earth and particularly with the forces and movements that have operated in a region to create these structures.

_____s is concerned with the orogenies and _____ development of cratons and _____ terranes as well as the earthquake and volcanic belts which directly affect much of the global population. _____ studies are also important for understanding erosion patterns in geomorphology and as guides for the economic geologist searching for petroleum and metallic ores.

    a. Fault trace   b. Cocos Plate
    c. Rivera Plate   d. Tectonic

36. _____ is a field of study within geology concerned generally with the structures within the lithosphere of the Earth and particularly with the forces and movements that have operated in a region to create these structures.

_____ is concerned with the orogenies and tectonic development of cratons and tectonic terranes as well as the earthquake and volcanic belts which directly affect much of the global population. Tectonic studies are also important for understanding erosion patterns in geomorphology and as guides for the economic geologist searching for petroleum and metallic ores.

   a. Rivera Plate
   c. Cocos Plate
   b. Fault trace
   d. Tectonics

37. In the natural sciences an _____, as contrasted with a open system, is a physical system that does not interact with its surroundings. It obeys a number of conservation laws: its total energy and mass stay constant. They cannot enter or exit, but can only move around inside.
   a. AL 129-1
   c. AASHTO Soil Classification System
   b. Isolated system
   d. AL 333

38. _____ is a layer of loose, heterogeneous material covering solid rock. It includes dust, soil, broken rock, and other related materials and is present on Earth, the Moon, some asteroids, and other planets. The term was first defined by George P. Merrill in 1897 who stated, 'In places this covering is made up of material originating through rock-weathering or plant growth in situ. In other instances it is of fragmental and more or less decomposed matter drifted by wind, water or ice from other sources. This entire mantle of unconsolidated material, whatever its nature or origin, it is proposed to call the _____.'
   a. 1700 Cascadia earthquake
   c. 1509 Istanbul earthquake
   b. 1703 Genroku earthquake
   d. Regolith

39. In ecology and Earth science, a _____ or nutrient cycle is a pathway by which a chemical element or molecule moves through both biotic (biosphere) and abiotic (lithosphere, atmosphere, and hydrosphere) compartments of Earth. In effect, the element is recycled, although in some cycles there may be places (called reservoirs) where the element is accumulated or held for a long period of time. Elements, chemical compounds, and other forms of matter are passed from one organism to another and from one part of the biosphere to another through the _____s.
   a. 1509 Istanbul earthquake
   c. Biogeochemical cycle
   b. 1703 Genroku earthquake
   d. 1700 Cascadia earthquake

40. The _____ describes the continuous movement of water on, above, and below the surface of the Earth. Since the _____ is truly a 'cycle,' there is no beginning or end. Water can change states among liquid, vapor, and ice at various places in the _____.
   a. Streamflow
   c. Flownet
   b. Water cycle
   d. Hydraulic conductivity

41. The _____ is a fundamental concept in geology that describes the dynamic transitions through geologic time among the three main rock types: sedimentary, metamorphic, and igneous. Each type of rock is altered or destroyed when it is forced out of its equilibrium conditions. An igneous rock such as basalt may break down and dissolve when exposed to the atmosphere, or melt as it is subducted under a continent.
   a. Metamorphic zone
   c. Felsic
   b. Vesicular texture
   d. Rock cycle

42. _____ is any particulate matter that can be transported by fluid flow, and which eventually is deposited.

They are most often transported by water (fluvial processes) transported by wind (aeolian processes) and glaciers. Beach sands and river channel deposits are examples of fluvial transport and deposition, though _____ also often settles out of slow-moving or standing water in lakes and oceans.

a. Sediment
b. Fech fech
c. Brickearth
d. Salt glacier

43. _____ is one of the three main rock types (the others being igneous and metamorphic rock.) _____ is formed by deposition and consolidation of mineral and organic material and from precipitation of minerals from solution. The processes that form _____ occur at the surface of the Earth and within bodies of water.

a. Serpentinite
b. Large igneous provinces
c. Felsic
d. Sedimentary rock

44. In thermodynamics, an _____ or an isocaloric process is a thermodynamic process in which no heat is transferred to or from the working fluid. Conversely, a process that involves heat transfer (addition or loss of heat to the surroundings) is generally called diabatic.

a. AASHTO Soil Classification System
b. AL 129-1
c. AL 333
d. Adiabatic process

45. The _____ is the biogeochemical cycle that describes the transformations of nitrogen and nitrogen-containing compounds in nature. It is a cycle which includes gaseous components.

Earth's atmosphere is approximately 79% nitrogen, making it the largest pool of nitrogen.

a. 1703 Genroku earthquake
b. 1700 Cascadia earthquake
c. 1509 Istanbul earthquake
d. Nitrogen cycle

46. _____ is a process that converts carbon dioxide into organic compounds, especially sugars, using the energy from sunlight. _____ occurs in plants, algae, and many species of bacteria. With the exception of some bacteria, all use water and carbon dioxide as initial substrates and release oxygen as a waste product.

a. 1700 Cascadia earthquake
b. 1509 Istanbul earthquake
c. 1703 Genroku earthquake
d. Photosynthesis

47. _____ is the solid-state recrystallization of pre-existing rocks due to changes in physical and chemical conditions, primarily heat, pressure, and the introduction of chemically active fluids. Both mineralogical, chemical and crystallographic changes can occur during this process.

Three types of _____ exist: dynamic, contact and regional.

a. Metamorphism
b. Lake capture
c. Pumice raft
d. Gibraltar Arc

Chapter 1. Meet Planet Earth

48. _____ is the name given to a rock consisting mainly of hornblende amphibole, the use of the term being restricted, however, to metamorphic rocks. The modern terminology for a holocrystalline plutonic igneous rocks composed primarily of hornblende amphibole is a hornblendite, which are usually crystal cumulates. Rocks with >90% amphibole which have a feldspar groundmass may be a lamprophyre.

   a. Amphibolite
   b. AASHTO Soil Classification System
   c. AL 333
   d. AL 129-1

49. _____ is the result of the transformation of an existing rock type, the protolith, in a process called metamorphism, which means 'change in form'. The protolith is subjected to heat and pressure (temperatures greater than 150 to 200 >°C and pressures of 1500 bars) causing profound physical and/or chemical change. The protolith may be sedimentary rock, igneous rock or another older _____.

   a. Laccolith
   b. Pluton
   c. Metamorphic rock
   d. Serpentinite

50. _____ is water located beneath the ground surface in soil pore spaces and in the fractures of lithologic formations. A unit of rock or an unconsolidated deposit is called an aquifer when it can yield a usable quantity of water. The depth at which soil pore spaces or fractures and voids in rock become completely saturated with water is called the water table.

   a. 1509 Istanbul earthquake
   b. Depression focused recharge
   c. 1700 Cascadia earthquake
   d. Groundwater

51. A _____ is a geological phenomenon which includes a wide range of ground movement, such as rock falls, deep failure of slopes and shallow debris flows, which can occur in offshore, coastal and onshore environments. Although the action of gravity is the primary driving force for a _____ to occur, there are other contributing factors affecting the original slope stability. Typically, pre-conditional factors build up specific sub-surface conditions that make the area/slope prone to failure, whereas the actual _____ often requires a trigger before being released.

   a. 1509 Istanbul earthquake
   b. Landslide
   c. Mass wasting
   d. 1700 Cascadia earthquake

52. A _____ is a marine landslide that transports sediment across the continental shelf and into the deep ocean. A _____ is initiated when the downwards driving stress (gravity and other factors) exceeds the resisting stress of the seafloor slope material causing movements along one or more concave to planer rupture surfaces. _____s take place in a variety of different settings including planes as low as 1>° and can cause significant damage to both life and property.

   a. 1700 Cascadia earthquake
   b. 1509 Istanbul earthquake
   c. 1703 Genroku earthquake
   d. Submarine landslide

Chapter 2. Global Tectonics: Our Dynamic Planet

1. The _____ is the biogeochemical cycle by which carbon is exchanged among the biosphere, pedosphere, geosphere, hydrosphere, and atmosphere of the Earth.

The _____ is usually thought of as four major reservoirs of carbon interconnected by pathways of exchange. These reservoirs are:

- The plants
- The terrestrial biosphere, which is usually defined to include fresh water systems and non-living organic material, such as soil carbon.
- The oceans, including dissolved inorganic carbon and living and non-living marine biota,
- The sediments including fossil fuels.

The annual movements of carbon, the carbon exchanges between reservoirs, occur because of various chemical, physical, geological, and biological processes. The ocean contains the largest active pool of carbon near the surface of the Earth, but the deep ocean part of this pool does not rapidly exchange with the atmosphere.

   a. Nanogeoscience
   c. 1509 Istanbul earthquake
   b. Cosmogenic isotopes
   d. Carbon cycle

2. _____ is the movement of the Earth's continents relative to each other. The hypothesis that continents 'drift' was first put forward by Abraham Ortelius in 1596 and was fully developed by Alfred Wegener in 1912. However, it was not until the development of the theory of plate tectonics in the 1960s, that a sufficient geological explanation of that movement was found.
   a. Convergent boundary
   c. Continental collision
   b. Nappe
   d. Continental drift

3. The terms _____ and icehouse Earth refer to the prevailing global climate on a timescale of millions of years.

During a _____ Earth period, the planet's atmosphere contains sufficient _____ gases such as carbon dioxide and methane for ice to be entirely absent from the planet's surface.

During icehouse periods, glaciers are present in fluctuating amounts; variations in the Earth's orbit may result in many ice ages, glacials, and interglacials.

   a. 1700 Cascadia earthquake
   c. 1703 Genroku earthquake
   b. 1509 Istanbul earthquake
   d. Greenhouse

4. In geology, _____ is transported rock debris overlying the solid bedrock. The term is also sometimes refers to organic debris so-transported. In the largest sense, it refers to the material left behind by retreating continental glaciers.
   a. Metamorphic reaction
   c. Riegel
   b. Geomechanics
   d. Drift

5. _____ is the study of underwater depth of the third dimension of lake or ocean floors. In other words, _____ is the underwater equivalent to hypsometry. Originally, _____ referred to the measurement of ocean depth through depth sounding. Early techniques used pre-measured heavy rope or cable lowered over a ship's side.

Chapter 2. Global Tectonics: Our Dynamic Planet

a. Bathymetry
b. 1703 Genroku earthquake
c. 1509 Istanbul earthquake
d. 1700 Cascadia earthquake

6. An _____ is a bulge which a planet may have around its equator, distorting it into an oblate spheroid. The Earth has an _____ of 42.72 km (26.5 miles) due to its rotation: its diameter measured across the equatorial plane (12756.28 km, 7,927 miles) is 42.72 km more than that measured between the poles (12713.56 km, 7,900 miles.)

An often-cited result of Earth's _____ is that the highest point on Earth, measured from the center outwards, is the peak of Mount Chimborazo in Ecuador, rather than Mount Everest.

a. AL 129-1
b. AL 333
c. AASHTO Soil Classification System
d. Equatorial bulge

7. _____ is a term used in geology to refer to the state of gravitational equilibrium between the earth's lithosphere and asthenosphere such that the tectonic plates 'float' at an elevation which depends on their thickness and density. This concept is invoked to explain how different topographic heights can exist at the Earth's surface. When a certain area of lithosphere reaches the state of _____, it is said to be in isostatic equilibrium.

a. Orientation Tensor
b. Economic geology
c. Isograd
d. Isostasy

8. _____ describes the large scale motions of Earth's lithosphere. The theory encompasses the older concepts of continental drift, developed during the first decades of the 20th century by Alfred Wegener, and seafloor spreading, understood during the 1960s.

The outermost part of the Earth's interior is made up of two layers: the lithosphere and the asthenosphere.

a. Mantle convection
b. Plate tectonics
c. Continental crust
d. Nappe

9. _____s is a field of study within geology concerned generally with the structures within the lithosphere of the Earth and particularly with the forces and movements that have operated in a region to create these structures.

_____s is concerned with the orogenies and _____ development of cratons and _____ terranes as well as the earthquake and volcanic belts which directly affect much of the global population. _____ studies are also important for understanding erosion patterns in geomorphology and as guides for the economic geologist searching for petroleum and metallic ores.

a. Tectonic
b. Fault trace
c. Rivera Plate
d. Cocos Plate

10. _____ is a field of study within geology concerned generally with the structures within the lithosphere of the Earth and particularly with the forces and movements that have operated in a region to create these structures.

_____ is concerned with the orogenies and tectonic development of cratons and tectonic terranes as well as the earthquake and volcanic belts which directly affect much of the global population. Tectonic studies are also important for understanding erosion patterns in geomorphology and as guides for the economic geologist searching for petroleum and metallic ores.

   a. Cocos Plate
   c. Fault trace
   b. Rivera Plate
   d. Tectonics

11. The _____ is the extended perimeter of each continent and associated coastal plain, and was part of the continent during the glacial periods, but is undersea during interglacial periods such as the current epoch by relatively shallow seas (known as shelf seas) and gulfs.

The continental rise is below the slope, but landward of the abyssal plains. Its gradient is intermediate between the slope and the shelf, on the order of 0.5-1°.

   a. Continental slope
   c. Surface runoff
   b. Mud
   d. Continental shelf

12. The shelf usually ends at a point of decreasing slope (called the shelf break.) The sea floor below the break is the _____. Below the slope is the continental rise, which finally merges into the deep ocean floor, the abyssal plain.
   a. Surface runoff
   c. Thermal pollution
   b. Mud
   d. Continental slope

13. The _____ of any physical feature such as a hill, stream, roof, railroad, or road refers to the amount of inclination of that surface where zero indicates level (with respect to gravity) and larger numbers indicate higher degrees of 'tilt'. Often slope is calculated as a ratio of 'rise over run' in which run is the horizontal distance and rise is the vertical distance.

There are several systems for expressing slope:

   1. as an angle of inclination from the horizontal of a right triangle. (This is the angle >α opposite the 'rise' side of the triangle.)
   2. as a percentage (also known as the _____), the formula for which is [×] > which could also be expressed as the tangent of the angle of inclination times 100. In the U.S., the _____ is the most commonly used unit for communicating slopes in transportation, surveying, construction, and civil engineering.
   3. as a per mille figure, the formula for which is [×] > which could also be expressed as the tangent of the angle of inclination times 1000. This is commonly used in Europe to denote the incline of a railway.
   4. as a ratio of one part rise per so many parts run. For example, a slope that has a rise of 5 feet for every 100 feet of run would have a slope ratio of 1 in 20.

Chapter 2. Global Tectonics: Our Dynamic Planet

Any one of these expressions may be used interchangeably to express the characteristics of a slope. _____ is usually expressed as a percentage, but this may easily be converted to the angle >α from horizontal since that carries the same information.

- a. Heavy metal
- b. Compaction
- c. Diamond Head
- d. Grade

14. _____ are flat or very gently sloping areas of the deep ocean basin floor. They are among the Earth's flattest and smoothest regions and the least explored. _____ cover approximately 40% of the ocean floor and reach depths between 2,200 and 5,500 m (7,200 and 18,000 ft).
    - a. Overland flow
    - b. Eutrophication
    - c. Abyssal plains
    - d. Upwelling

15. In plate tectonics, a _____ is an actively deforming region where two tectonic plates or fragments of lithosphere move toward one another and collide. As a result of pressure and friction and plate material melting in the mantle, earthquakes and volcanoes are common near convergent boundaries.
    - a. Convergent boundary
    - b. Mantle convection
    - c. Supercontinent cycle
    - d. Panthalassa

16. The shelf usually ends at a point of decreasing slope (called the shelf break.) The sea floor below the break is the continental slope. Below the slope is the _____, which finally merges into the deep ocean floor, the abyssal plain.
    - a. Continental rise
    - b. Continental slope
    - c. Continental shelf
    - d. Thermal pollution

17. In geology, _____ refers to heat sources within the planet. _____ is technically an adjective (e.g., _____ energy) but in U.S. English the word has attained frequent use as a noun.

The planet's internal heat was originally generated during its accretion, due to gravitational binding energy, and since then additional heat has continued to be generated by decay heat from the radioactive decay of elements.

- a. Cleavage
- b. Tarn
- c. Geothermal
- d. Grade

18. The _____ is the rate of increase in temperature per unit depth in the Earth. It varies with location and is typically measured by determining the bottom open-hole temperature after borehole drilling. To achieve accuracy the drilling fluid needs time to reach the ambient temperature.
    - a. Geothermal desalination
    - b. Geothermal power
    - c. Hot Dry Rock Geothermal Energy
    - d. Geothermal gradient

19. _____ in the most general terms refers to the movement of molecules within fluids (i.e. liquids, gases and rheids.) _____ is one of the major modes of heat transfer and mass transfer. In fluids, convective heat and mass transfer take place through both diffusion - the random Brownian motion of individual particles in the fluid - and by advection, in which matter or heat is transported by the larger-scale motion of currents in the fluid.

a. Convection
b. Turbulent flow
c. Power
d. Strong interaction

20. In materials science, _____ is a change in the shape or size of an object due to an applied force. This can be a result of tensile (pulling) forces, compressive (pushing) forces, shear, bending or torsion (twisting.) _____ is often described as strain.
a. Submersion
b. Deformation
c. Lingula
d. Stack

21. _____ is the difference between the greatest and the least compressive stress experienced by an object. For the geological convention, in which >σ_3 is the greatest compressive stress and >σ_1 is the weakest,

>.

For the engineering convention, >σ_1 is the greatest compressive stress and >σ_3 is the weakest, so

>.

a. Rill
b. Palynomorph
c. Cross-cutting relationships
d. Differential stress

22. _____ are waves that travel through the Earth or other elastic body, for example as the result of an earthquake, explosion, or some other process that imparts forces to the body. _____ are also continually excited on Earth by the incessant pounding of ocean waves (referred to as the microseism) and the wind. _____ are studied by seismologists, and measured by a seismograph, which records the output of a seismometer, or geophone.
a. Rayleigh waves
b. Seismic waves
c. Strong ground motion
d. Maximum magnitude

23. _____ is a measure of the resistance of a fluid which is being deformed by either shear stress or extensional stress. In everyday terms (and for fluids only), _____ is 'thickness'. Thus, water is 'thin', having a lower _____, while honey is 'thick' having a higher _____.
a. Thixotropy
b. Shear stress
c. Tensile stress
d. Viscosity

24. In thermodynamics, an _____ or an isocaloric process is a thermodynamic process in which no heat is transferred to or from the working fluid. Conversely, a process that involves heat transfer (addition or loss of heat to the surroundings) is generally called diabatic.
a. AL 129-1
b. AL 333
c. AASHTO Soil Classification System
d. Adiabatic process

25. In fluid mechanics, the _____ for a fluid is a dimensionless number associated with buoyancy driven flow. When the _____ is below the critical value for that fluid, heat transfer is primarily in the form of conduction; when it exceeds the critical value, heat transfer is primarily in the form of convection.

The _____ is defined as the product of the Grashof number, which describes the relationship between buoyancy and viscosity within a fluid, and the Prandtl number, which describes the relationship between momentum diffusivity and thermal diffusivity.

- a. Rayleigh number
- b. 1700 Cascadia earthquake
- c. 1509 Istanbul earthquake
- d. 1703 Genroku earthquake

26. In geology, _____ is the process that takes place at convergent boundaries by which one tectonic plate moves under another tectonic plate, sinking into the Earth's mantle, as the plates converge. A _____ zone is an area on Earth where two tectonic plates move towards one another and _____ occurs. Rates of _____ are typically measured in centimeters per year, with the average rate of convergence being approximately 2 to 8 centimeters per year (about the rate a fingernail grows.)

- a. Motagua Fault
- b. Mirovia
- c. Continental collision
- d. Subduction

27. _____ is the slow creeping motion of Earth's rocky mantle in response to perpetual gravitationally unstable variations in its density. Material near the surface of the Earth, particularly oceanic lithosphere, cools down by conduction of heat into the oceans and atmosphere, then thermally contracts to become dense, and then sinks under its own weight at convergent plate boundaries. This subducted material sinks to some depth in the Earth's interior where it is prohibited, by inherent density stratification, from sinking further.

- a. Divergent boundary
- b. Motagua Fault
- c. Mantle convection
- d. Plate tectonics

28. In plate tectonics, a _____ is a linear feature that exists between two tectonic plates that are moving away from each other. These areas can form in the middle of continents but eventually form ocean basins. Divergent boundaries within continents initially produce rifts which produce rift valleys. Therefore, most active divergent plate boundaries are between oceanic plates and are often called mid-oceanic ridges. Divergent boundaries also form Volcanic Islands which occur when the plates move apart to produce gaps which molten lava rises to fill. Thus creating a shield volcano which would eventually build up to become a volcanic island.

- a. Lithosphere
- b. Tectonic plates
- c. Thrust fault
- d. Divergent boundary

29. _____ a branch of earth sciences, is the scientific discipline that deals with the measurement and representation of the Earth, including its gravitational field, in a three-dimensional time-varying space. Geodesists also study geodynamical phenomena such as crustal motion, tides, and polar motion. For this they design global and national control networks, using space and terrestrial techniques while relying on datums and coordinate systems.

- a. 1700 Cascadia earthquake
- b. 1509 Istanbul earthquake
- c. 1703 Genroku earthquake
- d. Geodesy

30. A _____ or transform boundary is a fault which runs along the boundary of a tectonic plate. The relative motion of such plates is horizontal in either sinistral or dextral direction. Typically, some vertical motion may also exist, but the principal vectors in a _____ are oriented horizontally.

- a. Structural geology
- b. Michoud fault
- c. Molasse basin
- d. Transform fault

Chapter 2. Global Tectonics: Our Dynamic Planet

31. In geology, a _____ or _____ line is a planar fracture in rock in which the rock on one side of the fracture has moved with respect to the rock on the other side. Large _____s within the Earth's crust are the result of differential or shear motion and active _____ zones are the causal locations of most earthquakes. Earthquakes are caused by energy release during rapid slippage along a _____.
   a. Cleavage
   b. Drainage system
   c. Compaction
   d. Fault

32. The fault surface of _____ is usually near vertical and the footwall moves either left or right or laterally with very little vertical motion. _____ with left-lateral motion are also known as sinistral faults. Those with right-lateral motion are also known as dextral faults.
   a. Star dunes
   b. Strike-slip faults
   c. Suspended load
   d. Pahoehoe lava

33. A _____ is a type of fault in which rocks of lower stratigraphic position are pushed up and over higher strata. They are often recognized because they place older rocks above younger. _____s are the result of compressional forces.
   a. Convergent boundary
   b. Mantle convection
   c. Continental drift
   d. Thrust fault

34. An _____ is the result of a sudden release of energy in the Earth's crust that creates seismic waves. They are recorded with a seismometer or the related and mostly obsolete Richter magnitude, with a magnitude 3 or lower _____ being mostly imperceptible and magnitude 7 causing serious damage over large areas.
   a. AASHTO Soil Classification System
   b. AL 333
   c. AL 129-1
   d. Earthquake

35. _____ is molten rock that is found beneath the surface of the Earth, and may also exist on other terrestrial planets. Besides molten rock, _____ may also contain suspended crystals and gas bubbles. _____ often collects in a _____ chamber inside a volcano. _____ is capable of intrusion into adjacent rocks, extrusion onto the surface as lava, and explosive ejection as tephra to form pyroclastic rock.
   a. Large igneous provinces
   b. Magma
   c. Sedimentary rock
   d. Groundmass

36. _____ was the supercontinent that is theorized to have existed during the Paleozoic and Mesozoic eras about 250 million years ago, before the component continents were separated into their current configuration.

The name was first used by the German originator of the continental drift theory, Alfred Wegener, in the 1920 edition of his book The Origin of Continents and Oceans , in which a postulated supercontinent _____ played a key role.

The single enormous ocean which surrounded Pangaea is known as Panthalassa.

   a. 1700 Cascadia earthquake
   b. 1703 Genroku earthquake
   c. 1509 Istanbul earthquake
   d. Pangea

37. _____, originally Gondwanaland, is the name given to a southern precursor-supercontinent and then as a remnant separated from Laurasia 180-200 million years ago during the breakup of the Pangaea supercontinent that existed about 500 to 200 Ma ago into two large segments. While the corresponding northern hemisphere continent Laurasia moved further north, the nearly equal in area _____ included most of the landmasses in today's southern hemisphere, including Antarctica, South America, Africa, Madagascar, Australia-New Guinea, and New Zealand, as well as Arabia and the Indian subcontinent, which have now moved into the Northern Hemisphere.

a. 1700 Cascadia earthquake
b. Gondwana
c. Laurasia
d. 1509 Istanbul earthquake

38. _____ is water located beneath the ground surface in soil pore spaces and in the fractures of lithologic formations. A unit of rock or an unconsolidated deposit is called an aquifer when it can yield a usable quantity of water. The depth at which soil pore spaces or fractures and voids in rock become completely saturated with water is called the water table.

a. Depression focused recharge
b. 1509 Istanbul earthquake
c. 1700 Cascadia earthquake
d. Groundwater

39. The _____ is the rigid outermost shell of a rocky planet.

In the Earth, the _____ includes the crust and the uppermost mantle, which constitute the hard and rigid outer layer of the planet. The _____ is underlain by the asthenosphere, the weaker, hotter, and deeper part of the upper mantle.

a. Continental crust
b. Subduction
c. Mantle convection
d. Lithosphere

40. _____ is typically about 50-100 km thick (but beneath the mid-ocean ridges is no thicker than the crust), while continental lithosphere has a range in thickness from about 40 km to perhaps 200 km; the upper ~30 to ~50 km of typical continental lithosphere is crust. The mantle part of the lithosphere consists largely of peridotite. The crust is distinguished from the upper mantle by the change in chemical composition that takes place at the Moho discontinuity.

_____ consists mainly of mafic crust and ultramafic mantle (peridotite) and is denser than continental lithosphere, for which the mantle is associated with crust made of felsic rocks. _____ thickens as it ages and moves away from the mid-ocean ridge.

a. AL 129-1
b. AASHTO Soil Classification System
c. Oceanic lithosphere
d. AL 333

41. A _____ is a chain of volcanic islands or mountains formed by plate tectonics as an oceanic tectonic plate subducts under another tectonic plate and produces magma. There are two types of these: oceanic arcs (commonly called island arcs, a type of archipelago) and continental arcs. In the former, oceanic crust subducts beneath other oceanic crust on an adjacent plate, while in the latter case the oceanic crust subducts beneath continental crust. In some situations, a single subduction zone may show both aspects along its length, as part of a plate subducts beneath a continent and part beneath adjacent oceanic crust.

a. 1509 Istanbul earthquake
b. 1703 Genroku earthquake
c. Volcanic arc
d. 1700 Cascadia earthquake

42. A _____ is a mountain rising from the ocean seafloor that does not reach to the water's surface (sea level), and thus is not an island. These are typically formed from extinct volcanoes, that rise abruptly and are usually found rising from a seafloor of 1,000-4,000 meters depth. They are defined by oceanographers as independent features that rise to at least 1,000 meters above the seafloor.
   a. Seamount
   b. 1700 Cascadia earthquake
   c. 1703 Genroku earthquake
   d. 1509 Istanbul earthquake

43. A _____ is an opening in a planet's surface or crust, which allows hot, molten rock, ash, and gases to escape from below the surface. Volcanic activity involving the extrusion of rock tends to form mountains or features like mountains over a period of time.
   a. 1509 Istanbul earthquake
   b. 1703 Genroku earthquake
   c. 1700 Cascadia earthquake
   d. Volcano

44. A _____ is a deep active seismic area in a subduction zone. Differential motion along the zone produces deep-seated earthquakes, the foci of which may be as deep as about 700 kilometres (435 miles.) They develop beneath volcanic island arcs and continental margins above active subduction zones.
   a. Fissure vent
   b. Lava
   c. Volcanic pipes
   d. Wadati-Benioff zone

45. The _____ is a continental transform fault that runs a length of roughly 800 miles (1,300 km) through California in the United States. The fault's motion is right-lateral strike-slip (horizontal motion.) It forms the tectonic boundary between the Pacific Plate and the North American Plate.
   a. 1509 Istanbul earthquake
   b. San Andreas Fault
   c. 1703 Genroku earthquake
   d. 1700 Cascadia earthquake

46. In geology, a _____ is a location on the Earth's surface that has experienced active volcanism for a long period of time.

J. Tuzo Wilson came up with the idea in 1963 that volcanic chains like the Hawaiian Islands result from the slow movement of a tectonic plate across a 'fixed' _____ deep beneath the surface of the planet.

   a. 1700 Cascadia earthquake
   b. 1509 Istanbul earthquake
   c. 1703 Genroku earthquake
   d. Hotspot

47. A _____ is an upwelling of abnormally hot rock within the Earth's mantle. As the heads of _____s can partly melt when they reach shallow depths, they are thought to be the cause of volcanic centers known as hotspots and probably also to have caused flood basalts. It is a secondary way that Earth loses heat, much less important in this regard than is heat loss at plate margins.
   a. Seismic refraction
   b. Mantle plume
   c. Strainmeter
   d. Mazuku

48. _____ is the geomorphic process by which soil, regolith, and rock move downslope under the force of gravity. Types of _____ include creep, slides, flows, topples, and falls, each with its own characteristic features, and taking place over timescales from seconds to years. _____ occurs on both terrestrial and submarine slopes, and has been observed on Earth, Mars, and Venus.

Chapter 2. Global Tectonics: Our Dynamic Planet

a. Soil liquefaction
c. Mass wasting
b. 1700 Cascadia earthquake
d. 1509 Istanbul earthquake

49. A _____ is a type of intrusion in which a more mobile and ductily-deformable material is forced into brittle overlying rocks. Depending on the tectonic environment, they can range from idealized mushroom-shaped Rayleigh-Taylor instability-type structures in regions with low tectonic stress such as in the Gulf of Mexico to narrow dike (geology) dikes of material that move along tectonically-induced fractures in surrounding rock. The term was introduced by the Romanian geologist Ludovic Mrazek, who was the first to understand the principle of salt intrusion and plasticity.
   a. Drill cuttings
   c. Rockall Basin
   b. Phosphate rock
   d. Diapir

50. A _____ or sandstorm is a meteorological phenomenon common in arid and semi-arid regions and arises when a gust front passes or when the wind force exceeds the threshold value where loose sand and dust are removed from the dry surface. Particles are transported by saltation and suspension, causing soil erosion from one place and deposition in another. The Sahara and drylands around the Arabian peninsula are the main source of airborne dust, with some contributions from Iran, Pakistan and India into the Arabian Sea, and China's storms deposit dust in the Pacific.
   a. 1703 Genroku earthquake
   c. 1700 Cascadia earthquake
   b. 1509 Istanbul earthquake
   d. Dust storm

51. A _____ is a geological phenomenon which includes a wide range of ground movement, such as rock falls, deep failure of slopes and shallow debris flows, which can occur in offshore, coastal and onshore environments. Although the action of gravity is the primary driving force for a _____ to occur, there are other contributing factors affecting the original slope stability. Typically, pre-conditional factors build up specific sub-surface conditions that make the area/slope prone to failure, whereas the actual _____ often requires a trigger before being released.
   a. Landslide
   c. Mass wasting
   b. 1700 Cascadia earthquake
   d. 1509 Istanbul earthquake

52. A _____ is a marine landslide that transports sediment across the continental shelf and into the deep ocean. A _____ is initiated when the downwards driving stress (gravity and other factors) exceeds the resisting stress of the seafloor slope material causing movements along one or more concave to planer rupture surfaces. _____s take place in a variety of different settings including planes as low as 1>° and can cause significant damage to both life and property.
   a. 1509 Istanbul earthquake
   c. 1700 Cascadia earthquake
   b. 1703 Genroku earthquake
   d. Submarine landslide

Chapter 3. Atoms, Elements, Minerals, Rocks

1. A _____ is a mineral-like substance that does not demonstrate crystallinity. _____s possess chemical compositions that vary beyond the generally accepted ranges for specific minerals. For example, obsidian is an amorphous glass and not a crystal.
   a. 1509 Istanbul earthquake
   b. Mineraloid
   c. Chalcedony
   d. Silicate minerals

2. In thermodynamics, an _____ or an isocaloric process is a thermodynamic process in which no heat is transferred to or from the working fluid. Conversely, a process that involves heat transfer (addition or loss of heat to the surroundings) is generally called diabatic.
   a. Adiabatic process
   b. AL 333
   c. AASHTO Soil Classification System
   d. AL 129-1

3. _____ is water located beneath the ground surface in soil pore spaces and in the fractures of lithologic formations. A unit of rock or an unconsolidated deposit is called an aquifer when it can yield a usable quantity of water. The depth at which soil pore spaces or fractures and voids in rock become completely saturated with water is called the water table.
   a. Depression focused recharge
   b. 1700 Cascadia earthquake
   c. Groundwater
   d. 1509 Istanbul earthquake

4. In chemistry and physics, the _____ is the number of protons found in the nucleus of an atom and therefore identical to the charge number of the nucleus. It is conventionally represented by the symbol Z. The _____ uniquely identifies a chemical element. In an atom of neutral charge, _____ is equal to the number of electrons.
   a. AASHTO Soil Classification System
   b. AL 129-1
   c. AL 333
   d. Atomic number

5. The _____ is the total number of protons and neutrons in an atomic nucleus. Because protons and neutrons both are baryons, the _____ A is identical with the baryon number B as of the nucleus as of the whole atom or ion. The _____ is different for each different isotope of a chemical element.
   a. 1703 Genroku earthquake
   b. Mass number
   c. 1509 Istanbul earthquake
   d. 1700 Cascadia earthquake

6. A covalent bond is a form of chemical bonding that is characterized by the sharing of pairs of electrons between atoms, or between atoms and other covalent bonds. In short, attraction-to-repulsion stability that forms between atoms when they share electrons is known as _____.

   _____ includes many kinds of interaction, including >σ-bonding, >π-bonding, metal to non-metal bonding, agostic interactions, and three-center two-electron bonds.

   a. Van der Waals force
   b. 1700 Cascadia earthquake
   c. 1509 Istanbul earthquake
   d. Covalent bonding

7. An _____ is a type of chemical bond that involves a metal and a non-metal ion (or polyatomic ions such as ammonium) through electrostatic attraction. In short, it is a bond formed by the attraction between two oppositely charged ions. The metal donates one or more electrons, forming a positively charged ion or cation with a stable electron configuration.
   a. AASHTO Soil Classification System
   b. Ionic bond
   c. AL 129-1
   d. AL 333

8. _____ is the electromagnetic interaction between delocalized electrons, called conduction electrons, and the metallic nuclei within metals. Understood as the sharing of 'free' electrons among a lattice of positively-charged ions (cations), _____ is sometimes compared with that of molten salts; however, this simplistic view holds true for very few metals. In a more quantum-mechanical view, the conduction electrons divide their density equally over all atoms that function as neutral (non-charged) entities.

   a. 1509 Istanbul earthquake   b. 1700 Cascadia earthquake
   c. Van der Waals force   d. Metallic bonding

9. In physical chemistry, the _____ is the attractive or repulsive force between molecules (or between parts of the same molecule) other than those due to covalent bonds or to the electrostatic interaction of ions with one another or with neutral molecules. The term includes:

- permanent dipole-permanent dipole forces
- permanent dipole-induced dipole forces
- instantaneous induced dipole-induced dipole (London dispersion forces.)

It is also sometimes used loosely as a synonym for the totality of intermolecular forces. _____s are relatively weak compared to normal chemical bonds, but play a fundamental role in fields as diverse as supramolecular chemistry, structural biology, polymer science, nanotechnology, surface science, and condensed matter physics. _____s define the chemical character of many organic compounds.

   a. 1700 Cascadia earthquake   b. Van der Waals force
   c. Metallic bonding   d. 1509 Istanbul earthquake

10. An _____ is a solid in which there is no long-range order of the positions of the atoms. (Solids in which there is long-range atomic order are called crystalline solids or morphous). Most classes of solid materials can be found or prepared in an amorphous form.

   a. AASHTO Soil Classification System   b. AL 129-1
   c. AL 333   d. Amorphous solid

11. In mineralogy and crystallography, a _____ is a unique arrangement of atoms in a crystal. A _____ is composed of a motif, a set of atoms arranged in a particular way, and a lattice. Motifs are located upon the points of a lattice, which is an array of points repeating periodically in three dimensions.

   a. Crystal structure   b. 1700 Cascadia earthquake
   c. 1703 Genroku earthquake   d. 1509 Istanbul earthquake

12. The _____, r_{ion}, is a measure of the size of an ion in a crystal lattice. It is measured in either picometres (pm) or Angstrom (>Å), with 1 >Å = 100 pm. Typical values range from 30 pm (0.3 >Å) to over 200 pm (2 >Å).

The concept of _____ was developed independently by Goldschmidt and Pauling in the 1920s to summarize the data being generated by the (then) new technique of X-ray crystallography: it is Pauling's approach which proved to be the more influential.

   a. AASHTO Soil Classification System   b. AL 333
   c. AL 129-1   d. Ionic radius

Chapter 3. Atoms, Elements, Minerals, Rocks

13. The mineral _____ is a magnesium iron silicate with the formula $(Mg,Fe)_2SiO_4$. It is one of the most common minerals on Earth, and has also been identified in meteorites and on the Moon, Mars, and comet Wild 2.

The ratio of magnesium and iron varies between the two endmembers of the solid solution series: forsterite (Mg-endmember) and fayalite (Fe-endmember.)

    a. AL 129-1
    c. AL 333
    b. AASHTO Soil Classification System
    d. Olivine

14. _____ is the geomorphic process by which soil, regolith, and rock move downslope under the force of gravity. Types of _____ include creep, slides, flows, topples, and falls, each with its own characteristic features, and taking place over timescales from seconds to years. _____ occurs on both terrestrial and submarine slopes, and has been observed on Earth, Mars, and Venus.

    a. 1509 Istanbul earthquake
    c. Soil liquefaction
    b. 1700 Cascadia earthquake
    d. Mass wasting

15. _____, in structural geology and related disciplines, describes the tendency of a rock to break along preferred planes of weakness.

Rocks deformed under very low to low metamorphic grade often develop planes along which the rock can easily be split. Slates are an example of a rock with a penetrative _____ caused partly by the realignment of phyllosilicate minerals with increasing flattening strain.

    a. Diamond Head
    c. Geothermal
    b. Lingula
    d. Cleavage

16. The _____ of a mineral is the color of the powder produced when it is dragged across an unweathered surface. Unlike the apparent color of a mineral, which for most minerals can vary considerably, the trail of finely ground powder generally has a more consistent characteristic color, and is thus an important diagnostic tool in mineral identification. If no _____ seems to be made, the mineral's _____ is said to be white or colorless.

    a. Heavy metal
    c. Streak
    b. Geothermal
    d. Texture

17. _____ is defined as the ratio of the density of a given solid or liquid substance to the density of water at a specific temperature and pressure, typically at 4 >°C (39 >°F) and 1 atm (760.00 mmHg) , making it a dimensionless quantity Substances with a _____ greater than one are denser than water, and so (ignoring surface tension effects) will sink in it, and those with a _____ of less than one are less dense than water, and so will float in it. _____ is a special case of, or in some usages synonymous with, relative density, with the latter term often preferred in modern scientific writing.

    a. 1509 Istanbul earthquake
    c. 1703 Genroku earthquake
    b. 1700 Cascadia earthquake
    d. Specific gravity

18. In chemistry, a _____ is a salt or ester of carbonic acid.

To test for the presence of the _____ anion in a salt, the addition of dilute mineral acid (e.g. hydrochloric acid) will yield carbon dioxide gas.

Chapter 3. Atoms, Elements, Minerals, Rocks

_____-containing salts are industrially and mineralogically ubiquitous.

a. 1509 Istanbul earthquake
c. 1703 Genroku earthquake
b. 1700 Cascadia earthquake
d. Carbonate

19. An _____ is a type of rock that contains minerals such as gemstones and metals that can be extracted through mining and refined for use. Samples of _____ in the form of exceptionally beautiful crystals, exotic layering visible when sectioned or polished or metallic presentations such as large nuggets or crystalline formations of metals such as gold or copper may command a value far beyond their value as mere _____ or raw metal for subsequent reduction to utilitarian purposes.

The grade or concentration of an _____ mineral, or metal, as well as its form of occurrence, will directly affect the costs associated with mining the _____.

a. Ore genesis
c. AASHTO Soil Classification System
b. Iron ores
d. Ore

20. A _____, an inorganic chemical, is a salt of phosphoric acid. Inorganic _____s are mined to obtain phosphorus for use in agriculture and industry. In organic chemistry, a _____, or organophosphate, is an ester of phosphoric acid.

a. 1700 Cascadia earthquake
c. 1509 Istanbul earthquake
b. 1703 Genroku earthquake
d. Phosphate

21. A _____ is a compound containing an anion in which one or more central silicon atoms are surrounded by electronegative ligands. This definition is broad enough to include species such as hexafluorosilicate ('fluorosilicate'), $[SiF_6]^{2-}$, but the _____ species that are encountered most often consist of silicon with oxygen as the ligand. _____ anions, with a negative net electrical charge, must have that charge balanced by other cations to make an electrically neutral compound.

a. 1700 Cascadia earthquake
c. Silicate
b. 1509 Istanbul earthquake
d. 1703 Genroku earthquake

22. In inorganic chemistry, a _____ is a salt of sulfuric acid.

The _____ ion is a polyatomic anion with the empirical formula SO_4^{2-} and a molecular mass of 96.06 daltons; it consists of a central sulfur atom surrounded by four equivalent oxygen atoms in a tetrahedral arrangement. The sulfur atom is in the +6 oxidation state while the four oxygen atoms are each in the -2 state.

a. 1703 Genroku earthquake
c. Sulfate
b. 1700 Cascadia earthquake
d. 1509 Istanbul earthquake

Chapter 3. Atoms, Elements, Minerals, Rocks

23. _____ defines an important group of generally dark-colored rock-forming inosilicate minerals, composed of double chain SiO_4 tetrahedra, linked at the vertices and generally containing ions of iron and/or magnesium in their structures. They crystallize into two crystal systems, monoclinic and orthorhombic. In chemical composition and general characteristics they are similar to the pyroxenes. They are minerals of either igneous or metamorphic origin; in the former case occurring as constituents (hornblende) of igneous rocks, such as granite, diorite, andesite and others. Those of metamorphic origin include examples such as those developed in limestones by contact metamorphism (tremolite) and those formed by the alteration of other ferromagnesian minerals (hornblende).
   a. Amphibole
   b. AASHTO Soil Classification System
   c. AL 129-1
   d. AL 333

24. _____ is a naturally occurring material composed primarily of fine-grained minerals, which show plasticity through a variable range of water content, and which can be hardened when dried and/or fired. _____ deposits are mostly composed of _____ minerals (phyllosilicate minerals), minerals which impart plasticity and harden when fired and/or dried, and variable amounts of water trapped in the mineral structure by polar attraction. Organic materials which do not impart plasticity may also be a part of _____ deposits.
   a. 1509 Istanbul earthquake
   b. Clay
   c. 1703 Genroku earthquake
   d. 1700 Cascadia earthquake

25. The _____ are a group of important rock-forming silicate minerals found in many igneous and metamorphic rocks. They share a common structure consisting of single chains of silica tetrahedra and they crystallize in the monoclinic and orthorhombic systems. _____ have the general formula $XY(Si,Al)_2O_6$ (where X represents calcium, sodium, iron^{+2} and magnesium and more rarely zinc, manganese and lithium and Y represents ions of smaller size, such as chromium, aluminium, iron^{+3}, magnesium, manganese, scandium, titanium, vanadium and even iron^{+2}).
   a. 1700 Cascadia earthquake
   b. 1703 Genroku earthquake
   c. 1509 Istanbul earthquake
   d. Pyroxenes

26. _____ is a microcrystalline variety of quartz , chiefly chalcedony, characterised by its fineness of grain and brightness of color. Although _____s may be found in various kinds of rock, they are classically associated with volcanic rocks but can be common in certain metamorphic rocks.

Colorful _____s and other chalcedonies were obtained over 3,000 years ago from the Achates River, now called Dirillo, in Sicily.

   a. AL 129-1
   b. AL 333
   c. AASHTO Soil Classification System
   d. Agate

27. _____ is a cryptocrystalline form of silica, composed of very fine intergrowths of the minerals quartz and moganite. These are both silica minerals, but they differ in that quartz has a trigonal crystal structure, whilst moganite is monoclinic.

   _____ has a waxy luster, and may be semitransparent or translucent.

   a. Chalcedony
   b. 1509 Istanbul earthquake
   c. Silicate minerals
   d. Mineraloid

28. _____ are a group of rock-forming tectosilicate minerals which make up as much as 60% of the Earth's crust.

_____ crystallize from magma in both intrusive and extrusive igneous rocks, as veins, and are also present in many types of metamorphic rock. Rock formed entirely of plagioclase feldspar is known as anorthosite.

    a. 1509 Istanbul earthquake
    b. 1703 Genroku earthquake
    c. 1700 Cascadia earthquake
    d. Feldspars

29. _____ is the second most abundant mineral in the Earth's continental crust . It is made up of a framework of silicon-oxygen tetrahedra SiO_4, with each silicon shared between two oxygens to give the overall formula SiO_2. _____ has a hardness of 7 on the Mohs scale and a density of 2.65 g/cmÂ³.

    a. 1700 Cascadia earthquake
    b. Shocked quartz
    c. Quartz
    d. 1509 Istanbul earthquake

30. _____ is a group of phosphate minerals, usually referring to hydroxylapatite, fluorapatite, and chlorapatite $F^{>-}$, or $Cl^{>-}$ ions, respectively, in the crystal. The formula of the admixture of the three most common endmembers is written as $Ca_5(PO_4)_3(OH, F, Cl)$, and the formulae of the individual minerals are written as $Ca_5(PO_4)_3(OH)$, $Ca_5(PO_4)_3F$ and $Ca_5(PO_4)_3Cl$, respectively.

_____ is one of few minerals that are produced and used by biological micro-environmental systems.

    a. AASHTO Soil Classification System
    b. AL 129-1
    c. Aragonite
    d. Apatite

31. _____ is a carbonate mineral, one of the two common, naturally occurring polymorphs of calcium carbonate, $CaCO_3$. The other polymorph is the mineral calcite. _____'s crystal lattice differs from that of calcite, resulting in a different crystal shape, an orthorhombic system with acicular crystals.

    a. AL 129-1
    b. AASHTO Soil Classification System
    c. Apatite
    d. Aragonite

32. _____ is a carbonate mineral and the most stable polymorph of calcium carbonate ($CaCO_3$.) The other polymorphs are the minerals aragonite and vaterite. Aragonite will change to _____ at 470>°C, and vaterite is even less stable.

_____ is a common constituent of sedimentary rocks, limestone in particular, much of which is formed from the shells of dead marine organisms. Approximately 10% of sedimentary rock is limestone.

    a. 1703 Genroku earthquake
    b. 1700 Cascadia earthquake
    c. 1509 Istanbul earthquake
    d. Calcite

33. _____ is the name of a sedimentary carbonate rock and a mineral, both composed of calcium magnesium carbonate $CaMg_2$ found in crystals.

_____ rock (also dolostone) is composed predominantly of the mineral _____. Limestone that is partially replaced by _____ is referred to as dolomitic limestone, or in old U.S. geologic literature as magnesian limestone.

Chapter 3. Atoms, Elements, Minerals, Rocks 27

    a. Dolostone   b. Pelagic sediments
    c. Superficial deposits   d. Dolomite

34. _____ is a mineral - anhydrous calcium sulfate, $CaSO_4$. It is in the orthorhombic crystal system, with three directions of perfect cleavage parallel to the three planes of symmetry. It is not isomorphous with the orthorhombic barium (baryte) and strontium (celestine) sulfates, as might be expected from the chemical formulas.
    a. AASHTO Soil Classification System   b. Aragonite
    c. Anhydrite   d. AL 129-1

35. _____ is one of the three main rock types (the others being sedimentary and metamorphic rock.) _____ is formed by magma (molten rock) being cooled and becoming solid . They may form with or without crystallization, either below the surface as intrusive (plutonic) rocks or on the surface as extrusive (volcanic) rocks. They make up approximately 95% of the upper part of the Earth's crust, but their great abundance is hidden on the Earth's surface by a relatively thin but widespread layer of sedimentary and metamorphic rocks.
    a. Extrusive   b. Ignimbrite
    c. Igneous differentiation   d. Igneous rock

36. _____ is a layer of loose, heterogeneous material covering solid rock. It includes dust, soil, broken rock, and other related materials and is present on Earth, the Moon, some asteroids, and other planets. The term was first defined by George P. Merrill in 1897 who stated, 'In places this covering is made up of material originating through rock-weathering or plant growth in situ. In other instances it is of fragmental and more or less decomposed matter drifted by wind, water or ice from other sources. This entire mantle of unconsolidated material, whatever its nature or origin, it is proposed to call the _____.'
    a. 1509 Istanbul earthquake   b. 1703 Genroku earthquake
    c. 1700 Cascadia earthquake   d. Regolith

37. _____ is a mineral composed primarily of titanium dioxide, TiO_2.

_____ is the most common natural form of TiO_2. Two rarer polymorphs of TiO_2 are known:

- anatase (sometimes known by the obsolete name 'octahedrite'), a tetragonal mineral of pseudo-octahedral habit; and
- brookite, an orthorhombic mineral.

_____ has among the highest refractive indices of any known mineral and also exhibits high dispersion. Natural _____ may contain up to 10% iron and significant amounts of niobium and tantalum.

    a. 1509 Istanbul earthquake   b. Rutile
    c. 1700 Cascadia earthquake   d. 1703 Genroku earthquake

38. _____ is one of the three main rock types (the others being igneous and metamorphic rock.) _____ is formed by deposition and consolidation of mineral and organic material and from precipitation of minerals from solution. The processes that form _____ occur at the surface of the Earth and within bodies of water.
    a. Sedimentary rock   b. Large igneous provinces
    c. Serpentinite   d. Felsic

Chapter 3. Atoms, Elements, Minerals, Rocks

39. The _____ is a chronologic schema (or idealized model) relating stratigraphy to time that is used by geologists, paleontologists and other earth scientists to describe the timing and relationships between events that have occurred during the history of the Earth. The table of geologic time spans presented here agrees with the dates and nomenclature proposed by the International Commission on Stratigraphy, and uses the standard color codes of the United States Geological Survey.

Evidence from radiometric dating indicates that the Earth is about 4.570 billion years old.

- a. 1703 Genroku earthquake
- b. Geologic time scale
- c. 1700 Cascadia earthquake
- d. 1509 Istanbul earthquake

40. The _____ is a fundamental concept in geology that describes the dynamic transitions through geologic time among the three main rock types: sedimentary, metamorphic, and igneous. Each type of rock is altered or destroyed when it is forced out of its equilibrium conditions. An igneous rock such as basalt may break down and dissolve when exposed to the atmosphere, or melt as it is subducted under a continent.
- a. Felsic
- b. Rock cycle
- c. Metamorphic zone
- d. Vesicular texture

41. _____ is the result of the transformation of an existing rock type, the protolith, in a process called metamorphism, which means 'change in form'. The protolith is subjected to heat and pressure (temperatures greater than 150 to 200 >°C and pressures of 1500 bars) causing profound physical and/or chemical change. The protolith may be sedimentary rock, igneous rock or another older _____.
- a. Laccolith
- b. Pluton
- c. Serpentinite
- d. Metamorphic rock

42. _____ describes the large scale motions of Earth's lithosphere. The theory encompasses the older concepts of continental drift, developed during the first decades of the 20th century by Alfred Wegener, and seafloor spreading, understood during the 1960s.

The outermost part of the Earth's interior is made up of two layers: the lithosphere and the asthenosphere.

- a. Continental crust
- b. Nappe
- c. Mantle convection
- d. Plate tectonics

43. In materials science, _____ is the distribution of crystallographic orientations of a polycrystalline sample. A sample in which these orientations are fully random is said to have no _____. If the crystallographic orientations are not random, but have some preferred orientation, then the sample has a weak, strong, or moderate _____.
- a. Geothermal
- b. Diamond Head
- c. Platform
- d. Texture

44. _____s is a field of study within geology concerned generally with the structures within the lithosphere of the Earth and particularly with the forces and movements that have operated in a region to create these structures.

_____s is concerned with the orogenies and _____ development of cratons and _____ terranes as well as the earthquake and volcanic belts which directly affect much of the global population. _____ studies are also important for understanding erosion patterns in geomorphology and as guides for the economic geologist searching for petroleum and metallic ores.

a. Fault trace
b. Tectonic
c. Cocos Plate
d. Rivera Plate

45. _____ is a field of study within geology concerned generally with the structures within the lithosphere of the Earth and particularly with the forces and movements that have operated in a region to create these structures.

_____ is concerned with the orogenies and tectonic development of cratons and tectonic terranes as well as the earthquake and volcanic belts which directly affect much of the global population. Tectonic studies are also important for understanding erosion patterns in geomorphology and as guides for the economic geologist searching for petroleum and metallic ores.

a. Rivera Plate
b. Cocos Plate
c. Tectonics
d. Fault trace

Chapter 4. Igneous Rocks: Products of Earth's Internal Fire

1. A _____ is an opening in a planet's surface or crust, which allows hot, molten rock, ash, and gases to escape from below the surface. Volcanic activity involving the extrusion of rock tends to form mountains or features like mountains over a period of time.
   a. 1703 Genroku earthquake
   b. 1700 Cascadia earthquake
   c. 1509 Istanbul earthquake
   d. Volcano

2. _____ is one of the three main rock types (the others being sedimentary and metamorphic rock.) _____ is formed by magma (molten rock) being cooled and becoming solid . They may form with or without crystallization, either below the surface as intrusive (plutonic) rocks or on the surface as extrusive (volcanic) rocks. They make up approximately 95% of the upper part of the Earth's crust, but their great abundance is hidden on the Earth's surface by a relatively thin but widespread layer of sedimentary and metamorphic rocks.
   a. Extrusive
   b. Ignimbrite
   c. Igneous rock
   d. Igneous differentiation

3. In thermodynamics, an _____ or an isocaloric process is a thermodynamic process in which no heat is transferred to or from the working fluid. Conversely, a process that involves heat transfer (addition or loss of heat to the surroundings) is generally called diabatic.
   a. AL 333
   b. Adiabatic process
   c. AASHTO Soil Classification System
   d. AL 129-1

4. _____ is a name given to certain typically dark-coloured igneous rocks which are so fine-grained that their component mineral crystals are not detected by the unaided eye. This texture results from rapid cooling in volcanic or hypabyssal environments.

   They are commonly porphyritic, having large crystals embedded in the fine groundmass or matrix.

   a. AL 129-1
   b. AASHTO Soil Classification System
   c. Aphanite
   d. AL 333

5. _____ refers to the mode of igneous volcanic rock formation in which hot magma from inside the Earth flows out (extrudes) onto the surface as lava or explodes violently into the atmosphere to fall back as pyroclastics or tuff. This is opposed to intrusive rock formation, in which magma does not reach the surface.
   a. Ignimbrite
   b. Augen
   c. Igneous rock
   d. Extrusive

6. In geology, an _____ is a body of igneous rock that has crystallized from molten magma below the surface of the Earth. Bodies of magma that solidify underground before they reach the surface of the earth are called plutons the Roman god of the underworld. Correspondingly, rocks of this kind are also referred to as igneous plutonic rocks or igneous intrusive rocks.
   a. AASHTO Soil Classification System
   b. AL 333
   c. AL 129-1
   d. Intrusion

7. _____ is a very coarse-grained igneous rock that has a grain size of 20 mm or more; such rocks are referred to as pegmatitic.

Most _____ is composed of quartz, feldspar and mica; in essence a 'granite'. Rarer 'intermediate' and 'mafic' _____ containing amphibole, Ca-plagioclase feldspar, pyroxene and other minerals are known, found in recrystallised zones and apophyses associated with large layered intrusions.

   a. 1703 Genroku earthquake   b. Pegmatite
   c. 1509 Istanbul earthquake   d. 1700 Cascadia earthquake

8. A _____ is an igneous rock having the grains of its essential minerals large enough to be seen macroscopically, i.e. are distinguishable with the unaided eye. Synonymous with coarse grained or megascopically crystalline. Cf: aphanitic.

   a. Scoria   b. Phanerite
   c. Welded tuff   d. Lopolith

9. A _____ is a relatively large and usually conspicuous crystal distinctly larger than the grains of the rock groundmass of a porphyritic igneous rock. _____s often have euhedral forms either due to early growth within a magma or by post-emplacement recrystallization.

Plagioclase _____s often exhibit zoning with a more calcic core surrounded by progressively more sodic rinds.

   a. Sedimentary rock   b. Rock cycle
   c. Phenocryst   d. Migmatite

10. In materials science, _____ is the distribution of crystallographic orientations of a polycrystalline sample. A sample in which these orientations are fully random is said to have no _____. If the crystallographic orientations are not random, but have some preferred orientation, then the sample has a weak, strong, or moderate _____.

   a. Diamond Head   b. Geothermal
   c. Platform   d. Texture

11. _____ defines an important group of generally dark-colored rock-forming inosilicate minerals, composed of double chain SiO_4 tetrahedra, linked at the vertices and generally containing ions of iron and/or magnesium in their structures. They crystallize into two crystal systems, monoclinic and orthorhombic. In chemical composition and general characteristics they are similar to the pyroxenes. They are minerals of either igneous or metamorphic origin; in the former case occurring as constituents (hornblende) of igneous rocks, such as granite, diorite, andesite and others. Those of metamorphic origin include examples such as those developed in limestones by contact metamorphism (tremolite) and those formed by the alteration of other ferromagnesian minerals (hornblende).

   a. AL 129-1   b. AASHTO Soil Classification System
   c. AL 333   d. Amphibole

12. _____ are a group of rock-forming tectosilicate minerals which make up as much as 60% of the Earth's crust.

_____ crystallize from magma in both intrusive and extrusive igneous rocks, as veins, and are also present in many types of metamorphic rock. Rock formed entirely of plagioclase feldspar is known as anorthosite.

Chapter 4. Igneous Rocks: Products of Earth's Internal Fire

a. 1703 Genroku earthquake
b. 1700 Cascadia earthquake
c. Feldspars
d. 1509 Istanbul earthquake

13. _____ is a naturally occurring glass formed as an extrusive igneous rock. It is produced when felsic lava extruded from a volcano cools without crystal growth. _____ is commonly found within the margins of rhyolitic lava flows known as _____ flows, where the chemical composition (high silica content) induces a high viscosity and polymerization degree of the lava.

a. AL 333
b. Obsidian
c. AL 129-1
d. AASHTO Soil Classification System

14. The mineral _____ is a magnesium iron silicate with the formula $(Mg,Fe)_2SiO_4$. It is one of the most common minerals on Earth, and has also been identified in meteorites and on the Moon, Mars, and comet Wild 2.

The ratio of magnesium and iron varies between the two endmembers of the solid solution series: forsterite (Mg-endmember) and fayalite (Fe-endmember.)

a. AL 333
b. Olivine
c. AL 129-1
d. AASHTO Soil Classification System

15. The _____ are a group of important rock-forming silicate minerals found in many igneous and metamorphic rocks. They share a common structure consisting of single chains of silica tetrahedra and they crystallize in the monoclinic and orthorhombic systems. _____ have the general formula $XY(Si,Al)_2O_6$ (where X represents calcium, sodium, iron^{+2} and magnesium and more rarely zinc, manganese and lithium and Y represents ions of smaller size, such as chromium, aluminium, iron^{+3}, magnesium, manganese, scandium, titanium, vanadium and even iron^{+2}).

a. 1700 Cascadia earthquake
b. Pyroxenes
c. 1703 Genroku earthquake
d. 1509 Istanbul earthquake

16. _____ is the second most abundant mineral in the Earth's continental crust. It is made up of a framework of silicon-oxygen tetrahedra SiO_4, with each silicon shared between two oxygens to give the overall formula SiO_2. _____ has a hardness of 7 on the Mohs scale and a density of 2.65 g/cmÂ³.

a. 1700 Cascadia earthquake
b. 1509 Istanbul earthquake
c. Shocked quartz
d. Quartz

17. The _____ is a chronologic schema (or idealized model) relating stratigraphy to time that is used by geologists, paleontologists and other earth scientists to describe the timing and relationships between events that have occurred during the history of the Earth. The table of geologic time spans presented here agrees with the dates and nomenclature proposed by the International Commission on Stratigraphy, and uses the standard color codes of the United States Geological Survey.

Evidence from radiometric dating indicates that the Earth is about 4.570 billion years old.

a. 1700 Cascadia earthquake
b. 1703 Genroku earthquake
c. 1509 Istanbul earthquake
d. Geologic time scale

Chapter 4. Igneous Rocks: Products of Earth's Internal Fire

18. _____ is an igneous, volcanic rock, of intermediate composition, with aphanitic to porphyritic texture. The mineral assemblage is typically dominated by plagioclase plus pyroxene and/or hornblende. Magnetite, zircon, apatite, ilmenite, biotite, and garnet are common accessory minerals.

    a. AL 333
    b. AL 129-1
    c. Andesite
    d. AASHTO Soil Classification System

19. _____ refers to a large group of dark, coarse-grained, intrusive igneous rocks chemically equivalent to basalt. The rocks are plutonic, formed when molten magma is trapped beneath the Earth's surface and cools into a crystalline mass.

The vast majority of the Earth's surface is underlain by _____ within the oceanic crust, produced by basalt magmatism at mid-ocean ridges.

    a. 1703 Genroku earthquake
    b. 1700 Cascadia earthquake
    c. 1509 Istanbul earthquake
    d. Gabbro

20. _____ is a common and widely occurring type of intrusive, felsic, igneous rock. _____ has a medium to coarse texture, occasionally with some individual crystals larger than the groundmass forming a rock known as porphyry. _____s can be pink to dark gray or even black, depending on their chemistry and mineralogy.

    a. Granite
    b. 1700 Cascadia earthquake
    c. 1509 Istanbul earthquake
    d. 1703 Genroku earthquake

21. _____ is an intrusive igneous rock similar to granite, but contains more plagioclase than potassium feldspar. It usually contains abundant biotite mica and hornblende, giving it a darker appearance than true granite. Mica may be present in well-formed hexagonal crystals, and hornblende may appear as needle-like crystals.

    a. 1703 Genroku earthquake
    b. 1700 Cascadia earthquake
    c. Granodiorite
    d. 1509 Istanbul earthquake

22. A _____ is a dense, coarse-grained igneous rock, consisting mostly of the minerals olivine and pyroxene. _____ is ultramafic, as the rock contains less than 45% silica. It is high in magnesium, reflecting the high proportions of magnesium-rich olivine, with appreciable iron.

_____ is the dominant rock of the upper part of the Earth's mantle. The compositions of _____ nodules found in certain basalts and diamond pipes (kimberlites) are of special interest, because they provide samples of the Earth's Mantle roots of continents brought up from depths from about 30 km or so to depths at least as great as about 200 km.

    a. 1703 Genroku earthquake
    b. 1700 Cascadia earthquake
    c. 1509 Istanbul earthquake
    d. Peridotite

23. _____ is an igneous, volcanic (extrusive) rock, of felsic (silicon-rich) composition. It may have any texture from aphanitic to porphyritic. The mineral assemblage is usually quartz, alkali feldspar and plagioclase. Biotite and hornblende are common accessory minerals.

Chapter 4. Igneous Rocks: Products of Earth's Internal Fire

_____ can be considered as the extrusive equivalent to the plutonic granite rock, and consequently, outcroppings of it often bear a resemblance to granite. Due to their high content of silica and low iron and magnesium contents, _____ melts are highly polymerized and form highly viscous lavas.

- a. 1509 Istanbul earthquake
- b. 1700 Cascadia earthquake
- c. 1703 Genroku earthquake
- d. Rhyolite

24. _____ are coarse accumulations of large blocks of volcanic material that contain at least 75% bombs. Volcanic bombs differ from volcanic blocks in that their shape records fluidal surfaces: they may, for example, have ropy, cauliform, scoriaceous, or folded, chilled margins and spindle, spatter, ribbon, ragged, or amoeboid shapes. Globular masses of lava may have been shot from the crater at a time when partly molten lava was exposed, and was frequently shattered by sudden outbursts of steam.

- a. AL 333
- b. AL 129-1
- c. AASHTO Soil Classification System
- d. Agglomerates

25. _____ is a common extrusive volcanic rock. It is usually grey to black and fine-grained due to rapid cooling of lava at the surface of a planet. It may be porphyritic containing larger crystals in a fine matrix, or vesicular, or frothy scoria.

- a. 1700 Cascadia earthquake
- b. Basalt
- c. 1509 Istanbul earthquake
- d. 1703 Genroku earthquake

26. _____ are clastic rocks composed solely or primarily of volcanic materials. Where the volcanic material has been transported and reworked through mechanical action, such as by wind or water, these rocks are termed volcaniclastic. Commonly associated with explosive volcanic activity - such as Plinian or krakatoan eruption styles, or phreatomagmatic eruptions - pyroclastic deposits are commonly formed from airborne ash, lapilli and bombs or blocks ejected from the volcano itself, mixed in with shattered country rock.

- a. Welded tuff
- b. Great Dyke
- c. Pyroclastic rocks
- d. Lopolith

27. _____ is air-fall material produced by a volcanic eruption regardless of composition or fragment size. _____ is typically rhyolitic in composition, as most explosive volcanoes are the product of the more viscous felsic or high silica magmas.

Volcanologists also refer to airborne fragments as pyroclasts.

- a. Large igneous provinces
- b. Tephra
- c. Laccolith
- d. Sedimentary rock

28. _____ is a type of rock consisting of consolidated volcanic ash ejected from vents during a volcanic eruption. _____ is sometimes called tufa, particularly when used as construction material, although tufa also refers to a quite different rock.

Chapter 4. Igneous Rocks: Products of Earth's Internal Fire   35

The products of a volcanic eruption are volcanic gases, lava, steam, and tephra. Magma is blown apart when it interacts violently with volcanic gases and steam. Solid material produced and thrown into the air by such volcanic eruptions is called tephra, regardless of composition or fragment size. If the resulting pieces of ejecta are small enough, the material is called volcanic ash, defined as such particles less than 2 mm in diameter, sand-sized or smaller.

 a. Tuff
 b. Lopolith
 c. Phanerite
 d. Pyroclastic rocks

29. A _____ in geology is an intrusive igneous rock body that crystallized from a magma slowly cooling below the surface of the Earth. _____s include batholiths, dikes, sills, laccoliths, lopoliths, and other igneous bodies. In practice, '_____' usually refers to a distinctive mass of igneous rock, typically kilometers in dimension, without a tabular shape like those of dikes and sills.
 a. Matrix
 b. Tephra
 c. Petrology
 d. Pluton

30. _____ is a pyroclastic rock, of any origin, that was sufficiently hot at the time of deposition to weld together. Strictly speaking, if the rock contains scattered pea-sized fragments or fiamme in it, it is called a welded lapilli-tuff. They (and welded lapilli-tuffs) can be of fallout origin, or deposited from pyroclastic density currents, as in the case of ignimbrites.
 a. Country rock
 b. Flood basalt
 c. Pyroclastic rocks
 d. Welded tuff

31. A _____ or dyke in geology is a type of sheet intrusion referring to any geologic body that cuts discordantly across

- planar wall rock structures, such as bedding or foliation
- massive rock formations, like igneous/magmatic intrusions and salt diapirs.

They can therefore be either intrusive or sedimentary in origin.

An intrusive _____ is an igneous body with a very high aspect ratio, which means that its thickness is usually much smaller than the other two dimensions. Thickness can vary from sub-centimeter scale to many meters and the lateral dimensions can extend over many kilometers. A _____ is an intrusion into an opening cross-cutting fissure, shouldering aside other pre-existing layers or bodies of rock; this implies that a _____ is always younger than the rocks that contain it.

 a. Detritus
 b. Type locality
 c. Gradualism
 d. Dike

32. A _____ is a large emplacement of igneous intrusive rock that forms from cooled magma deep in the Earth's crust. they are almost always made mostly of felsic or intermediate rock-types, such as granite, quartz monzonite, or diorite

Although they may appear uniform, _____s are in fact structures with complex histories and compositions.

a. Welded tuff
b. Litchfieldite
c. Country rock
d. Batholith

33. A _____ is an igneous intrusion (or concordant pluton) that has been injected between two layers of sedimentary rock. The pressure of the magma is high enough that the overlying strata are forced upward, giving the _____ a dome or mushroom-like form with a generally planar base.

They tend to form at relatively shallow depths and are typically formed by relatively viscous magmas, such as those that crystallize to diorite, granodiorite, and granite. Cooling underground takes place slowly, giving time for larger crystals to form in the cooling magma. The surface rock above the _____ often erodes away completely, leaving the core mound of igneous rock.

a. Metavolcanic rock
b. Laccolith
c. Pluton
d. Serpentinite

34. A _____ is a volcanic landform created when magma hardens within a vent on an active volcano. When forming, a _____ can cause an extreme build-up of pressure if volatile-charged magma is trapped beneath it, and this can sometimes lead to an explosive eruption. If a plug is preserved, erosion may remove the surrounding rock while the erosion-resistant plug remains, producing a distinctive landform.

a. 1703 Genroku earthquake
b. 1700 Cascadia earthquake
c. 1509 Istanbul earthquake
d. Volcanic plug

35. _____ are subterranean geological structures formed by the violent, supersonic eruption of deep-origin volcanoes. They are considered to be a type of diatreme. _____ are composed of a deep, narrow cone of solidified magma (described as 'carrot-shaped'), and are usually largely composed of one of two characteristic rock types -- kimberlite or lamproite.

a. Volcanic pipes
b. Supervolcano
c. Pyroclastic flow
d. Pit crater

36. _____ is a process accommodating the ascent of magmatic bodies from their sources in the mantle (geology) or lower crust to the surface. The process involves the mechanical disintegration of the surrounding country/host rock, typically through fracturing due to pressure increases associated with thermal expansion of the host rock in proximity of the interface with the melt. Once fractures are formed, melt and/or volatiles will typically invade, widening the fracture and promoting the foundering of host rock blocks (i.e. stoped blocks.)

a. Transgression
b. Permineralization
c. Hydrothermal
d. Stoping

37. The _____ is the most significant regional geologic distinction in the Pacific Ocean basin. It separates the mafic basaltic volcanic rocks of the Central Pacific Basin from the partially submerged continental areas of more felsic andesitic volcanic rock on its margins. The _____ parallels the subduction zones and deep oceanic trenches around the Pacific basin.

a. AASHTO Soil Classification System
b. AL 333
c. Andesite Line
d. AL 129-1

Chapter 4. Igneous Rocks: Products of Earth's Internal Fire

38. _____ is molten rock that is found beneath the surface of the Earth, and may also exist on other terrestrial planets. Besides molten rock, _____ may also contain suspended crystals and gas bubbles. _____ often collects in a _____ chamber inside a volcano. _____ is capable of intrusion into adjacent rocks, extrusion onto the surface as lava, and explosive ejection as tephra to form pyroclastic rock.

a. Magma
b. Sedimentary rock
c. Large igneous provinces
d. Groundmass

39. _____ is the solid-state recrystallization of pre-existing rocks due to changes in physical and chemical conditions, primarily heat, pressure, and the introduction of chemically active fluids. Both mineralogical, chemical and crystallographic changes can occur during this process.

Three types of _____ exist: dynamic, contact and regional.

a. Lake capture
b. Pumice raft
c. Gibraltar Arc
d. Metamorphism

40. _____ is a process of melting that takes place in the Earth's mantle. The melting temperatures are unlikely high enough to melt the entire source rock, and only portions of or some of the minerals they contain melt.

a. Submarine eruption
b. Volcanic blocks
c. Raton hotspot
d. Partial melting

41. _____ is one of the most important geochemical and physical processes operating within the Earth's crust and mantle. _____ is the removal and segregation from a melt of mineral precipitates; except in special cases, removal of the crystals changes the composition of the magma. _____ in silicate melts (magmas) is complex compared to crystallization in chemical systems at constant pressure and composition, because changes in pressure and composition can have dramatic effects on magma evolution.

a. Combe
b. Deformation
c. Fractional crystallization
d. Texture

42. _____ is the (natural or artificial) process of formation of solid crystals precipitating from a solution, melt or more rarely deposited directly from a gas. _____ is also a chemical solid-liquid separation technique, in which mass transfer of a solute from the liquid solution to a pure solid crystalline phase occurs.

The _____ process consists of two major events, nucleation and crystal growth.

a. 1509 Istanbul earthquake
b. 1700 Cascadia earthquake
c. 1703 Genroku earthquake
d. Crystallization

43. _____ circulation in its most general sense is the circulation of hot water; 'hydros' in the Greek meaning water and 'thermos' meaning heat. _____ circulation occurs most often in the vicinity of sources of heat within the Earth's crust. This generally occurs near volcanic activity, but can occur in the deep crust related to the intrusion of granite, or as the result of orogeny or metamorphism.

a. Transgression
b. Headward erosion
c. Hydrothermal
d. Seafloor spreading

Chapter 4. Igneous Rocks: Products of Earth's Internal Fire

44. An _____ is a section of the Earth's oceanic crust and the underlying upper mantle that has been uplifted or emplaced to be exposed within continental crustal rocks. Ophio is Greek for 'snake', lite means 'stone' from the Greek lithos.

The term _____ was originally used by Alexandre Brongniart for an assemblage of green rocks (serpentine, diabase) in the Alps; Steinmann (1927) later modified its use to include serpentine, pillow lava, and chert ('Steinmann's trinity'), again based on occurrences in the Alps.

    a. AASHTO Soil Classification System
    b. AL 129-1
    c. AL 333
    d. Ophiolite

45. In materials science, _____ is a change in the shape or size of an object due to an applied force. This can be a result of tensile (pulling) forces, compressive (pushing) forces, shear, bending or torsion (twisting.) _____ is often described as strain.

    a. Lingula
    b. Stack
    c. Submersion
    d. Deformation

46. _____ describes the large scale motions of Earth's lithosphere. The theory encompasses the older concepts of continental drift, developed during the first decades of the 20th century by Alfred Wegener, and seafloor spreading, understood during the 1960s.

The outermost part of the Earth's interior is made up of two layers: the lithosphere and the asthenosphere.

    a. Continental crust
    b. Mantle convection
    c. Nappe
    d. Plate tectonics

47. _____s is a field of study within geology concerned generally with the structures within the lithosphere of the Earth and particularly with the forces and movements that have operated in a region to create these structures.

_____s is concerned with the orogenies and _____ development of cratons and _____ terranes as well as the earthquake and volcanic belts which directly affect much of the global population. _____ studies are also important for understanding erosion patterns in geomorphology and as guides for the economic geologist searching for petroleum and metallic ores.

    a. Tectonic
    b. Fault trace
    c. Cocos Plate
    d. Rivera Plate

48. _____ is a field of study within geology concerned generally with the structures within the lithosphere of the Earth and particularly with the forces and movements that have operated in a region to create these structures.

_____ is concerned with the orogenies and tectonic development of cratons and tectonic terranes as well as the earthquake and volcanic belts which directly affect much of the global population. Tectonic studies are also important for understanding erosion patterns in geomorphology and as guides for the economic geologist searching for petroleum and metallic ores.

a. Cocos Plate
b. Fault trace
c. Tectonics
d. Rivera Plate

Chapter 5. Magmas and Volcanoes

1. _____ is molten rock expelled by a volcano during eruption. When first expelled from a volcanic vent, it is a liquid at temperatures from 700 >°C to 1,200 >°C (1,300 >°F to 2,200 >°F.) Although _____ is quite viscous, with about 100,000 times the viscosity of water, it can flow great distances before cooling and solidifying, because of both its thixotropic and shear thinning properties.
   a. Lava
   b. Volcanic ash
   c. Cinder
   d. Pyroclastic flow

2. _____ is molten rock that is found beneath the surface of the Earth, and may also exist on other terrestrial planets. Besides molten rock, _____ may also contain suspended crystals and gas bubbles. _____ often collects in a _____ chamber inside a volcano. _____ is capable of intrusion into adjacent rocks, extrusion onto the surface as lava, and explosive ejection as tephra to form pyroclastic rock.
   a. Large igneous provinces
   b. Magma
   c. Sedimentary rock
   d. Groundmass

3. _____ is a common extrusive volcanic rock. It is usually grey to black and fine-grained due to rapid cooling of lava at the surface of a planet. It may be porphyritic containing larger crystals in a fine matrix, or vesicular, or frothy scoria.
   a. 1703 Genroku earthquake
   b. Basalt
   c. 1509 Istanbul earthquake
   d. 1700 Cascadia earthquake

4. _____ is one of the most important geochemical and physical processes operating within the Earth's crust and mantle. _____ is the removal and segregation from a melt of mineral precipitates; except in special cases, removal of the crystals changes the composition of the magma. _____ in silicate melts (magmas) is complex compared to crystallization in chemical systems at constant pressure and composition, because changes in pressure and composition can have dramatic effects on magma evolution.
   a. Texture
   b. Deformation
   c. Fractional crystallization
   d. Combe

5. _____ is the solid-state recrystallization of pre-existing rocks due to changes in physical and chemical conditions, primarily heat, pressure, and the introduction of chemically active fluids. Both mineralogical, chemical and crystallographic changes can occur during this process.

   Three types of _____ exist: dynamic, contact and regional.

   a. Pumice raft
   b. Lake capture
   c. Gibraltar Arc
   d. Metamorphism

6. _____ is a measure of the resistance of a fluid which is being deformed by either shear stress or extensional stress. In everyday terms (and for fluids only), _____ is 'thickness'. Thus, water is 'thin', having a lower _____, while honey is 'thick' having a higher _____.
   a. Tensile stress
   b. Viscosity
   c. Thixotropy
   d. Shear stress

7. _____ are natural conduits through which lava travels beneath the surface of a lava flow, expelled by a volcano during an eruption. They can be actively draining lava from a source, or can be extinct, meaning the lava flow has ceased and the rock has cooled and left a long, cave-like channel.

Chapter 5. Magmas and Volcanoes

_____ are formed when an active low-viscosity lava flow develops a continuous and hard crust, which thickens and forms a roof above the still-flowing lava stream.

   a. 1703 Genroku earthquake
   b. Lava tubes
   c. 1509 Istanbul earthquake
   d. 1700 Cascadia earthquake

8. The chemical compound silicon dioxide, also known as _____ , is an oxide of silicon with a chemical formula of SiO_2 and has been known for its hardness since antiquity. _____ is most commonly found in nature as sand or quartz, as well as in the cell walls of diatoms. It is a principal component of most types of glass and substances such as concrete.
   a. Silica
   b. 1703 Genroku earthquake
   c. 1509 Istanbul earthquake
   d. 1700 Cascadia earthquake

9. In geology, _____ is the process that takes place at convergent boundaries by which one tectonic plate moves under another tectonic plate, sinking into the Earth's mantle, as the plates converge. A _____ zone is an area on Earth where two tectonic plates move towards one another and _____ occurs. Rates of _____ are typically measured in centimeters per year, with the average rate of convergence being approximately 2 to 8 centimeters per year (about the rate a fingernail grows.)
   a. Mirovia
   b. Continental collision
   c. Subduction
   d. Motagua Fault

10. _____ form when the vesicular cavities (created by expanding gas bubbles in volcanic lava) are filled with a secondary mineral such as calcite, quartz, chlorite or one of the zeolites, which are deposited by having minerals 'wash' through the pores in the rock They are filled from the outside, making some _____ concentrically layered.
   a. Igneous rock
   b. Extrusive
   c. Augen
   d. Amygdules

11. _____ consists of small tephra, which are bits of pulverized rock and glass created by volcanic eruptions, less than 2 millimetres (0.079 in) in diameter. There are three mechanisms of _____ formation: gas release under decompression causing magmatic eruptions; thermal contraction from chilling on contact with water causing phreatomagmatic eruptions and ejection of entrained particles during steam eruptions causing phreatic eruptions. The violent nature of volcanic eruptions involving steam results in the magma and solid rock surrounding the vent being torn into particles of clay to sand size.
   a. Supervolcano
   b. Wadati-Benioff zone
   c. Cinder
   d. Volcanic ash

12. An _____ is a volcanic term to describe a violent, explosive type of eruption. Mount St. Helens in 1980 was an example. Such an eruption is driven by gas accumulating under great pressure.
   a. AL 129-1
   b. AL 333
   c. AASHTO Soil Classification System
   d. Explosive eruption

13. _____ is a textural term for a volcanic rock that is a solidified frothy lava typically created when super-heated, highly pressurized rock is violently ejected from a volcano. It can be formed when lava and water are mixed. This unusual formation is due to the simultaneous actions of rapid cooling and rapid depressurization.

Chapter 5. Magmas and Volcanoes

    a. Fissure vent
    b. Pumice
    c. Pyroclastic flow
    d. Wadati-Benioff zone

14. _____ is a volcanic rock texture characterised by, or containing many vesicles. The texture is often found in extrusive aphanitic igneous rock. The vesicles are small cavities formed by the expansion of bubbles of gas or steam during the solidification of the rock.

    a. Rock cycle
    b. Pluton
    c. Large igneous provinces
    d. Vesicular texture

15. In materials science, _____ is the distribution of crystallographic orientations of a polycrystalline sample. A sample in which these orientations are fully random is said to have no _____. If the crystallographic orientations are not random, but have some preferred orientation, then the sample has a weak, strong, or moderate _____.

    a. Texture
    b. Geothermal
    c. Platform
    d. Diamond Head

16. An _____ consists of hot volcanic ash emitted during an explosive volcanic eruption. The ash forms a column rising many kilometres into the air above the peak of the volcano. In the most explosive eruptions, the _____ may rise over 40 km, penetrating the stratosphere.

    a. AL 333
    b. AL 129-1
    c. AASHTO Soil Classification System
    d. Eruption column

17. _____ are volcanic eruptions marked by their similarity to the eruption of Mount Vesuvius in AD 79 (as described in a letter written by Pliny the Younger), which killed Pliny the Elder.

_____ are marked by columns of gas and volcanic ash extending high into the stratosphere, a high layer of the atmosphere. The key characteristics are ejection of large amount of pumice and very powerful continuous gas blast eruptions.

    a. Limnic eruption
    b. Phreatic eruption
    c. Plinian eruptions
    d. Phreatomagmatic eruptions

18. _____ is air-fall material produced by a volcanic eruption regardless of composition or fragment size. _____ is typically rhyolitic in composition, as most explosive volcanoes are the product of the more viscous felsic or high silica magmas.

Volcanologists also refer to airborne fragments as pyroclasts.

    a. Sedimentary rock
    b. Large igneous provinces
    c. Laccolith
    d. Tephra

19. An _____ is the deposit of a pyroclastic density current a hot suspension of particles and gases that flows rapidly from a volcano, driven by a greater density than the surrounding atmosphere. _____s are often of dacitic or rhyolitic composition.

_____s are made of a very poorly sorted mixture of volcanic ash (or tuff when lithified) and pumice lapilli, commonly with scattered lithic fragments.

Chapter 5. Magmas and Volcanoes

a. Augen
b. Igneous differentiation
c. Ignimbrite
d. Extrusive

20. A _____ is a common and devastating result of some explosive volcanic eruptions. The flows are fast-moving currents of hot gas and rock (collectively known as tephra), which travel away from the volcano at speeds generally as great as 700 km/hr (450 mi/h.) The gas can reach temperatures of about 1,000 >°C (1,830 >°F). The flows normally hug the ground and travel downhill, or spread laterally under gravity. Their speed depends upon the density of the current, the volcanic output rate, and the gradient of the slope.
   a. Lava
   b. Pyroclastic flow
   c. Volcanic ash
   d. Pumice

21. A _____ is generally a large area of exposed Precambrian crystalline igneous and high-grade metamorphic rocks that form tectonically stable areas. In all cases, the age of these rocks is greater than 570 million years and sometimes dates back 2 to 3.5 billion years. They have been little affected by tectonic events following the end of the Precambrian Era, and are relatively flat regions where mountain building, faulting, and other tectonic processes are greatly diminished compared with the activity that occurs at the margins of the _____s and the boundaries between tectonic plates.
   a. 1509 Istanbul earthquake
   b. 1703 Genroku earthquake
   c. 1700 Cascadia earthquake
   d. Shield

22. A _____ is a large volcano with shallow-sloping sides.

They are formed by lava flows of low viscosity - lava that flows easily. Consequently, a volcanic mountain having a broad profile is built up over time by flow after flow of relatively fluid basaltic lava issuing from vents or fissures on the surface of the volcano

   a. Shield volcano
   b. 1703 Genroku earthquake
   c. 1509 Istanbul earthquake
   d. 1700 Cascadia earthquake

23. A _____ is a geological phenomenon which includes a wide range of ground movement, such as rock falls, deep failure of slopes and shallow debris flows, which can occur in offshore, coastal and onshore environments. Although the action of gravity is the primary driving force for a _____ to occur, there are other contributing factors affecting the original slope stability. Typically, pre-conditional factors build up specific sub-surface conditions that make the area/slope prone to failure, whereas the actual _____ often requires a trigger before being released.
   a. 1700 Cascadia earthquake
   b. Mass wasting
   c. 1509 Istanbul earthquake
   d. Landslide

24. A _____ is a marine landslide that transports sediment across the continental shelf and into the deep ocean. A _____ is initiated when the downwards driving stress (gravity and other factors) exceeds the resisting stress of the seafloor slope material causing movements along one or more concave to planer rupture surfaces. _____s take place in a variety of different settings including planes as low as 1>° and can cause significant damage to both life and property.
   a. 1509 Istanbul earthquake
   b. 1700 Cascadia earthquake
   c. 1703 Genroku earthquake
   d. Submarine landslide

Chapter 5. Magmas and Volcanoes

25. A _____ is an opening in a planet's surface or crust, which allows hot, molten rock, ash, and gases to escape from below the surface. Volcanic activity involving the extrusion of rock tends to form mountains or features like mountains over a period of time.
    a. Volcano
    b. 1509 Istanbul earthquake
    c. 1703 Genroku earthquake
    d. 1700 Cascadia earthquake

26. A _____, sometimes called a composite volcano, is a tall, conical volcano with many layers (strata) of hardened lava, tephra, and volcanic ash. They are characterized by a steep profile and periodic, explosive eruptions. The lava that flows from a _____ tends to be viscous; it cools and hardens before spreading far.
    a. Broken Top
    b. Mount Overlord
    c. Mount Baker
    d. Stratovolcano

27. A _____ is a circular depression in the ground caused by volcanic activity. It is typically a basin, circular in form within which occurs a vent (or vents) from which magma erupts as gases, lava, and ejecta. A _____ can be of large dimensions, and sometimes of great depth.
    a. Volcanic crater
    b. 1700 Cascadia earthquake
    c. 1703 Genroku earthquake
    d. 1509 Istanbul earthquake

28. A _____ is a cauldron-like volcanic feature usually formed by the collapse of land following a volcanic eruption such as the one at Yellowstone National Park. They are sometimes confused with volcanic craters.
    a. 1509 Istanbul earthquake
    b. Caldera
    c. 1700 Cascadia earthquake
    d. 1703 Genroku earthquake

29. In volcanology, a _____ is a roughly circular mound-shaped protrusion resulting from the slow extrusion of viscous lava from a volcano. The geochemistry of _____s can vary from basalt to rhyolite although most preserved domes tend to have high silica content.

The characteristic dome shape is attributed to high viscosity that prevents the lava from flowing very far. This high viscosity can be obtained in two ways: by high levels of silica in the magma, or by degassing of fluid magma.

    a. Lava dome
    b. 1700 Cascadia earthquake
    c. 1703 Genroku earthquake
    d. 1509 Istanbul earthquake

30. A _____ is a linear volcanic vent through which lava erupts, usually without any explosive activity. The vent is usually a few meters wide and may be many kilometers long. _____s can cause large flood basalts and lava channels. This type of volcano is usually hard to recognize from the ground and from outer space because it has no central caldera and the surface is mostly flat. The volcano can usually be seen as a crack in the ground or on the ocean floor.
    a. Lava
    b. Cinder
    c. Pyroclastic flow
    d. Fissure vent

31. In geology and earth science, a _____ is an area of highland, usually consisting of relatively flat terrain. A highly eroded _____ is called a dissected _____. A volcanic _____ is a _____ produced by volcanic activity.
    a. 1700 Cascadia earthquake
    b. Plateau
    c. 1703 Genroku earthquake
    d. 1509 Istanbul earthquake

Chapter 5. Magmas and Volcanoes

32. In geology, _____ refers to heat sources within the planet. _____ is technically an adjective (e.g., _____ energy) but in U.S. English the word has attained frequent use as a noun.

The planet's internal heat was originally generated during its accretion, due to gravitational binding energy, and since then additional heat has continued to be generated by decay heat from the radioactive decay of elements.

    a. Cleavage   b. Tarn
    c. Grade   d. Geothermal

33. _____ is power extracted from heat stored in the earth. This geothermal energy originates from the original formation of the planet, from radioactive decay of minerals, and from solar energy absorbed at the surface. It has been used for space heating and bathing since ancient roman times, but is now better known for generating electricity.

    a. Geothermal heat pump   b. Geothermal desalination
    c. Geothermal gradient   d. Geothermal power

34. A _____ is a type of mudflow or landslide composed of pyroclastic material and water that flows down from a volcano, typically along a river valley. The term '_____' originated in the Javanese language of Indonesia. They can be best described as volcanic mudflows. They may not necessarily be caused by volcanic activity, but at the very least do originate from some type of volcanism.

    a. 1703 Genroku earthquake   b. 1700 Cascadia earthquake
    c. 1509 Istanbul earthquake   d. Lahar

35. A _____ or mudslide is the most rapid (up to 80 km/h, or 50 mph) and fluid type of downhill mass wasting. It is a rapid movement of a large mass of mud formed from loose earth and water. Similar terms are mudslide (not very liquid), mud stream, debris flow (e.g. in high mountains), jökulhlaup, and lahar

    a. 1509 Istanbul earthquake   b. 1700 Cascadia earthquake
    c. 1703 Genroku earthquake   d. Mudflow

36. _____ is the principle that the same scientific laws and processes are constant throughout space and time. It applies specifically to sciences that require a long timescale such as geology, astronomy, and paleontology. It was first defined by Charles Lyell (1797 - 1875), who incorporated James Hutton's gradualism into the idea of _____.

    a. Uniformitarianism   b. AASHTO Soil Classification System
    c. AL 333   d. AL 129-1

37. _____ describes the large scale motions of Earth's lithosphere. The theory encompasses the older concepts of continental drift, developed during the first decades of the 20th century by Alfred Wegener, and seafloor spreading, understood during the 1960s.

The outermost part of the Earth's interior is made up of two layers: the lithosphere and the asthenosphere.

    a. Mantle convection   b. Nappe
    c. Continental crust   d. Plate tectonics

38. _____s is a field of study within geology concerned generally with the structures within the lithosphere of the Earth and particularly with the forces and movements that have operated in a region to create these structures.

_____s is concerned with the orogenies and _____ development of cratons and _____ terranes as well as the earthquake and volcanic belts which directly affect much of the global population. _____ studies are also important for understanding erosion patterns in geomorphology and as guides for the economic geologist searching for petroleum and metallic ores.

a. Rivera Plate
c. Tectonic
b. Cocos Plate
d. Fault trace

39. _____ is a field of study within geology concerned generally with the structures within the lithosphere of the Earth and particularly with the forces and movements that have operated in a region to create these structures.

_____ is concerned with the orogenies and tectonic development of cratons and tectonic terranes as well as the earthquake and volcanic belts which directly affect much of the global population. Tectonic studies are also important for understanding erosion patterns in geomorphology and as guides for the economic geologist searching for petroleum and metallic ores.

a. Fault trace
c. Rivera Plate
b. Cocos Plate
d. Tectonics

40. _____ is water located beneath the ground surface in soil pore spaces and in the fractures of lithologic formations. A unit of rock or an unconsolidated deposit is called an aquifer when it can yield a usable quantity of water. The depth at which soil pore spaces or fractures and voids in rock become completely saturated with water is called the water table.

a. Groundwater
c. 1509 Istanbul earthquake
b. Depression focused recharge
d. 1700 Cascadia earthquake

Chapter 6. Weathering and Soils

1. _____ is the naturally occurring, unconsolidated or loose covering on the Earth's surface. _____ is composed of particles of broken rock that have been altered by chemical, biological and environmental processes including weathering and erosion. _____ is different from its parent rock(s) source(s), altered by interactions between the lithosphere, hydrosphere, atmosphere, and the biosphere.
   a. Slump
   b. 1509 Istanbul earthquake
   c. Soil
   d. Topsoil

2. _____ is the decomposition of Earth rocks, soils and their minerals through direct contact with the planet's atmosphere. _____ occurs in situ, or 'with no movement', and thus should not be confused with erosion, which involves the movement of rocks and minerals by agents such as water, ice, wind and gravity.

   Two important classifications of _____ processes exist -- physical and chemical _____.
   a. Physical weathering
   b. 1509 Istanbul earthquake
   c. 1700 Cascadia earthquake
   d. Weathering

3. In thermodynamics, an _____ or an isocaloric process is a thermodynamic process in which no heat is transferred to or from the working fluid. Conversely, a process that involves heat transfer (addition or loss of heat to the surroundings) is generally called diabatic.
   a. AL 333
   b. AL 129-1
   c. AASHTO Soil Classification System
   d. Adiabatic process

4. _____ is a homogeneous, typically nonstratified, porous, friable, slightly coherent, often calcareous, fine-grained, silty, pale yellow or buff, windblown (aeolian) sediment. It generally occurs as a widespread blanket deposit that covers areas of hundreds of square kilometers and tens of meters thick. _____ often stands in either steep or vertical faces.
   a. 1509 Istanbul earthquake
   b. 1703 Genroku earthquake
   c. 1700 Cascadia earthquake
   d. Loess

5. Two important classifications of weathering processes exist -- physical and _____. Mechanical or physical weathering involves the breakdown of rocks and soils through direct contact with atmospheric conditions, such as heat, water, ice and pressure. The second classification, _____, involves the direct effect of atmospheric chemicals or biologically produced chemicals (also known as biological weathering) in the breakdown of rocks, soils and minerals.
   a. 1700 Cascadia earthquake
   b. Chemical weathering
   c. Physical weathering
   d. 1509 Istanbul earthquake

6. In geology the term _____ refers to a fracture in rock where there has been no lateral movement in the plane of the fracture (up, down or sideways) of one side relative to the other. This makes it different from a fault which is defined as a fracture in rock where one side slides laterally past to the other. _____s normally have a regular spacing related to either the mechanical properties of the individual rock or the thickness of the layer involved.
   a. 1509 Istanbul earthquake
   b. 1700 Cascadia earthquake
   c. 1703 Genroku earthquake
   d. Joint

7. Two important classifications of weathering processes exist -- _____ and chemical weathering. Mechanical or _____ involves the breakdown of rocks and soils through direct contact with atmospheric conditions, such as heat, water, ice and pressure. The second classification, chemical weathering, involves the direct effect of atmospheric chemicals or biologically produced chemicals (also known as biological weathering) in the breakdown of rocks, soils and minerals.

Chapter 6. Weathering and Soils

a. Weathering
c. 1700 Cascadia earthquake
b. 1509 Istanbul earthquake
d. Physical weathering

8. _____ can also be called frost shattering or frost-wedging. This type of weathering is common in mountain areas where the temperature is around freezing point. Frost induced weathering, although often attributed to the expansion of freezing water captured in cracks, is generally independent of the water-to-ice expansion. It has long been known that moist soils expand or frost heave upon freezing as a result of water migrating along from unfrozen areas via thin films to collect at growing ice lenses. This same phenomena occurs within pore spaces of rocks.
   a. Weathering
   c. Physical weathering
   b. 1509 Istanbul earthquake
   d. Frost disintegration

9. _____ are flakes of a material that are broken off a larger solid body and can be produced by a variety of mechanisms, including as a result of projectile impact, corrosion, weathering, cavitation, or excessive rolling pressure (as in a ball bearing.) Spalling and spallation both describe the process of surface failure in which _____ is shed.

The terms _____ and spalling have been adopted by particle physicists; in neutron scattering instruments, neutrons are generated by bombarding a uranium target with a stream of atoms.

   a. 1700 Cascadia earthquake
   c. 1703 Genroku earthquake
   b. 1509 Istanbul earthquake
   d. Spall

10. _____ is a chemical reaction during which one or more water molecules are split into hydrogen and hydroxide ions which may go on to participate in further reactions. It is the type of reaction that is used to break down certain polymers, especially those made by step-growth polymerization. Such polymer degradation is usually catalysed by either acid e.g. concentrated sulphuric acid [H_2SO_4] or alkali e.g. sodium hydroxide [NaOH] attack, often increasing with their strength or pH.
    a. 1700 Cascadia earthquake
    c. 1703 Genroku earthquake
    b. 1509 Istanbul earthquake
    d. Hydrolysis

11. _____ is a clay mineral with the chemical composition $Al_2Si_2O_5(OH)_4$. It is a layered silicate mineral, with one tetrahedral sheet linked through oxygen atoms to one octahedral sheet of alumina octahedra. Rocks that are rich in _____ are known as china clay or kaolin. _____ clay occurs in abundance in soils that have formed from the chemical weathering of rocks in hot, moist climates - for example in tropical rainforest areas
    a. Clay minerals
    c. Kaolinite
    b. 1509 Istanbul earthquake
    d. Glauconite

12. In pedology, _____ is the loss of mineral and organic solutes due to percolation. It is a mechanism of soil formation. It is distinct from the soil forming process of eluviation, which is the loss of mineral and organic colloids.
    a. Fault
    c. Depression
    b. Melange
    d. Leaching

13. _____, a branch of geology, studies rock layers and layering (stratification.) It is primarily used in the study of sedimentary and layered volcanic rocks. _____ includes two related subfields: lithologic or lithostratigraphy and biologic _____ or biostratigraphy.
    a. 1703 Genroku earthquake
    c. 1509 Istanbul earthquake
    b. 1700 Cascadia earthquake
    d. Stratigraphy

Chapter 6. Weathering and Soils

14. _____ is a type of chemical weathering that creates rounded boulders and helps to create domed monoliths. This should not be confused with stream abrasion, a physical process which also creates rounded rocks on a much smaller scale. A good example of _____ can be found in the Alabama Hills area of eastern California.
    a. Spheroidal weathering
    b. Hydrothermal
    c. Diagenesis
    d. Headward erosion

15. _____ is the difference in degree of discoloration, disintegration, etc., of rocks of different kinds exposed to the same environment. Quartz deposits in basaltic flows will weather slower than the surrounding rock, while being exposed to the same forces of weathering.

    _____ occurs when some parts of a rock weathers at different rates than others.

    a. Differential weathering
    b. Gravitational erosion
    c. Coastal erosion
    d. Toreva block

16. _____ is the process by which the removal of material, through means of erosion and weathering, leads to a reduction of elevation and relief in landforms and landscapes. Exogenic processes, including the action of water, ice, and wind, predominantly involve _____. Denudation can involve the removal of both solid particles and dissolved material.
    a. Denudation
    b. Palustrine
    c. 1509 Istanbul earthquake
    d. Mesa

17. The _____ is a chronologic schema (or idealized model) relating stratigraphy to time that is used by geologists, paleontologists and other earth scientists to describe the timing and relationships between events that have occurred during the history of the Earth. The table of geologic time spans presented here agrees with the dates and nomenclature proposed by the International Commission on Stratigraphy, and uses the standard color codes of the United States Geological Survey.

    Evidence from radiometric dating indicates that the Earth is about 4.570 billion years old.

    a. 1509 Istanbul earthquake
    b. 1700 Cascadia earthquake
    c. 1703 Genroku earthquake
    d. Geologic time scale

18. _____, in soil science, means the underlying geological material (generally bedrock or a superficial or drift deposit) in which soil horizons form. Soils typically get a great deal of structure and minerals from their _____. Parent materials are made up of consolidated or unconsolidated mineral material that has undergone some degree of physical or chemical weathering.
    a. Parent material
    b. 1509 Istanbul earthquake
    c. 1703 Genroku earthquake
    d. 1700 Cascadia earthquake

19. A _____ is a specific layer in the soil which measures parallel to the soil surface and possesses physical characteristics which differ from the layers above and beneath. Horizon formation is a function of a range of geological, chemical, and biological processes and occurs over long time periods. Soils vary in the degree to which horizons are expressed.
    a. Soil horizon
    b. Mollisols
    c. Paleosol
    d. Soil type

20. _____ are a soil order in USDA soil taxonomy. _____ form in semiarid to humid areas, typically under a hardwood forest cover. They have a clay-enriched subsoil and relatively high native fertility. Because of their productivity and abundance, the _____ represent one of the more important soil orders for food and fiber production. They are widely used both in agriculture and forestry and are generally easier to keep fertile than other humid-climate soils, though those in Australia and Africa are still very deficient in Nitrogen and available Phosphorus.
   a. Illuvium
   b. Entisols
   c. Ultisols
   d. Alfisols

21. In USA soil taxonomy, _____ are soils formed in volcanic ash and defined as soils containing high proportions of glass and amorphous colloidal materials, including allophane, imogolite and ferrihydrite. In the FAO soil classification, _____ are known as Andosols.

Because they are generally quite young, _____ typically are very fertile except in cases where phosphorus is easily fixed (this sometimes occurs in the tropics).

   a. AL 333
   b. AASHTO Soil Classification System
   c. Andisols
   d. AL 129-1

22. In USA soil taxonomy, _____ are defined as soils that do not show any profile development other than an A horizon. They have no diagnostic horizons, and most are basically unaltered from their parent material, which can be unconsolidated sediment or rock. _____ are the second most abundant soil order (after Inceptisols), occupying ~16% of the global ice-free land area.
   a. Ultisols
   b. Illuvium
   c. Oxisols
   d. Entisols

23. In both the FAO soil classification and the USA soil taxonomy, a _____ is a soil comprised primarily of organic materials. They are defined as having 40 centimetres (16 in) or more of organic soil material in the upper 80 centimetres (31 in.) Organic soil material has an organic carbon content (by weight) of 12 to 18 percent, or more, depending on the clay content of the soil.
   a. Soil type
   b. Histosol
   c. Soil horizon
   d. Mollisols

24. _____ are a soil order in USDA soil taxonomy. They form quickly through alteration of parent material. They are older than entisols. They have no accumulation of clays, Fe, Al or organic matter. They have an Ochric or Umbric horizon and a cambic subsurface horizon.
   a. AL 129-1
   b. AL 333
   c. AASHTO Soil Classification System
   d. Inceptisols

25. In soil science, _____ are the typical soils of coniferous, or Boreal forests. They are also the typical soils of eucalypt forests and heathlands in southern Australia. These soils are found in areas that are wet and cold and also in warm areas such as Florida where sandy soils have fluctuating water tables. An example of a warm-climate _____ is the Myakka fine sand, state soil of Florida.
   a. Soil horizon
   b. Mollisols
   c. Soil type
   d. Podsol

26. _____ are a soil order in USA soil taxonomy. _____ form in semi-arid to semi-humid areas, typically under a grassland cover. They are most commonly found latitudinally in a band of 50 degrees north of the equator, although there are some in South America, South-Eastern Australia (mainly South Australia) and South Africa. Their parent material is generally limestone, loess, or wind-blown sand. The main processes that lead to the formation of grassland _____ are melanisation, decomposition, humification and pedoturbation.

   a. Pedogenesis   b. Slickenside
   c. Mollisols   d. Soil type

27. _____ are an order in USDA soil taxonomy, best known for their occurrence in tropical rain forest, 15-25 degrees north and south of the Equator. Some _____ have been previously classified as laterite soils.

The main processes of soil formation of _____ are weathering, humification and pedoturbation due to animals.

   a. Illuvium   b. Entisols
   c. Ultisols   d. Oxisols

28. _____ are an order in USDA soil taxonomy. They are defined as mineral soils which contain no calcareous material anywhere within the soil, have less than 10% weatherable minerals in the extreme top layer of soil, and have less the 35% base saturation throughout the soil.

In the FAO soil classification system, most _____ are known as Acrisols.

   a. Illuvium   b. Ultisols
   c. Oxisols   d. Entisols

29. In both the FAO and USA soil taxonomy, a _____ is a soil in which there is a high content of expansive clay known as montmorillonite that forms deep cracks in drier seasons or years. Alternate shrinking and swelling causes self-mulching, where the soil material consistently mixes itself, causing them to have an extremely deep A horizon and no B horizon. (A soil with no B horizon is called an A/C soil).

   a. Slickenside   b. Vertisol
   c. Paleosol   d. Mollisols

30. _____ is a fine-grained, heavy and compact sedimentary rock. Its main components are the carbonate or oxide of iron, clay and/or sand. It can be thought of as a concretionary form of siderite.

Freshly cleaved _____ is usually grey. The brown external appearance is due to oxidation of its surface. _____, being a sedimentary rock is not always homogeneous, and can be found in a red and black banded form called tiger iron, sometimes used for jewelry purposes.

   a. AL 333   b. Ironstone
   c. AASHTO Soil Classification System   d. AL 129-1

Chapter 6. Weathering and Soils

31. _____ is a surface formation in hot and wet tropical areas which is enriched in iron and aluminium and develops by intensive and long lasting weathering of the underlying parent rock. Nearly all kinds of rocks can be deeply decomposed by the action of high rainfall and elevated temperatures. The percolating rain water causes dissolution of primary rock minerals and decrease of easily soluble elements as sodium, potassium, calcium, magnesium and silicon.
   a. Soil horizon
   b. Pedogenesis
   c. Slickenside
   d. Laterite

32. In the geosciences, _____ can have two meanings. The first meaning, common in geology and paleontology, refers to a former soil preserved by burial underneath either sediments (alluvium or loess) or volcanic deposits (Volcanic ash), which in case of older deposits have lithified into rock. In Quaternary geology, sedimentology, paleoclimatology, and geology in general, it is the typical and accepted practice to use the term '_____' to designate such 'fossil' soils found buried within either sedimentary or volcanic deposits exposed in all continents as illustrated by Rettallack (2001), Kraus (1999), and innumerable other published papers and books.
   a. Soil structure
   b. Paleosol
   c. Slickenside
   d. Soil horizon

33. _____ is the removal of solids (sediment, soil, rock and other particles) in the natural environment. It usually occurs due to transport by wind, water, or ice; by down-slope creep of soil and other material under the force of gravity; or by living organisms, such as burrowing animals, in the case of bioerosion.

   _____ is distinguished from weathering, which is the process of chemical or physical breakdown of the minerals in the rocks, although the two processes may occur concurrently.

   a. AASHTO Soil Classification System
   b. AL 129-1
   c. AL 333
   d. Erosion

34. _____ is the principle that the same scientific laws and processes are constant throughout space and time. It applies specifically to sciences that require a long timescale such as geology, astronomy, and paleontology. It was first defined by Charles Lyell (1797 - 1875), who incorporated James Hutton's gradualism into the idea of _____.
   a. AL 129-1
   b. AASHTO Soil Classification System
   c. AL 333
   d. Uniformitarianism

35. _____ describes the large scale motions of Earth's lithosphere. The theory encompasses the older concepts of continental drift, developed during the first decades of the 20th century by Alfred Wegener, and seafloor spreading, understood during the 1960s.

   The outermost part of the Earth's interior is made up of two layers: the lithosphere and the asthenosphere.

   a. Mantle convection
   b. Nappe
   c. Continental crust
   d. Plate tectonics

36. _____s is a field of study within geology concerned generally with the structures within the lithosphere of the Earth and particularly with the forces and movements that have operated in a region to create these structures.

_____s is concerned with the orogenies and _____ development of cratons and _____ terranes as well as the earthquake and volcanic belts which directly affect much of the global population. _____ studies are also important for understanding erosion patterns in geomorphology and as guides for the economic geologist searching for petroleum and metallic ores.

a. Cocos Plate
c. Fault trace
b. Rivera Plate
d. Tectonic

37. _____ is a field of study within geology concerned generally with the structures within the lithosphere of the Earth and particularly with the forces and movements that have operated in a region to create these structures.

_____ is concerned with the orogenies and tectonic development of cratons and tectonic terranes as well as the earthquake and volcanic belts which directly affect much of the global population. Tectonic studies are also important for understanding erosion patterns in geomorphology and as guides for the economic geologist searching for petroleum and metallic ores.

a. Fault trace
c. Rivera Plate
b. Tectonics
d. Cocos Plate

Chapter 7. Sediments and Sedimentary Rocks: Archives of Earth History

1. _____ is any particulate matter that can be transported by fluid flow, and which eventually is deposited.

They are most often transported by water (fluvial processes) transported by wind (aeolian processes) and glaciers. Beach sands and river channel deposits are examples of fluvial transport and deposition, though _____ also often settles out of slow-moving or standing water in lakes and oceans.

- a. Fech fech
- b. Salt glacier
- c. Brickearth
- d. Sediment

2. _____ is one of the three main rock types (the others being igneous and metamorphic rock.) _____ is formed by deposition and consolidation of mineral and organic material and from precipitation of minerals from solution. The processes that form _____ occur at the surface of the Earth and within bodies of water.
- a. Serpentinite
- b. Sedimentary rock
- c. Large igneous provinces
- d. Felsic

3. In thermodynamics, an _____ or an isocaloric process is a thermodynamic process in which no heat is transferred to or from the working fluid. Conversely, a process that involves heat transfer (addition or loss of heat to the surroundings) is generally called diabatic.
- a. AL 333
- b. AL 129-1
- c. Adiabatic process
- d. AASHTO Soil Classification System

4. In geology, _____ refers to inclined sedimentary structures in a horizontal unit of rock. These tilted structures are deposits from bedforms such as ripples and dunes, and they indicate that the depositional environment contained a flowing fluid (typically, water or wind.) This is a case in geology when original depositional layering is tilted, and that the tilting is not a result of post-depositional deformation.
- a. Cross-bedding
- b. Gibraltar Arc
- c. Contact metamorphism
- d. Geomicrobiology

5. _____ is the tendency for particles in suspension or molecules in solution to settle out of the fluid in which they are entrained, and come to rest against a wall. This is due to their motion through the fluid in response to the forces acting on them: these forces can be due to gravity, centrifugal acceleration or electromagnetism.

_____ may pertain to objects of various sizes, ranging from large rocks in flowing water to suspensions of dust and pollen particles to cellular suspensions to solutions of single molecules such as proteins and peptides.

- a. 1509 Istanbul earthquake
- b. 1700 Cascadia earthquake
- c. 1703 Genroku earthquake
- d. Sedimentation

6. _____ is a paramount and base concept in archaeology, especially in the course of excavation. It is largely based on the Law of Superposition. When archaeological finds are below the surface of the ground (as is most commonly the case), the identification of the context of each find is vital in enabling the archaeologist to draw conclusions about the site and about the nature and date of its occupation.
- a. Submersion
- b. Streak
- c. Stratification
- d. Fractional crystallization

Chapter 7. Sediments and Sedimentary Rocks: Archives of Earth History

7. The _____ is a fundamental concept in geology that describes the dynamic transitions through geologic time among the three main rock types: sedimentary, metamorphic, and igneous. Each type of rock is altered or destroyed when it is forced out of its equilibrium conditions. An igneous rock such as basalt may break down and dissolve when exposed to the atmosphere, or melt as it is subducted under a continent.

  a. Metamorphic zone
  b. Felsic
  c. Vesicular texture
  d. Rock cycle

8. In geology a _____ is the smallest division of a geologic formation or stratigraphic rock series marked by well-defined divisional planes (bedding planes) separating it from layers above and below. A _____ is the smallest lithostratigraphic unit, usually ranging in thickness from a centimeter to several meters and distinguishable from _____s above and below it. _____s can be differentiated in various ways, including rock or mineral type and particle size.

  a. Sequence stratigraphy
  b. Cyclostratigraphy
  c. Biozones
  d. Bed

9. A _____ is a substance produced by life processes. It may be either constituents, or secretions, of plants or animals.

Examples

- Coal and oil are possible examples of constituents which may have undergone changes over geologic time periods.
- Chalk and limestone are examples of secretions (marine animal shells) which are of geologic age.
- Cotton and wood are biogenic constituents of contemporary origin.
- Pearls, silk and ambergris are examples of secretions of contemporary origin.

  a. Hydrothermal circulation
  b. Hydrothermal
  c. Permineralization
  d. Biogenic substance

10. _____ rocks are composed of fragments of pre-existing rock. The term is most commonly, but not uniquely, applied to sedimentary rocks.

_____ metamorphic rocks include breccias formed in faults, as well as some protomylonite and pseudotachylite.

  a. 1509 Istanbul earthquake
  b. Clastic
  c. 1703 Genroku earthquake
  d. 1700 Cascadia earthquake

11. In geology and related fields, a _____ is a layer of rock or soil with internally consistent characteristics that distinguishes it from contiguous layers. Each layer is generally one of a number of parallel layers that lie one upon another, laid down by natural forces. They may extend over hundreds of thousands of square kilometers of the Earth's surface.

  a. 1509 Istanbul earthquake
  b. Stratum
  c. 1700 Cascadia earthquake
  d. 1703 Genroku earthquake

Chapter 7. Sediments and Sedimentary Rocks: Archives of Earth History

12. _____ refers to the diameter of individual grains of sediment, or the lithified particles in clastic rocks. The term may also be applied to other granular materials. This is different from the crystallite size, which is the size of a single crystal inside the particles or grains.

   a. Particle size
   b. 1509 Istanbul earthquake
   c. 1703 Genroku earthquake
   d. 1700 Cascadia earthquake

13. Sorting indicates the distribution of grain size of sediments, either in unconsolidated deposits or in sedimentary rocks. _____ indicates that the sediment sizes are mixed (large variance); whereas well sorted indicates that the sediment sizes are similar (low variance.)

The degree of sorting may also indicate the energy and/or duration of deposition.

   a. Poorly sorted
   b. Wave-cut platform
   c. Rill
   d. Planar deformation features

14. A _____ is an annual layer of sediment or sedimentary rock. Initially, _____ was used to describe the separate components of annual layers in glacial lake sediments, but at the 1910 Geological Congress, the Swedish geologist Gerard De Geer (1858-1943) proposed a new formal definition where _____ described the whole of any annual sedimentary layer.

   a. 1703 Genroku earthquake
   b. 1509 Istanbul earthquake
   c. 1700 Cascadia earthquake
   d. Varve

15. In geology, a _____ is one characterized by a systematic change in grain or clast size from the base of the bed to the top. Most commonly this takes the form of normal grading, with coarser sediments at the base, which grade upward into progressively finer ones. Normally _____s generally represent depositional environments which decrease in transport energy as time passes, but also form during rapid depositional events.

   a. Graded bed
   b. 1700 Cascadia earthquake
   c. 1703 Genroku earthquake
   d. 1509 Istanbul earthquake

16. _____ are skeletal fragments of marine or land organisms that are found in sedimentary rocks laid down in a marine environment--especially limestone varieties, some of which take on distinct textures and coloration from their predominate _____--that geologists, archaeologists and paleontologists use to date a rock strata to a particular geological era.

_____ used for such relative dating purposes can be whole fossils or broken fragments of organisms. Their preponderance can give a rough guide to life diversity in the historic biosphere, but absolute counts much depend on water conditions such as the depth of the deposition, local currents, as well as wave strength in large body of water such as lake.

   a. Fasciculus
   b. Xanioascus
   c. Turgai Sea
   d. Bioclasts

17. _____ refers to a sediment, sedimentary rock, or soil type which is formed from or contains a high proportion of calcium carbonate in the form of calcite or aragonite.

Chapter 7. Sediments and Sedimentary Rocks: Archives of Earth History

It can also be used as an adjectival term applied to anatomical structures which are made of calcium carbonate in animals such as gastropods, when referring to such structures as the operculum, the clausilium, and the love dart.

_____ sediments are usually deposited in shallow water near land, since the carbonate is precipitated by marine organisms that need land-derived nutrients.

a. 1509 Istanbul earthquake
b. 1700 Cascadia earthquake
c. 1703 Genroku earthquake
d. Calcareous

18. In geology, _____ are a body of rock with specified characteristics. Ideally, a _____ is a distinctive rock unit that forms under certain conditions of sedimentation, reflecting a particular process or environment.

The term _____ was introduced by the Swiss geologist Amanz Gressly in 1838 and was part of his significant contribution to the foundations of modern stratigraphy, [Cross and Homewood (1997)] which replaced the earlier notions of Neptunism.

a. Greenstone belts
b. Metaconglomerate
c. Metamorphic facies
d. Facies

19. _____ is composed of the debris of plankton with silica shells, such as diatoms and radiolaria. This ooze is limited to areas with high biological productivity, such as the polar oceans, and upwelling zones near the equator. The least common type of sediment, it covers only 15% of the ocean floor.

a. Cap carbonates
b. Bediasite
c. Siliceous ooze
d. Differential stress

20. In geology, sedimentary _____ describes the combination of physical, chemical and biological processes associated with the deposition of a particular type of sediment and, therefore, the rock types that will be formed after lithification, if the sediment is preserved in the rock record. In most cases the environments associated with particular rock types or associations of rock types can be matched to existing analogues. However, the further back in geological time sediments were deposited, the more likely that direct modern analogues are not available (e.g. banded iron formations.)

a. 1703 Genroku earthquake
b. 1700 Cascadia earthquake
c. 1509 Istanbul earthquake
d. Depositional environment

21. The _____ is the extended perimeter of each continent and associated coastal plain, and was part of the continent during the glacial periods, but is undersea during interglacial periods such as the current epoch by relatively shallow seas (known as shelf seas) and gulfs.

The continental rise is below the slope, but landward of the abyssal plains. Its gradient is intermediate between the slope and the shelf, on the order of 0.5-1°.

a. Continental slope
b. Surface runoff
c. Mud
d. Continental shelf

Chapter 7. Sediments and Sedimentary Rocks: Archives of Earth History

22. An _____ is a semi-enclosed coastal body of water with one or more rivers or streams flowing into it, and with a free connection to the open sea. They are affected by both marine influences, such as tides, waves, and the influx of saline water; and riverine influences, such as flows of fresh water and sediment. As a result they may contain many biological niches within a small area, and so are associated with high biological diversity.

    a. AL 333
    b. AASHTO Soil Classification System
    c. AL 129-1
    d. Estuary

23. In chemistry, a _____ is a salt or ester of carbonic acid.

To test for the presence of the _____ anion in a salt, the addition of dilute mineral acid (e.g. hydrochloric acid) will yield carbon dioxide gas.

_____-containing salts are industrially and mineralogically ubiquitous.

    a. 1509 Istanbul earthquake
    b. 1700 Cascadia earthquake
    c. 1703 Genroku earthquake
    d. Carbonate

24. _____ are water-soluble mineral sediments that result from the evaporation of bodies of surficial water. _____ are considered sedimentary rocks.

Although all water bodies on the surface and in aquifers contain dissolved salts, the water must evaporate into the atmosphere for the minerals to precipitate.

    a. AL 333
    b. AL 129-1
    c. AASHTO Soil Classification System
    d. Evaporites

25. _____ geological formations have their origins in turbidity current deposits, which are deposits from a form of underwater avalanche that are responsible for distributing vast amounts of clastic sediment into the deep ocean.

They were first properly described by Bouma (1962), who studied deepwater sediments and recognized particular fining up intervals within deep water, fine grained shales, which were anomalous because they started at pebble conglomerates and terminated in shales.

This was anomalous because within the deep ocean it had historically been assumed that there was no mechanism by which tractional flow could carry and deposit coarse-grained sediments into the abyssal depths.

    a. Turbidite
    b. 1700 Cascadia earthquake
    c. 1509 Istanbul earthquake
    d. 1703 Genroku earthquake

26. In geology, _____ is transported rock debris overlying the solid bedrock. The term is also sometimes refers to organic debris so-transported. In the largest sense, it refers to the material left behind by retreating continental glaciers.

    a. Metamorphic reaction
    b. Riegel
    c. Geomechanics
    d. Drift

Chapter 7. Sediments and Sedimentary Rocks: Archives of Earth History

27. _____ refers to the process by which a sediment progressively loses its porosity due to the effects of loading. This forms part of the process of lithification. When a layer of sediment is originally deposited, it contains an open framework of particles with the pore space being usually filled with water.
   a. Combe
   b. Drainage system
   c. Cohesion
   d. Compaction

28. In geology and oceanography, _____ is any chemical, physical or biological change undergone by a sediment after its initial deposition and during and after its lithification, exclusive of surface alteration (weathering) and metamorphism. These changes happen at relatively low temperatures and pressures and result in changes to the rock's original mineralogy and texture. The boundary between _____ and metamorphism, which occurs under conditions of higher temperature and pressure, is gradational.
   a. Transgression
   b. Spheroidal weathering
   c. Mid-ocean ridge
   d. Diagenesis

29. _____ is the process in which sediments compact under pressure, expel connate fluids, and gradually become solid rock. Essentially, _____ is a process of porosity destruction through compaction and cementation. _____ includes all the processes which convert unconsolidated sediments into sedimentary rocks.
   a. Dolostone
   b. Mudstone
   c. Claystone
   d. Lithification

30. _____ is an accumulation of partially decayed vegetation matter. _____ forms in wetlands or peatlands, variously called bogs, moors, muskegs, pocosins, mires, and _____ swamp forests. By volume there are about 4 trillion mÂÂ³ of _____ in the world covering a total of around 2% of global land mass (about 3 million km^2), containing about 8 billion terajoules of energy.
   a. 1700 Cascadia earthquake
   b. 1703 Genroku earthquake
   c. 1509 Istanbul earthquake
   d. Peat

31. In geology, solid-state _____ is a metamorphic process that occurs under situations of intense temperature and pressure where grains, atoms or molecules of a rock or mineral are packed closer together, creating a new crystal structure. The basic composition remains the same. This process can be illustrated by observing how snow recrystallizes to ice without melting.
   a. Vitrification
   b. 1509 Istanbul earthquake
   c. Recrystallization
   d. 1700 Cascadia earthquake

32. _____ is a detrital sedimentary rock, specifically a type of sandstone containing at least 25% feldspar., Arkosic sand is sand that is similarly rich in feldspar, and thus the potential precursor of _____. The other mineral components may vary, but quartz is commonly dominant, and some mica is often present. Apart from the mineral content, rock fragments may also be a significant component.
   a. AASHTO Soil Classification System
   b. AL 129-1
   c. Arkose
   d. AL 333

33. _____ is a rock composed of angular fragments of minerals or rocks in a matrix (cementing material), that may be similar or different in composition to the fragments. A _____ may have a variety of different origins, as indicated by the named types including sedimentary _____, tectonic _____, igneous _____, impact _____ and hydrothermal _____.

Sedimentary _____s are a type of clastic sedimentary rock which are composed of angular to subangular, randomly oriented clasts of other sedimentary rocks.

a. Fault breccia
b. Breccia
c. 1509 Istanbul earthquake
d. Ventifacts

34. A _____ is a rock consisting of individual stones that have become cemented together. They are sedimentary rocks consisting of rounded fragments and are thus differentiated from breccias, which consist of angular clasts. Both _____s and breccias are characterized by clasts larger than sand (>2 mm).

a. Pelagic sediments
b. Conglomerate
c. Concretion
d. Keystone

35. _____ are the preserved remains or traces of animals, plants, and other organisms from the remote past. The totality of _____, both discovered and undiscovered, and their placement in fossiliferous rock formations and sedimentary layers (strata) is known as the fossil record. The study of _____ across geological time, how they were formed, and the evolutionary relationships between taxa (phylogeny) are some of the most important functions of the science of paleontology.

a. Fossils
b. 1703 Genroku earthquake
c. 1509 Istanbul earthquake
d. 1700 Cascadia earthquake

36. _____ is a variety of sandstone generally characterized by its hardness, dark color, and poorly-sorted, angular grains of quartz, feldspar, and small rock fragments set in a compact, clay-fine matrix. It is a texturally-immature sedimentary rock generally found in Palaeozoic strata. The larger grains can be sand-to-gravel-sized, and matrix materials generally constitute more than 15% of the rock by volume.

a. Diatomaceous earth
b. Sandstone
c. Greywacke
d. Coquina

37. The _____ or groundmass of rock is the fine-grained mass of material in which larger grains or crystals are embedded.

The _____ of an igneous rock consists of fine-grained, often microscopic, crystals in which larger crystals (phenocrysts) are embedded. This porphyritic texture is indicative of multi-stage cooling of magma.

a. Lithology
b. Magma
c. Rock cycle
d. Matrix

38. _____ is a sedimentary rock composed mainly of sand-size mineral or rock grains. Most _____ is composed of quartz and/or feldspar because these are the most common minerals in the Earth's crust. Like sand, _____ may be any color, but the most common colors are tan, brown, yellow, red, gray and white.

a. Claystone
b. Sandstone
c. Superficial deposits
d. Shale

39. _____ is a sedimentary rock which has a composition intermediate in grain size between the coarser sandstones and the finer mudstones and shales.

Chapter 7. Sediments and Sedimentary Rocks: Archives of Earth History

As its name implies, it is primarily composed (greater than 2/3) of silt sized particles, defined as grains between 3.9 and 62.5 micrometres or 4 to 8 on the Krumbein phi (>φ) scale. _____s differ significantly from sandstones due to their smaller pores and higher propensity for containing a significant clay fraction.

a. Sedimentary deposits
b. Siltstone
c. Pelagic sediments
d. Keystone

40. _____ is a fine grained sedimentary rock whose original constituents were clays or muds. Grain size is up to 0.0625 mm with individual grains too small to be distinguished without a microscope. With increased pressure over time the platey clay minerals may become aligned, with the appearance of fissility or parallel layering.

a. Diatomaceous earth
b. Dolostone
c. Porcellanite
d. Mudstone

41. A _____ is a type of structural dome formed when a thick bed of evaporite minerals found at depth intrudes vertically into surrounding rock strata, forming a diapir.

The salt that forms these domes was deposited within restricted marine basins. Due to restricted flow of water into a basin, evaporation occurs resulting in the precipitation of salts from solution, depositing evaporites.

a. 1509 Istanbul earthquake
b. Salt dome
c. 1703 Genroku earthquake
d. 1700 Cascadia earthquake

42. _____ is a fine-grained sedimentary rock whose original constituents were clay minerals or muds. It is characterized by thin laminae breaking with an irregular curving fracture, often splintery and usually parallel to the often-indistinguishable bedding plane. This property is called fissility.

a. Claystone
b. Concretion
c. Shale
d. Jasperoid

43. _____ is a fine-grained silica-rich microcrystalline, cryptocrystalline or microfibrous sedimentary rock that may contain small fossils. It varies greatly in color (from white to black), but most often manifests as gray, brown, grayish brown and light green to rusty red; its color is an expression of trace elements present in the rock, and both red and green are most often related to traces of iron (in its oxidized and reduced forms respectively.)

_____ occurs as oval to irregular nodules in greensand, limestone, chalk, and dolostone formations as a replacement mineral, where it is formed as a result of some type of diagenesis.

a. Chert
b. 1509 Istanbul earthquake
c. 1703 Genroku earthquake
d. 1700 Cascadia earthquake

44. _____ is a sedimentary rock composed largely of the mineral calcite (calcium carbonate: $CaCO_3$.) The deposition of _____ strata is often a by-product and indicator of biological activity in the geologic record. Calcium (along with nitrogen, phosphorus, and potassium) is a key mineral to plant nutrition: soils overlying _____ bedrock tend to be pre-fertilized with calcium.

Chapter 7. Sediments and Sedimentary Rocks: Archives of Earth History

a. Limestone
b. 1703 Genroku earthquake
c. 1509 Istanbul earthquake
d. 1700 Cascadia earthquake

45. _____ is a relatively soft coal containing a tarlike substance called bitumen. It is of higher quality than lignite coal but of poorer quality than anthracite coal.

_____ is a sedimorphic rock formed by diagenetic and submetamorphic compression of peat bog material.

a. 1700 Cascadia earthquake
b. 1703 Genroku earthquake
c. 1509 Istanbul earthquake
d. Bituminous coal

46. _____ is a soft, white, porous sedimentary rock, a form of limestone composed of the mineral calcite. It forms under relatively deep marine conditions from the gradual accumulation of minute calcite plates shed from micro-organisms called coccolithophores. It is common to find flint and chert nodules embedded in _____.

a. 1703 Genroku earthquake
b. 1509 Istanbul earthquake
c. 1700 Cascadia earthquake
d. Chalk

47. _____ is an incompletely consolidated sedimentary rock. _____ was formed in association with marine reefs and is a variety of 'coral rag', technically a subset of limestone.

_____ is mainly composed of mineral calcite, often including some phosphate, in the form of seashells or coral.

a. Shale
b. Mudstone
c. Superficial deposits
d. Coquina

48. _____ or dolomite rock is a sedimentary carbonate rock that contains a high percentage of the mineral dolomite. In old U.S.G.S. publications it was referred to as magnesian limestone. Most _____ formed as a magnesium replacement of limestone or lime mud prior to lithification.

a. Sedimentary deposits
b. Mudstone
c. Dolostone
d. Jasperoid

49. _____ is a sedimentary rock formed from ooids, spherical grains composed of concentric layers. The name derives from the Hellenic word >òoion for egg. Strictly, _____s consist of ooids of diameter 0.25-2 mm: rocks composed of ooids larger than 2 mm are called pisolites.

a. Oolite
b. AL 333
c. AASHTO Soil Classification System
d. AL 129-1

50. The _____ is a chronologic schema (or idealized model) relating stratigraphy to time that is used by geologists, paleontologists and other earth scientists to describe the timing and relationships between events that have occurred during the history of the Earth. The table of geologic time spans presented here agrees with the dates and nomenclature proposed by the International Commission on Stratigraphy, and uses the standard color codes of the United States Geological Survey.

Evidence from radiometric dating indicates that the Earth is about 4.570 billion years old.

Chapter 7. Sediments and Sedimentary Rocks: Archives of Earth History

a. 1703 Genroku earthquake
b. 1509 Istanbul earthquake
c. Geologic time scale
d. 1700 Cascadia earthquake

51. _____ is an organic-rich fine-grained sedimentary rock. It contains significant amounts of kerogen, a solid mixture of organic chemical compounds from which liquid hydrocarbons can be extracted. Deposits of _____ occur around the world, including major deposits in the United States of America. Estimates of global deposits range from 2.8 trillion to 3.3 trillion barrels >(450 >× 10^9 to 520 >× 10^9 m^3) of recoverable oil.
   a. AL 129-1
   b. Oil shale
   c. AASHTO Soil Classification System
   d. AL 333

52. _____ or kerogen oil is a non-conventional oil produced by the destructive distillation of oil shale. This process, a controlled form of pyrolysis, converts the organic matter within the rock (kerogen) into synthetic oil and gas. The resulting oil can be used immediately as a fuel or upgraded to meet refinery feedstock specifications by adding hydrogen and removing impurities such as sulfur and nitrogen.
   a. 1703 Genroku earthquake
   b. 1700 Cascadia earthquake
   c. 1509 Istanbul earthquake
   d. Shale oil

53. A _____ is a mountain rising from the ocean seafloor that does not reach to the water's surface (sea level), and thus is not an island. These are typically formed from extinct volcanoes, that rise abruptly and are usually found rising from a seafloor of 1,000-4,000 meters depth. They are defined by oceanographers as independent features that rise to at least 1,000 meters above the seafloor.
   a. Seamount
   b. 1703 Genroku earthquake
   c. 1700 Cascadia earthquake
   d. 1509 Istanbul earthquake

54. In geology, _____ are sedimentary structures that indicate agitation by water (current or waves) or wind. _____ formed by water consist of two basic types:

   1. Current _____ are asymmetrical in profile, with a gentle up-current slope and a steeper down-current slope. The down-current slope depends on the shape of the sediment, with 33>° being typical.
   2. Wave-formed _____ have a symmetrical, almost sinusoidal profile; they indicate an environment with weak currents where water motion is dominated by wave oscillations.

Ripples will not form in sediment larger than course sand.

   a. 1703 Genroku earthquake
   b. Ripple marks
   c. 1509 Istanbul earthquake
   d. 1700 Cascadia earthquake

55. _____ is a phenomenon of the plate tectonics of Earth that occurs at convergent boundaries. _____ is a variation on the fundamental process of subduction, whereby the subduction zone is destroyed, mountains produced, and two continents sutured together. _____ is known only from this planet and is an interesting example of how our different crusts, oceanic and continental, behave during subduction.
   a. Continental collision
   b. Mirovia
   c. Copperbelt Province
   d. Supercontinent cycle

56. The _____ is the zone of the ocean floor that separates the thin oceanic crust from thick continental crust. _____s constitute about 28% of the oceanic area.

Chapter 7. Sediments and Sedimentary Rocks: Archives of Earth History

The transition from continental to oceanic crust commonly occurs within the outer part of the margin, called continental rise.

a. Swash
b. 1509 Istanbul earthquake
c. Cuspate forelands
d. Continental margin

57. _____ describes the large scale motions of Earth's lithosphere. The theory encompasses the older concepts of continental drift, developed during the first decades of the 20th century by Alfred Wegener, and seafloor spreading, understood during the 1960s.

The outermost part of the Earth's interior is made up of two layers: the lithosphere and the asthenosphere.

a. Continental crust
b. Mantle convection
c. Nappe
d. Plate tectonics

58. In geology, _____ refers to heat sources within the planet. _____ is technically an adjective (e.g., _____ energy) but in U.S. English the word has attained frequent use as a noun.

The planet's internal heat was originally generated during its accretion, due to gravitational binding energy, and since then additional heat has continued to be generated by decay heat from the radioactive decay of elements.

a. Geothermal
b. Grade
c. Cleavage
d. Tarn

59. _____s is a field of study within geology concerned generally with the structures within the lithosphere of the Earth and particularly with the forces and movements that have operated in a region to create these structures.

_____s is concerned with the orogenies and _____ development of cratons and _____ terranes as well as the earthquake and volcanic belts which directly affect much of the global population. _____ studies are also important for understanding erosion patterns in geomorphology and as guides for the economic geologist searching for petroleum and metallic ores.

a. Rivera Plate
b. Tectonic
c. Cocos Plate
d. Fault trace

60. _____ is a field of study within geology concerned generally with the structures within the lithosphere of the Earth and particularly with the forces and movements that have operated in a region to create these structures.

_____ is concerned with the orogenies and tectonic development of cratons and tectonic terranes as well as the earthquake and volcanic belts which directly affect much of the global population. Tectonic studies are also important for understanding erosion patterns in geomorphology and as guides for the economic geologist searching for petroleum and metallic ores.

a. Rivera Plate
b. Tectonics
c. Fault trace
d. Cocos Plate

61. The terms _____ and icehouse Earth refer to the prevailing global climate on a timescale of millions of years.

During a _____ Earth period, the planet's atmosphere contains sufficient _____ gases such as carbon dioxide and methane for ice to be entirely absent from the planet's surface.

During icehouse periods, glaciers are present in fluctuating amounts; variations in the Earth's orbit may result in many ice ages, glacials, and interglacials.

a. 1703 Genroku earthquake
b. 1509 Istanbul earthquake
c. 1700 Cascadia earthquake
d. Greenhouse

62. _____ are gases in an atmosphere that absorb and emit radiation within the thermal infrared range. This process is the fundamental cause of the greenhouse effect. Common _____ in the Earth's atmosphere include water vapor, carbon dioxide, methane, nitrous oxide, ozone, and chlorofluorocarbons.

a. Climate models
b. Greenhouse gases
c. Deforestation
d. Glacier

63. The _____ is the biogeochemical cycle by which carbon is exchanged among the biosphere, pedosphere, geosphere, hydrosphere, and atmosphere of the Earth.

The _____ is usually thought of as four major reservoirs of carbon interconnected by pathways of exchange. These reservoirs are:

- The plants
- The terrestrial biosphere, which is usually defined to include fresh water systems and non-living organic material, such as soil carbon.
- The oceans, including dissolved inorganic carbon and living and non-living marine biota,
- The sediments including fossil fuels.

The annual movements of carbon, the carbon exchanges between reservoirs, occur because of various chemical, physical, geological, and biological processes. The ocean contains the largest active pool of carbon near the surface of the Earth, but the deep ocean part of this pool does not rapidly exchange with the atmosphere.

a. Nanogeoscience
b. Cosmogenic isotopes
c. 1509 Istanbul earthquake
d. Carbon cycle

Chapter 8. Metamorphism and Metamorphic Rocks: New Rocks from Old

1. _____ is the result of the transformation of an existing rock type, the protolith, in a process called metamorphism, which means 'change in form'. The protolith is subjected to heat and pressure (temperatures greater than 150 to 200 >°C and pressures of 1500 bars) causing profound physical and/or chemical change. The protolith may be sedimentary rock, igneous rock or another older _____.
   a. Laccolith
   b. Serpentinite
   c. Pluton
   d. Metamorphic rock

2. _____ is the solid-state recrystallization of pre-existing rocks due to changes in physical and chemical conditions, primarily heat, pressure, and the introduction of chemically active fluids. Both mineralogical, chemical and crystallographic changes can occur during this process.

   Three types of _____ exist: dynamic, contact and regional.

   a. Pumice raft
   b. Lake capture
   c. Gibraltar Arc
   d. Metamorphism

3. In thermodynamics, an _____ or an isocaloric process is a thermodynamic process in which no heat is transferred to or from the working fluid. Conversely, a process that involves heat transfer (addition or loss of heat to the surroundings) is generally called diabatic.
   a. Adiabatic process
   b. AL 129-1
   c. AL 333
   d. AASHTO Soil Classification System

4. _____ is the difference between the greatest and the least compressive stress experienced by an object. For the geological convention, in which $>\sigma_3$ is the greatest compressive stress and $>\sigma_1$ is the weakest,

   [×] >.

   For the engineering convention, $>\sigma_1$ is the greatest compressive stress and $>\sigma_3$ is the weakest, so

   [×] >.

   a. Cross-cutting relationships
   b. Rill
   c. Palynomorph
   d. Differential stress

5. In materials science, _____ is the distribution of crystallographic orientations of a polycrystalline sample. A sample in which these orientations are fully random is said to have no _____. If the crystallographic orientations are not random, but have some preferred orientation, then the sample has a weak, strong, or moderate _____.
   a. Geothermal
   b. Platform
   c. Diamond Head
   d. Texture

6. _____ is the name given to a rock consisting mainly of hornblende amphibole, the use of the term being restricted, however, to metamorphic rocks. The modern terminology for a holocrystalline plutonic igneous rocks composed primarily of hornblende amphibole is a hornblendite, which are usually crystal cumulates. Rocks with >90% amphibole which have a feldspar groundmass may be a lamprophyre.

Chapter 8. Metamorphism and Metamorphic Rocks: New Rocks from Old

a. AASHTO Soil Classification System
b. AL 333
c. AL 129-1
d. Amphibolite

7. _____s is a field of study within geology concerned generally with the structures within the lithosphere of the Earth and particularly with the forces and movements that have operated in a region to create these structures.

_____s is concerned with the orogenies and _____ development of cratons and _____ terranes as well as the earthquake and volcanic belts which directly affect much of the global population. _____ studies are also important for understanding erosion patterns in geomorphology and as guides for the economic geologist searching for petroleum and metallic ores.

a. Cocos Plate
b. Rivera Plate
c. Fault trace
d. Tectonic

8. _____ is a common and widely distributed type of rock formed by high-grade regional metamorphic processes from pre-existing formations that were originally either igneous or sedimentary rocks. Gneissic rocks are usually medium to coarse foliated and largely recrystallized but do not carry large quantities of micas, chlorite or other platy minerals. _____es that are metamorphosed igneous rocks or their equivalent are termed granite _____es, diorite _____es, etc.

a. 1700 Cascadia earthquake
b. 1509 Istanbul earthquake
c. Gneiss
d. 1703 Genroku earthquake

9. In geology, a _____ or _____ line is a planar fracture in rock in which the rock on one side of the fracture has moved with respect to the rock on the other side. Large _____s within the Earth's crust are the result of differential or shear motion and active _____ zones are the causal locations of most earthquakes. Earthquakes are caused by energy release during rapid slippage along a _____.

a. Drainage system
b. Compaction
c. Cleavage
d. Fault

10. The _____ is a chronologic schema (or idealized model) relating stratigraphy to time that is used by geologists, paleontologists and other earth scientists to describe the timing and relationships between events that have occurred during the history of the Earth. The table of geologic time spans presented here agrees with the dates and nomenclature proposed by the International Commission on Stratigraphy, and uses the standard color codes of the United States Geological Survey.

Evidence from radiometric dating indicates that the Earth is about 4.570 billion years old.

a. 1509 Istanbul earthquake
b. 1703 Genroku earthquake
c. Geologic time scale
d. 1700 Cascadia earthquake

11. _____ is water located beneath the ground surface in soil pore spaces and in the fractures of lithologic formations. A unit of rock or an unconsolidated deposit is called an aquifer when it can yield a usable quantity of water. The depth at which soil pore spaces or fractures and voids in rock become completely saturated with water is called the water table.

a. 1509 Istanbul earthquake
b. Depression focused recharge
c. 1700 Cascadia earthquake
d. Groundwater

68 *Chapter 8. Metamorphism and Metamorphic Rocks: New Rocks from Old*

12. _____ is a rock at the frontier between igneous and metamorphic rocks. They can also be known as diatexite.

_____ forms under extreme temperature conditions during prograde metamorphism, where partial melting occurs in pre-existing rocks.

 a. Large igneous provinces
 b. Metamorphic zone
 c. Magma
 d. Migmatite

13. _____ is the geomorphic process by which soil, regolith, and rock move downslope under the force of gravity. Types of _____ include creep, slides, flows, topples, and falls, each with its own characteristic features, and taking place over timescales from seconds to years. _____ occurs on both terrestrial and submarine slopes, and has been observed on Earth, Mars, and Venus.
 a. 1509 Istanbul earthquake
 b. Soil liquefaction
 c. 1700 Cascadia earthquake
 d. Mass wasting

14. _____, in structural geology and related disciplines, describes the tendency of a rock to break along preferred planes of weakness.

Rocks deformed under very low to low metamorphic grade often develop planes along which the rock can easily be split. Slates are an example of a rock with a penetrative _____ caused partly by the realignment of phyllosilicate minerals with increasing flattening strain.

 a. Diamond Head
 b. Geothermal
 c. Cleavage
 d. Lingula

15. _____ is a feature of rocks containing platy minerals. Platy minerals include clay minerals and micas, with a long thin shape. When these align, they form a series of planes along which the rock tends to split.
 a. Marine clay
 b. Slaty cleavage
 c. Palynomorph
 d. Basin and Range

16. _____ is a type of foliated metamorphic rock primarily composed of quartz, sericite mica, and chlorite; the rock represents a gradation in the degree of metamorphism between slate and mica schist. Minute crystals of graphite, sericite, or chlorite impart a silky, sometimes golden sheen to the surfaces of cleavage (or schistosity.) _____ is formed from the continued metamorphism of slate.
 a. 1509 Istanbul earthquake
 b. 1700 Cascadia earthquake
 c. Phyllite
 d. 1703 Genroku earthquake

17. _____ is a fine-grained, foliated, homogeneous metamorphic rock derived from an original shale-type sedimentary rock composed of clay or volcanic ash through low grade regional metamorphism. The result is a foliated rock in which the foliation may not correspond to the original sedimentary layering. _____ is frequently grey in colour especially when seen en masse covering roofs.
 a. Cataclasite
 b. Talc carbonate
 c. Slate
 d. Shock metamorphism

18. _____ is a common extrusive volcanic rock. It is usually grey to black and fine-grained due to rapid cooling of lava at the surface of a planet. It may be porphyritic containing larger crystals in a fine matrix, or vesicular, or frothy scoria.

Chapter 8. Metamorphism and Metamorphic Rocks: New Rocks from Old

    a. Basalt
    b. 1509 Istanbul earthquake
    c. 1703 Genroku earthquake
    d. 1700 Cascadia earthquake

19. _____ - also known as greenstone - is a general field petrologic term applied to metamorphic and/or altered mafic volcanic rock. The green is due to abundant green chlorite, actinolite and epidote minerals that dominate the rock. However, basalts may remain quite black if primary pyroxene does not revert to chlorite or actinolite.
    a. Greenstone belts
    b. Prehnite-pumpellyite facies
    c. Greenschist
    d. Metasomatism

20. _____ forms a group of medium-grade metamorphic rocks, chiefly notable for the preponderance of lamellar minerals such as micas, chlorite, talc, hornblende, graphite, and others. Quartz often occurs in drawn-out grains to such an extent that a particular form called quartz _____ is produced. By definition, _____ contains more than 50% platy and elongated minerals, often finely interleaved with quartz and feldspar.
    a. Porphyroblast
    b. Schist
    c. Talc carbonate
    d. Hornfels

21. _____ are fine to medium-grained metamorphic rocks that have experienced high temperatures of metamorphism, composed mainly of feldspars sometimes associated with quartz and anhydrous ferromagnesian minerals, with granoblastic texture and gneissose to massive structure. They are of particular interest to geologists because many _____ represent samples of the deep continental crust. Some _____ experienced decompression from deep in the Earth to shallower crustal levels at high temperature; others cooled while remaining at depth in the Earth.
    a. Granulites
    b. Hornfels
    c. Slate
    d. Greenschist facies

22. _____ is a sedimentary rock composed largely of the mineral calcite (calcium carbonate: $CaCO_3$.) The deposition of _____ strata is often a by-product and indicator of biological activity in the geologic record. Calcium (along with nitrogen, phosphorus, and potassium) is a key mineral to plant nutrition: soils overlying _____ bedrock tend to be pre-fertilized with calcium.
    a. 1509 Istanbul earthquake
    b. Limestone
    c. 1703 Genroku earthquake
    d. 1700 Cascadia earthquake

23. _____ is a hard metamorphic rock which was originally sandstone. Sandstone is converted into _____ through heating and pressure usually related to tectonic compression within orogenic belts. Pure _____ is usually white to grey, though _____s often occur in various shades of pink and red due to varying amounts of iron oxide .
    a. Quartzite
    b. Slate
    c. Hornfels
    d. Talc carbonate

24. _____ is a sedimentary rock composed mainly of sand-size mineral or rock grains. Most _____ is composed of quartz and/or feldspar because these are the most common minerals in the Earth's crust. Like sand, _____ may be any color, but the most common colors are tan, brown, yellow, red, gray and white.
    a. Shale
    b. Claystone
    c. Superficial deposits
    d. Sandstone

25. _____ rocks are composed of fragments of pre-existing rock. The term is most commonly, but not uniquely, applied to sedimentary rocks.

_____ metamorphic rocks include breccias formed in faults, as well as some protomylonite and pseudotachylite.

a. 1509 Istanbul earthquake
b. 1700 Cascadia earthquake
c. 1703 Genroku earthquake
d. Clastic

26. _____ is one of the three main rock types (the others being igneous and metamorphic rock.) _____ is formed by deposition and consolidation of mineral and organic material and from precipitation of minerals from solution. The processes that form _____ occur at the surface of the Earth and within bodies of water.

a. Serpentinite
b. Felsic
c. Large igneous provinces
d. Sedimentary rock

27. In materials science, _____ is a change in the shape or size of an object due to an applied force. This can be a result of tensile (pulling) forces, compressive (pushing) forces, shear, bending or torsion (twisting.) _____ is often described as strain.

a. Stack
b. Deformation
c. Submersion
d. Lingula

28. In geology, solid-state _____ is a metamorphic process that occurs under situations of intense temperature and pressure where grains, atoms or molecules of a rock or mineral are packed closer together, creating a new crystal structure. The basic composition remains the same. This process can be illustrated by observing how snow recrystallizes to ice without melting.

a. Vitrification
b. 1700 Cascadia earthquake
c. 1509 Istanbul earthquake
d. Recrystallization

29. _____ rocks contain angular fragments formed by cataclasis. Cataclasis is a deformation of the rock caused by fracture and rotation of aggregates or mineral grains.

The term _____ refers to the structure produced in a rock by the actions of severe mechanical stresses that occur during metamorphism.

a. Metamorphic rock
b. Phenocryst
c. Metavolcanic rock
d. Cataclastic

30. _____ occurs typically around intrusive igneous rocks as a result of the temperature increase caused by the intrusion of magma into cooler country rock. The area surrounding the intrusion (called aureoles) where the _____ effects are present is called the metamorphic aureole. Contact metamorphic rocks are usually known as hornfels.

a. Dispersion
b. Sea-level curve
c. Georeactor
d. Contact metamorphism

Chapter 8. Metamorphism and Metamorphic Rocks: New Rocks from Old

31. _____ is the group designation for a series of contact metamorphic rocks that have been baked and indurated by the heat of intrusive igneous masses and have been rendered massive, hard, splintery, and in some cases exceedingly tough and durable. Most _____ are fine-grained, and while the original rocks may have been more or less fissile owing to the presence of bedding or cleavage planes, this structure is effaced or rendered inoperative in the _____. Though they may show banding, due to bedding, etc., they break across this as readily as along it; in fact, they tend to separate into cubical fragments rather than into thin plates.
   a. Quartzite
   b. Hornfels
   c. Metasomatism
   d. Greenstone belts

32. Contact metamorphism occurs typically around intrusive igneous rocks as a result of the temperature increase caused by the intrusion of magma into cooler country rock. The area surrounding the intrusion (called aureoles) where the contact metamorphism effects are present is called the _____. Contact metamorphic rocks are usually known as hornfels.
   a. Reading Prong
   b. Metamorphic aureole
   c. Perched coastline
   d. Fulgurites

33. An _____ is used in geology to determine the degree of metamorphism a rock has experienced. Depending on the original composition of and the pressure and temperature experienced by the protolith (parent rock), chemical reactions between minerals in the solid state produce new minerals. When an _____ is found in a metamorphosed rock, it indicates the minimum pressure and temperature the protolith must have achieved in order for that mineral to form.
   a. AL 129-1
   b. Index mineral
   c. AASHTO Soil Classification System
   d. AL 333

34. _____ is the chemical alteration of a rock by hydrothermal and other fluids.

   _____ can occur via the action of hydrothermal fluids from an igneous or metamorphic source.

   In the igneous environment, _____ creates skarns, greisen, and may affect hornfels in the contact metamorphic aureole adjacent to an intrusive rock mass.

   a. Metasomatism
   b. Greenstone belts
   c. Geothermobarometry
   d. Quartzite

35. _____s are microporous, aluminosilicate minerals commonly used as commercial adsorbents. The term _____ was originally coined in 1756 by Swedish mineralogist Axel Fredrik Cronstedt, who observed that upon rapidly heating the material stilbite, it produced large amounts of steam from water that had been adsorbed by the material. Based on this, he called the material _____, from the Greek ζἰω , meaning 'boil' and λῖθος (lithos), meaning 'stone'.
   a. 1703 Genroku earthquake
   b. 1509 Istanbul earthquake
   c. 1700 Cascadia earthquake
   d. Zeolite

36. In geology, an _____ is a plane of constant metamorphic grade in the field; it separates metamorphic zones of different metamorphic index minerals. On geologic maps focusing on metamorphic terranes (or landscapes underlain by metamorphic rocks), the boundaries between rocks of different metamorphic grade are commonly demarcated by _____ lines. The garnet _____, for example, would mark the first occurrence of garnet in the rocks.
   a. Ostwald ripening
   b. Exner equation
   c. Espresso crema effect
   d. Isograd

Chapter 8. Metamorphism and Metamorphic Rocks: New Rocks from Old

37. The _____ are groups of mineral compositions in metamorphic rocks, that are typical for a certain field in pressure-temperature space. Rocks which contain certain minerals can therefore be linked to certain tectonic settings.

The name facies was first used for specific sedimentary environments in sedimentary rocks by Swiss geologist Amanz Gressly in 1838.

   a. Mylonite
   b. Metamorphic facies
   c. Prehnite-pumpellyite facies
   d. Facies

38. A _____ is in geology an area where, as a result of metamorphism, the same combination of minerals occur in the bed rocks. These zones occur because most metamorphic minerals are only stable in certain intervals of temperature and pressure.

The temperature and pressure at which the mineralogical composition of a rock equilibrated can vary laterally through a metamorphic terrane.

   a. Volcanic rock
   b. Petrology
   c. Phenocryst
   d. Metamorphic zone

39. In geology, _____ are a body of rock with specified characteristics. Ideally, a _____ is a distinctive rock unit that forms under certain conditions of sedimentation, reflecting a particular process or environment.

The term _____ was introduced by the Swiss geologist Amanz Gressly in 1838 and was part of his significant contribution to the foundations of modern stratigraphy, [Cross and Homewood (1997)] which replaced the earlier notions of Neptunism.

   a. Greenstone belts
   b. Metaconglomerate
   c. Metamorphic facies
   d. Facies

40. _____ describes the large scale motions of Earth's lithosphere. The theory encompasses the older concepts of continental drift, developed during the first decades of the 20th century by Alfred Wegener, and seafloor spreading, understood during the 1960s.

The outermost part of the Earth's interior is made up of two layers: the lithosphere and the asthenosphere.

   a. Nappe
   b. Mantle convection
   c. Continental crust
   d. Plate tectonics

41. _____ is a field of study within geology concerned generally with the structures within the lithosphere of the Earth and particularly with the forces and movements that have operated in a region to create these structures.

_____ is concerned with the orogenies and tectonic development of cratons and tectonic terranes as well as the earthquake and volcanic belts which directly affect much of the global population. Tectonic studies are also important for understanding erosion patterns in geomorphology and as guides for the economic geologist searching for petroleum and metallic ores.

Chapter 8. Metamorphism and Metamorphic Rocks: New Rocks from Old

a. Fault trace
b. Cocos Plate
c. Tectonics
d. Rivera Plate

42. _____ is a rock that forms by the metamorphism of basalt and rocks with similar composition at high pressures and low temperatures, approximately corresponding to a depth of 15 to 30 kilometers and 200 to ~500 degrees Celsius. The blue color of the rock comes from the presence of the mineral glaucophane.

They are typically found within orogenic belts as terranes of lithology in faulted contact with greenschist or rarely eclogite facies rocks.

a. Geothermobarometry
b. Metamorphic facies
c. Blueschist
d. Porphyroblast

43. _____ is a coarse-grained mafic metamorphic rock. _____ is of special interest for at least two reasons. First, it forms at pressures greater than those typical of the crust of the Earth. Second, being unusually dense rock, _____ can play an important role in driving convection within the solid Earth.
a. Eclogite
b. Epidosite
c. AL 129-1
d. AASHTO Soil Classification System

44. _____ circulation in its most general sense is the circulation of hot water; 'hydros' in the Greek meaning water and 'thermos' meaning heat. _____ circulation occurs most often in the vicinity of sources of heat within the Earth's crust. This generally occurs near volcanic activity, but can occur in the deep crust related to the intrusion of granite, or as the result of orogeny or metamorphism.
a. Seafloor spreading
b. Headward erosion
c. Transgression
d. Hydrothermal

45. The _____ is a fundamental concept in geology that describes the dynamic transitions through geologic time among the three main rock types: sedimentary, metamorphic, and igneous. Each type of rock is altered or destroyed when it is forced out of its equilibrium conditions. An igneous rock such as basalt may break down and dissolve when exposed to the atmosphere, or melt as it is subducted under a continent.
a. Metamorphic zone
b. Rock cycle
c. Felsic
d. Vesicular texture

1. Study of geological _____ is related to the study of structural geology, rock microstructure or rock texture and fault mechanics.

_____ is the response of a rock to deformation usually by compressive stress and forms particular textures. _____ can be homogeneous or non-homogeneous, and may be pure _____ or simple _____.

   a. Syncline   b. Tectonites
   c. Molasse basin   d. Shear

2. A _____, denoted τ (tau), is defined as a stress which is applied parallel or tangential to a face of a material, as opposed to a normal stress which is applied perpendicularly. In other words, considering that weight is a force, hanging something from a wall creates a _____ on the wall, since the weight of the object is acting parallel to the wall, as opposed to hanging something from the ceiling which creates a normal stress on the ceiling, since the weight is acting perpendicular to the ceiling.

The formula to calculate average _____ is:

$$\tau = \frac{F}{A}$$

where

      τ = the _____
      F = the force applied
      A = the cross sectional area

Beam shear is defined as the internal _____ of a beam caused by the shear force applied to the beam.

   a. Thixotropy   b. Viscosity
   c. Shear stress   d. Tensile stress

3. In materials science, _____ is a change in the shape or size of an object due to an applied force. This can be a result of tensile (pulling) forces, compressive (pushing) forces, shear, bending or torsion (twisting.) _____ is often described as strain.

   a. Submersion   b. Stack
   c. Lingula   d. Deformation

4. In chronostratigraphy, a _____ is a succession of rock strata laid down in an single age on the geologic timescale, which usually represents millions of years of deposition. A given _____ of rock and the corresponding age of time will by convention have the same name, and the same boundaries.

   a. Paleomagnetism   b. Lichenometry
   c. Relative dating   d. Stage

Chapter 9. How Rock Bends, Buckles, and Breaks

5. The _____ is a chronologic schema (or idealized model) relating stratigraphy to time that is used by geologists, paleontologists and other earth scientists to describe the timing and relationships between events that have occurred during the history of the Earth. The table of geologic time spans presented here agrees with the dates and nomenclature proposed by the International Commission on Stratigraphy, and uses the standard color codes of the United States Geological Survey.

Evidence from radiometric dating indicates that the Earth is about 4.570 billion years old.

   a. 1700 Cascadia earthquake
   b. 1509 Istanbul earthquake
   c. 1703 Genroku earthquake
   d. Geologic time scale

6. _____ is the naturally occurring, unconsolidated or loose covering on the Earth's surface. _____ is composed of particles of broken rock that have been altered by chemical, biological and environmental processes including weathering and erosion. _____ is different from its parent rock(s) source(s), altered by interactions between the lithosphere, hydrosphere, atmosphere, and the biosphere.

   a. Topsoil
   b. Slump
   c. 1509 Istanbul earthquake
   d. Soil

7. The _____ is the rigid outermost shell of a rocky planet.

In the Earth, the _____ includes the crust and the uppermost mantle, which constitute the hard and rigid outer layer of the planet. The _____ is underlain by the asthenosphere, the weaker, hotter, and deeper part of the upper mantle.

   a. Continental crust
   b. Subduction
   c. Mantle convection
   d. Lithosphere

8. _____, with regards to materials science, is the change in strain over the change in time and is denoted as $\hat{\imath}$.

$\hat{\imath} = >\delta>\varepsilon/>\delta t$

We have

$\hat{\imath} = >\delta>\varepsilon/>\delta t \,\square\, >$

where $\square >$ is the original length and v is the speed of deformation.

In a Newtonian fluid, the relation between the shear stress and the rate of strain is linear, the constant of proportionality being the coefficient of viscosity.

   a. 1509 Istanbul earthquake
   b. Kinematics
   c. 1700 Cascadia earthquake
   d. Strain rate

9. The _____ is the strongest part of the Earth's crust. For quartz and feldspar rich rocks in continental crust this occurs at an approximate depth of 13-18 km (roughly equivalent to temperatures in the range 250-400>°C.) At this depth rock becomes less likely to fracture, and more likely to deform ductilely by creep.
   a. Core-mantle boundary
   b. Brittle-ductile transition zone
   c. 1509 Istanbul earthquake
   d. Seismogenic layer

10. In geology, a _____ or _____ line is a planar fracture in rock in which the rock on one side of the fracture has moved with respect to the rock on the other side. Large _____s within the Earth's crust are the result of differential or shear motion and active _____ zones are the causal locations of most earthquakes. Earthquakes are caused by energy release during rapid slippage along a _____.
   a. Drainage system
   b. Compaction
   c. Cleavage
   d. Fault

11. A _____ is a special-purpose map made to show geological features.

The stratigraphic contour lines are drawn on the surface of a selected deep stratum, so that they can show the topographic trends of the strata under the ground. It is not always possible to properly show this when the strata are extremely fractured, mixed, in some discontinuities, or where they are otherwise disturbed.

   a. Geologic map
   b. 1700 Cascadia earthquake
   c. 1703 Genroku earthquake
   d. 1509 Istanbul earthquake

12. _____ is the study of the three-dimensional distribution of rock units with respect to their deformational histories. The primary goal of _____ is to use measurements of present-day rock geometries to uncover information about the history of deformation (strain) in the rocks, and ultimately, to understand the stress field that resulted in the observed strain and geometries. This understanding of the dynamics of the stress field can be linked to important events in the regional geologic past; a common goal is to understand the structural evolution of a particular area with respect to regionally widespread patterns of rock deformation (e.g., mountain building, rifting) due to plate tectonics.
   a. Strike and dip
   b. Petermann Orogeny
   c. Monocline
   d. Structural geology

13. In geology the term _____ refers to a fracture in rock where there has been no lateral movement in the plane of the fracture (up, down or sideways) of one side relative to the other. This makes it different from a fault which is defined as a fracture in rock where one side slides laterally past to the other. _____s normally have a regular spacing related to either the mechanical properties of the individual rock or the thickness of the layer involved.
   a. 1509 Istanbul earthquake
   b. 1703 Genroku earthquake
   c. 1700 Cascadia earthquake
   d. Joint

14. In geology, a _____ is a place where the Earth's crust and lithosphere are being pulled apart and is an example of extensional tectonics.

Typical _____ features are a central linear downdropped fault segment, called a graben, with parallel normal faulting and _____-flank uplifts on either side forming a _____ valley, where the _____ remains above sea level. The axis of the _____ area commonly contains volcanic rocks and active volcanism is a part of many, but not all active _____ systems.

a. 1700 Cascadia earthquake
b. 1703 Genroku earthquake
c. 1509 Istanbul earthquake
d. Rift

15. A _____ is the opposite of a normal fault -- the hanging wall moves up relative to the footwall. They are indicative of shortening of the crust. The dip of a _____ is relatively steep, greater than 45>°.
   a. Fault plane
   b. 1509 Istanbul earthquake
   c. Hanging wall
   d. Reverse fault

16. A _____ is a type of fault in which rocks of lower stratigraphic position are pushed up and over higher strata. They are often recognized because they place older rocks above younger. _____s are the result of compressional forces.
   a. Continental drift
   b. Thrust fault
   c. Mantle convection
   d. Convergent boundary

17. The fault surface of _____ is usually near vertical and the footwall moves either left or right or laterally with very little vertical motion. _____ with left-lateral motion are also known as sinistral faults. Those with right-lateral motion are also known as dextral faults.
   a. Pahoehoe lava
   b. Star dunes
   c. Strike-slip faults
   d. Suspended load

18. A _____ or transform boundary is a fault which runs along the boundary of a tectonic plate. The relative motion of such plates is horizontal in either sinistral or dextral direction. Typically, some vertical motion may also exist, but the principal vectors in a _____ are oriented horizontally.
   a. Structural geology
   b. Transform fault
   c. Michoud fault
   d. Molasse basin

19. In pedology, the study of soils in their natural environments, a _____ is a surface of the cracks produced in soils containing a high proportion of swelling clays. _____s are a type of cutan.

In geology, the term refers to a smoothly polished surface caused by frictional movement between rocks along the two sides of a fault.

   a. Soil horizon
   b. Pedogenesis
   c. Soil type
   d. Slickenside

20. In structural geology, an _____ is a fold that is convex up and has its oldest beds at its core. The term is not to be confused with antiform, which is a purely descriptive term for any fold that is convex up. Therefore if age relationships (i.e. younging direction) between various strata are unknown, the term antiform must be used.
   a. AASHTO Soil Classification System
   b. Anticline
   c. AL 129-1
   d. AL 333

21. _____, or tectonic breccia is a breccia (a rock type consisting of angular clasts) that was formed by tectonic forces. _____ has no cohesion, it is normally an unconsolidated rock type, unless cementation took place at a later stage. Sometimes a distinction is made between fault gouge and _____, the first has a smaller grain size.
   a. 1509 Istanbul earthquake
   b. Coprolite
   c. Ventifacts
   d. Fault breccia

22. The term _____ is used in geology when one or a stack of originally flat and planar surfaces, such as sedimentary strata, are bent or curved as a result of plastic (i.e. permanent) deformation. Synsedimentary _____s are those due to slumping of sedimentary material before it is lithified. _____s in rocks vary in size from microscopic crinkles to mountain-sized _____s.

- a. 1509 Istanbul earthquake
- b. 1700 Cascadia earthquake
- c. 1703 Genroku earthquake
- d. Fold

23. A _____ is a step-like fold consisting of a zone of steeper dip within an otherwise horizontal or gently-dipping sequence.

_____s may be formed in several different ways

- By differential compaction over an underlying structure, particularly a large fault at the edge of a basin due to the greater compactibility of the basin fill, the amplitude of the fold will die out gradually upwards e.g.

- By mild reactivation of an earlier extensional fault during a phase of inversion causing folding in the overlying sequence e.g.

- As a form of fault propagation fold during upward propagation of an extensional fault in basement into an overlying cover sequence e.g.

- As a form of fault propagation fold during upward propagation of a reverse fault in basement into an overlying cover sequence e.g.

- a. Structural geology
- b. Crenulation
- c. Syncline
- d. Monocline

24. In structural geology, a _____ is a downward-curving fold, with layers that dip toward the center of the structure. A synclinorium is a large _____ with superimposed smaller folds.

On a geologic map, they are recognized by a sequence of rock layers that grow progressively younger, followed by the youngest layer at the fold's center or hinge, and by a reverse sequence of the same rock layers on the opposite side of the hinge.

- a. Structural geology
- b. Shear
- c. Syncline
- d. Sag pond

25. _____ is a rock composed of angular fragments of minerals or rocks in a matrix (cementing material), that may be similar or different in composition to the fragments. A _____ may have a variety of different origins, as indicated by the named types including sedimentary _____, tectonic _____, igneous _____, impact _____ and hydrothermal _____.

Sedimentary _____s are a type of clastic sedimentary rock which are composed of angular to subangular, randomly oriented clasts of other sedimentary rocks.

Chapter 9. How Rock Bends, Buckles, and Breaks

    a. Fault breccia
    c. Ventifacts
    b. Breccia
    d. 1509 Istanbul earthquake

26. In petroleum geology _____ refers to rocks from which hydrocarbons have been generated or are capable of being generated. They form one of the necessary elements of a working hydrocarbon system. They are organic rich sediments that may have been deposited in a variety of environments including deepwater marine, lacustrine and deltaic.
    a. 1703 Genroku earthquake
    c. Source rock
    b. 1700 Cascadia earthquake
    d. 1509 Istanbul earthquake

27. _____ describes the large scale motions of Earth's lithosphere. The theory encompasses the older concepts of continental drift, developed during the first decades of the 20th century by Alfred Wegener, and seafloor spreading, understood during the 1960s.

The outermost part of the Earth's interior is made up of two layers: the lithosphere and the asthenosphere.

    a. Plate tectonics
    c. Continental crust
    b. Mantle convection
    d. Nappe

28. The _____ is a continental transform fault that runs a length of roughly 800 miles (1,300 km) through California in the United States. The fault's motion is right-lateral strike-slip (horizontal motion.) It forms the tectonic boundary between the Pacific Plate and the North American Plate.
    a. San Andreas Fault
    c. 1703 Genroku earthquake
    b. 1509 Istanbul earthquake
    d. 1700 Cascadia earthquake

29. _____ is the process by which the removal of material, through means of erosion and weathering, leads to a reduction of elevation and relief in landforms and landscapes. Exogenic processes, including the action of water, ice, and wind, predominantly involve _____. Denudation can involve the removal of both solid particles and dissolved material.
    a. Denudation
    c. 1509 Istanbul earthquake
    b. Mesa
    d. Palustrine

30. _____s is a field of study within geology concerned generally with the structures within the lithosphere of the Earth and particularly with the forces and movements that have operated in a region to create these structures.

_____s is concerned with the orogenies and _____ development of cratons and _____ terranes as well as the earthquake and volcanic belts which directly affect much of the global population. _____ studies are also important for understanding erosion patterns in geomorphology and as guides for the economic geologist searching for petroleum and metallic ores.

    a. Rivera Plate
    c. Cocos Plate
    b. Fault trace
    d. Tectonic

31. _____ is a field of study within geology concerned generally with the structures within the lithosphere of the Earth and particularly with the forces and movements that have operated in a region to create these structures.

_____ is concerned with the orogenies and tectonic development of cratons and tectonic terranes as well as the earthquake and volcanic belts which directly affect much of the global population. Tectonic studies are also important for understanding erosion patterns in geomorphology and as guides for the economic geologist searching for petroleum and metallic ores.

a. Cocos Plate
c. Fault trace
b. Rivera Plate
d. Tectonics

Chapter 10. Earthquakes and Earth's Interior

1. An _____ is the result of a sudden release of energy in the Earth's crust that creates seismic waves. They are recorded with a seismometer or the related and mostly obsolete Richter magnitude, with a magnitude 3 or lower _____ being mostly imperceptible and magnitude 7 causing serious damage over large areas.
   a. AL 333
   b. AASHTO Soil Classification System
   c. AL 129-1
   d. Earthquake

2. _____ are waves that travel through the Earth or other elastic body, for example as the result of an earthquake, explosion, or some other process that imparts forces to the body. _____ are also continually excited on Earth by the incessant pounding of ocean waves (referred to as the microseism) and the wind. _____ are studied by seismologists, and measured by a seismograph, which records the output of a seismometer, or geophone.
   a. Rayleigh waves
   b. Maximum magnitude
   c. Seismic waves
   d. Strong ground motion

3. _____ is the scientific study of earthquakes and the propagation of elastic waves through the Earth. The field also includes studies of earthquake effects, such as tsunamis as well as diverse seismic sources such as volcanic, tectonic, oceanic, atmospheric, and artificial processes . A related field that uses geology to infer information regarding past earthquakes is paleoseismology.
   a. 1509 Istanbul earthquake
   b. Seismology
   c. 1703 Genroku earthquake
   d. 1700 Cascadia earthquake

4. _____ are instruments that measure and record motions of the ground, including those of seismic waves generated by earthquakes, nuclear explosions, and other seismic sources. Records of seismic waves allow seismologists to map the interior of the Earth, and locate and measure the size of these different sources. Seismograph is another Greek term from seismós and γρÎ¬φω, gráphÀ , to draw.
   a. 1700 Cascadia earthquake
   b. 1703 Genroku earthquake
   c. Seismometers
   d. 1509 Istanbul earthquake

5. The _____ or epicentre is the point on the Earth's surface that is directly above the hypocenter or focus, the point where an earthquake or underground explosion originates.

   The _____ is usually the location of greatest damage. However, in some cases the _____ is above the start of a much larger event.

   a. AASHTO Soil Classification System
   b. AL 129-1
   c. AL 333
   d. Epicenter

6. In seismology, _____ are surface seismic waves that cause horizontal shifting of the earth during an earthquake. A.E.H. Love predicted the existence of _____ mathematically in 1911. They form a distinct class, different from other types of seismic waves, such as P-waves and S-waves (both body waves), or Rayleigh waves (another type of surface wave). _____ travel with a slower velocity than P- or S- waves, but faster than Rayleigh waves.
   a. Mazuku
   b. Seismic refraction
   c. Mantle plume
   d. Love waves

7. In physics, a _____ is a mechanical wave that propagates along the interface between differing media, usually two fluids with different densities. A _____ can also be an electromagnetic wave guided by a refractive index gradient. In radio transmission, a ground wave is a _____ that propagates close to the surface of the Earth.

Chapter 10. Earthquakes and Earth's Interior

a. 1700 Cascadia earthquake
c. 1703 Genroku earthquake
b. 1509 Istanbul earthquake
d. Surface wave

8. The _____, also known as the local magnitude (M_L) scale, assigns a single number to quantify the amount of seismic energy released by an earthquake. It is a base-10 logarithmic scale obtained by calculating the logarithm of the combined horizontal amplitude of the largest displacement from zero on a Wood-Anderson torsion seismometer output. So, for example, an earthquake that measures 5.0 on the Richter scale has a shaking amplitude 10 times larger than one that measures 4.0.

a. Mercalli intensity scale
c. Seismic scale
b. Moment magnitude scale
d. Richter magnitude Scale

9. _____ is a quantity used by earthquake seismologists to measure the size of an earthquake. The scalar _____ M_0 is defined by the equation $M_0 = >\mu A u$, where

- $>\mu$ is the shear modulus of the rocks involved in the earthquake, typically 30 gigapascals
- A is the area of the rupture along the geologic fault where the earthquake occurred, and
- u is the average displacement on A.

The _____ of an earthquake is typically estimated using whatever information is available to constrain its factors. For modern earthquakes, moment is usually estimated from ground motion recordings of earthquakes known as seismograms. For earthquakes that occurred in times before modern instruments were available, moment may be estimated from geologic estimates of the size of the fault rupture and the displacement.

a. Passive seismic
c. Gutenberg-Richter law
b. Reflection seismology
d. Seismic moment

10. _____ are type of elastic wave, also called seismic waves, that can travel through gases, elastic solids and liquids, including the Earth. _____ can be produced by earthquakes and recorded by seismometers.

a. 1700 Cascadia earthquake
c. 1703 Genroku earthquake
b. 1509 Istanbul earthquake
d. P-waves

11. A type of seismic wave, the _____, secondary wave or shear wave (sometimes called an elastic _____) is one of the two main types of elastic body waves, so named because they move through the body of an object, unlike surface waves.

The _____ move as a shear or transverse wave, so motion is perpendicular to the direction of wave propagation: _____ s, like waves in a rope, as opposed to waves moving through a slinky, the P-wave. The wave moves through elastic media, and the main restoring force comes from shear effects.

a. 1700 Cascadia earthquake
c. 1703 Genroku earthquake
b. 1509 Istanbul earthquake
d. S-wave

12. _____ occurs when a soil is sodic. When a sodic soil is wetted the clay particles are forced apart. This is generally a major cause of erosion.

a. Geomicrobiology
b. Seismic inversion
c. Dispersion
d. Schreyerite

13. The _____ is a scale used for measuring the intensity of an earthquake. The scale quantifies the effects of an earthquake on the Earth's surface, humans, objects of nature, and man-made structures on a scale of I through XII, with I denoting not felt, and XII one that causes almost complete destruction. The values will differ based on the distance to the earthquake, with the highest intensities being around the epicentral area.
   a. Richter magnitude scale
   b. Seismic scale
   c. Moment magnitude scale
   d. Mercalli intensity scale

14. In 1902 the ten-degree Mercalli scale was expanded to twelve degrees by Italian physicist Adolfo Cancani. It was later completely re-written by German geophysicist August Heinrich Sieberg and became known as the _____ scale. The _____ scale was later modified and published in English by Harry O. Wood and Frank Neumann in 1931 as the Mercalli-Wood-Neuman (MWN) scale.
   a. China Seismic Intensity Scale
   b. Mercalli-Cancani-Sieberg
   c. Moment magnitude scale
   d. Surface wave magnitude

15. _____ are a type of elastic surface wave that travel on solids. They are produced on the Earth by earthquakes, in which case they are also known as 'ground roll', or by other sources of seismic energy such as an explosion or even a sledgehammer impact. They are also produced in materials by acoustic transducers, and are used in non-destructive testing for detecting defects.
   a. Strong ground motion
   b. Hypocenter
   c. Seismic gap
   d. Rayleigh waves

16. A _____ is a deep active seismic area in a subduction zone. Differential motion along the zone produces deep-seated earthquakes, the foci of which may be as deep as about 700 kilometres (435 miles.) They develop beneath volcanic island arcs and continental margins above active subduction zones.
   a. Lava
   b. Fissure vent
   c. Volcanic pipes
   d. Wadati-Benioff zone

17. In geology, a _____ or _____ line is a planar fracture in rock in which the rock on one side of the fracture has moved with respect to the rock on the other side. Large _____s within the Earth's crust are the result of differential or shear motion and active _____ zones are the causal locations of most earthquakes. Earthquakes are caused by energy release during rapid slippage along a _____.
   a. Drainage system
   b. Compaction
   c. Cleavage
   d. Fault

18. Since faults do not usually consist of a single, clean fracture, the term fault zone is used when referring to the zone of complex deformation that is associated with the _____. The two sides of a non-vertical fault are called the hanging wall and footwall. By definition, the hanging wall occurs above the fault and the footwall occurs below the fault.
   a. 1509 Istanbul earthquake
   b. Hanging wall
   c. Reverse fault
   d. Fault plane

Chapter 10. Earthquakes and Earth's Interior

19. The _____ is an explanation for how energy is spread during earthquakes. As plates shift on opposite sides of a fault are subjected to force, they accumulate energy and slowly deform until their internal strength is exceeded. At that time, a sudden movement occurs along the fault, releasing the accumulated energy, and the rocks snap back to their original undeformed shape.
    a. Elastic rebound theory
    b. Azores-Gibraltar Transform Fault
    c. East Pacific Rise
    d. Obduction

20. _____ earthquakes occur at subduction zones at destructive plate boundaries (convergent boundaries), where one tectonic plate is forced (or subducts) under another. Due to the shallow dip of the plate boundary, these earthquakes are among the world's largest, with moment magnitudes (M_w) that can exceed 9.0.

    The major subduction zone is associated with the Pacific and Indian Oceans and are responsible for the volcanic activity associated with the Pacific Ring of Fire.

    a. Sonoma orogeny
    b. Tectonics
    c. Megathrust
    d. Cocos Plate

21. A _____ is a segment of an active fault that has not slipped in an unusually long time when compared with other segments along the same structure. _____ hypothesis/theory states that, over long periods of time, the displacement on any segment must be equal to that experienced by all the other parts of the fault. Any large and longstanding gap is therefore considered to be the fault segment most likely to suffer future earthquakes.
    a. Paleoliquefaction
    b. Receiver function
    c. Tornillo event
    d. Seismic gap

22. An _____ is an earthquake that occurs after a previous earthquake (the main shock.) An _____ is in the same region of the main shock but is always of smaller magnitude strength. If an _____ is larger than the main shock, the _____ is redesignated as the main shock and the original main shock is redesignated as a foreshock.
    a. AL 333
    b. Aftershock
    c. AL 129-1
    d. AASHTO Soil Classification System

23. The _____ is a continental transform fault that runs a length of roughly 800 miles (1,300 km) through California in the United States. The fault's motion is right-lateral strike-slip (horizontal motion.) It forms the tectonic boundary between the Pacific Plate and the North American Plate.
    a. 1700 Cascadia earthquake
    b. 1509 Istanbul earthquake
    c. San Andreas Fault
    d. 1703 Genroku earthquake

24. _____ is water located beneath the ground surface in soil pore spaces and in the fractures of lithologic formations. A unit of rock or an unconsolidated deposit is called an aquifer when it can yield a usable quantity of water. The depth at which soil pore spaces or fractures and voids in rock become completely saturated with water is called the water table.
    a. Groundwater
    b. 1700 Cascadia earthquake
    c. 1509 Istanbul earthquake
    d. Depression focused recharge

25. _____ is the result of the transformation of an existing rock type, the protolith, in a process called metamorphism, which means 'change in form'. The protolith is subjected to heat and pressure (temperatures greater than 150 to 200 >°C and pressures of 1500 bars) causing profound physical and/or chemical change. The protolith may be sedimentary rock, igneous rock or another older _____.
   a. Serpentinite
   b. Laccolith
   c. Metamorphic rock
   d. Pluton

26. The _____, usually referred to as the Moho, is the boundary between the Earth's crust and the mantle. The Moho serves to separate both oceanic crust and continental crust from underlying mantle. The Moho mostly lies entirely within the lithosphere; only beneath mid-ocean ridges does it define the lithosphere-asthenosphere boundary.
   a. Mohorovičić discontinuity
   b. Copperbelt Province
   c. Panthalassa
   d. Gorda Ridge

27. _____ is the geomorphic process by which soil, regolith, and rock move downslope under the force of gravity. Types of _____ include creep, slides, flows, topples, and falls, each with its own characteristic features, and taking place over timescales from seconds to years. _____ occurs on both terrestrial and submarine slopes, and has been observed on Earth, Mars, and Venus.
   a. 1509 Istanbul earthquake
   b. Soil liquefaction
   c. Mass wasting
   d. 1700 Cascadia earthquake

28. _____ is a type of potassic volcanic rock best known for sometimes containing diamonds. It is named after the town of Kimberley in South Africa, where the discovery of an 83.5 carats (16.7 g) diamond in 1871 spawned a diamond rush, eventually creating the Big Hole.

   _____ occurs in the Earth's crust in vertical structures known as _____ pipes.
   a. 1509 Istanbul earthquake
   b. Kimberlite
   c. 1700 Cascadia earthquake
   d. 1703 Genroku earthquake

29. A _____ is a sand- to boulder-sized particle of debris in the Solar System. The visible path of a _____ that enters Earth's (or another body's) atmosphere is called a meteor, or commonly a 'shooting star' or 'falling star.' If a _____ reaches the ground, it is then called a meteorite. Many meteors are part of a meteor shower.
   a. Meteoroid
   b. 1703 Genroku earthquake
   c. 1509 Istanbul earthquake
   d. 1700 Cascadia earthquake

30. A _____ is an area in which an S-Wave (secondary seismic wave) is not detected due to it not being able to pass through the outer core of the earth due to it being liquid. When an earthquake occurs, seismographs near the epicenter, out to about 90° distance, are able to record both Primary and Secondary waves, but those at a greater distance no longer detect the S-wave. This is because shear waves cannot pass through liquids.
   a. Receiver function
   b. Fault friction
   c. Seismic waves
   d. Shadow zone

31. _____ is the idea that Earth has been affected in the past by sudden, short-lived, violent events, possibly worldwide in scope.

The dominant paradigm of modern geology, in contrast, is uniformitarianism (also sometimes described as gradualism), in which slow incremental changes, such as erosion, create the Earth's appearance. This view holds that the present is the key to the past, and that all things continue as they were from the beginning of the world.

a. 1509 Istanbul earthquake
c. 1703 Genroku earthquake
b. 1700 Cascadia earthquake
d. Catastrophism

32. The _____ is the mechanically weak ductilly-deforming region of the upper mantle of the Earth. It lies below the lithosphere, at depths between 100 and 200 km (~ 62 and 124 miles) below the surface, but perhaps extending as deep as 400 km (~ 249 miles.)

The _____ is a portion of the upper mantle just below the lithosphere that is involved in plate movements and isostatic adjustments. In spite of its heat, pressures keep it plastic, and it has a relatively low density. Seismic waves pass relatively slowly through the _____, compared to the overlying lithospheric mantle, thus it has been called the low-velocity zone. This was the observation that originally alerted seismologists to its presence and gave some information about its physical properties, as the speed of seismic waves decreases with decreasing rigidity.

a. AL 333
c. AL 129-1
b. AASHTO Soil Classification System
d. Asthenosphere

33. The _____ of the Earth, its innermost hottest part as detected by seismological studies, is a primarily solid sphere about 1,220 km (758 mi) in radius, only about 70% that of the Moon. It is believed to consist of an iron-nickel alloy, and it may have a temperature similar to the Sun's surface.

The existence of an _____ distinct from the liquid outer core was discovered in 1936 by seismologist Inge Lehmann using observations of earthquake-generated seismic waves that partly reflect from its boundary and can be detected by sensitive seismographs on the Earth's surface.

a. AL 129-1
c. AASHTO Soil Classification System
b. AL 333
d. Inner core

34. _____, is a calcium titanium oxide mineral species with the chemical formula $CaTiO_3$.

The mineral was discovered in the Ural mountains of Russia by Gustav Rose in 1839 and is named after Russian mineralogist, L. A. Perovski .

It lends its name to the class of compounds which have the same type of crystal structure as $CaTiO_3$, known as the _____ structure.

a. 1700 Cascadia earthquake
c. Perovskite
b. Wollastonite
d. 1509 Istanbul earthquake

Chapter 10. Earthquakes and Earth's Interior

35. _____ describes the large scale motions of Earth's lithosphere. The theory encompasses the older concepts of continental drift, developed during the first decades of the 20th century by Alfred Wegener, and seafloor spreading, understood during the 1960s.

The outermost part of the Earth's interior is made up of two layers: the lithosphere and the asthenosphere.

   a. Nappe
   b. Plate tectonics
   c. Continental crust
   d. Mantle convection

36. _____s is a field of study within geology concerned generally with the structures within the lithosphere of the Earth and particularly with the forces and movements that have operated in a region to create these structures.

_____s is concerned with the orogenies and _____ development of cratons and _____ terranes as well as the earthquake and volcanic belts which directly affect much of the global population. _____ studies are also important for understanding erosion patterns in geomorphology and as guides for the economic geologist searching for petroleum and metallic ores.

   a. Fault trace
   b. Tectonic
   c. Cocos Plate
   d. Rivera Plate

37. _____ is a field of study within geology concerned generally with the structures within the lithosphere of the Earth and particularly with the forces and movements that have operated in a region to create these structures.

_____ is concerned with the orogenies and tectonic development of cratons and tectonic terranes as well as the earthquake and volcanic belts which directly affect much of the global population. Tectonic studies are also important for understanding erosion patterns in geomorphology and as guides for the economic geologist searching for petroleum and metallic ores.

   a. Rivera Plate
   b. Cocos Plate
   c. Fault trace
   d. Tectonics

Chapter 11. Geologic Time and the Rock Record

1. The _____ is a chronologic schema (or idealized model) relating stratigraphy to time that is used by geologists, paleontologists and other earth scientists to describe the timing and relationships between events that have occurred during the history of the Earth. The table of geologic time spans presented here agrees with the dates and nomenclature proposed by the International Commission on Stratigraphy, and uses the standard color codes of the United States Geological Survey.

Evidence from radiometric dating indicates that the Earth is about 4.570 billion years old.

  a. 1700 Cascadia earthquake
  b. 1703 Genroku earthquake
  c. 1509 Istanbul earthquake
  d. Geologic time scale

2. _____, a branch of geology, studies rock layers and layering (stratification.) It is primarily used in the study of sedimentary and layered volcanic rocks. _____ includes two related subfields: lithologic or lithostratigraphy and biologic _____ or biostratigraphy.
  a. 1509 Istanbul earthquake
  b. Stratigraphy
  c. 1703 Genroku earthquake
  d. 1700 Cascadia earthquake

3. _____ is a term used in geology to refer to the state of gravitational equilibrium between the earth's lithosphere and asthenosphere such that the tectonic plates 'float' at an elevation which depends on their thickness and density. This concept is invoked to explain how different topographic heights can exist at the Earth's surface. When a certain area of lithosphere reaches the state of _____, it is said to be in isostatic equilibrium.
  a. Isograd
  b. Orientation Tensor
  c. Economic geology
  d. Isostasy

4. In geology and related fields, a _____ is a layer of rock or soil with internally consistent characteristics that distinguishes it from contiguous layers. Each layer is generally one of a number of parallel layers that lie one upon another, laid down by natural forces. They may extend over hundreds of thousands of square kilometers of the Earth's surface.
  a. 1703 Genroku earthquake
  b. Stratum
  c. 1509 Istanbul earthquake
  d. 1700 Cascadia earthquake

5. An _____ is a buried erosion surface separating two rock masses or strata of different ages, indicating that sediment deposition was not continuous. In general, the older layer was exposed to erosion for an interval of time before deposition of the younger, but the term is used to describe any break in the sedimentary geologic record. The phenomenon of angular unconformities was discovered by James Hutton, who found examples at Jedburgh in 1787 and at Siccar Point in 1788.
  a. AL 129-1
  b. AL 333
  c. AASHTO Soil Classification System
  d. Unconformity

6. _____ is an unconformity between parallel layers of sedimentary rocks which represents a period of erosion or non-deposition. Paraconformity is a type of _____ in which the separation is a simple bedding plane; i.e., there is no obvious buried erosional surface. Blended unconformity is a type of _____ or nonconformity with no distinct separation plane or contact, sometimes consisting of soils, paleosols, or beds of pebbles derived from the underlying rock.
  a. 1700 Cascadia earthquake
  b. 1703 Genroku earthquake
  c. 1509 Istanbul earthquake
  d. Disconformity

7. _____ are fossils used to define and identify geologic periods They work on the premise that, although different sediments may look different depending on the conditions under which they were laid down, they may include the remains of the same species of fossil. If the species concerned were short-lived, then it is certain that the sediments in question were deposited within that narrow time period.
   a. Indian bead
   b. Allotrioceras
   c. Invertebrate paleontology
   d. Index fossils

8. In geology, a _____ is a widespread sedimentary layer that formed at a single time, such that it is useful for geologic correlations and dating over a large area. Examples of these are massive ashfalls, such as those produced by nearby normal volcanic eruptions, and far away in supervolcanic eruptions, as well as tills deposited by continental glaciers, and the global iridium layer deposited at the K-T boundary.
   a. Bedrock
   b. Key bed
   c. Sequence stratigraphy
   d. Principle of original horizontality

9. In geology a _____ is the smallest division of a geologic formation or stratigraphic rock series marked by well-defined divisional planes (bedding planes) separating it from layers above and below. A _____ is the smallest lithostratigraphic unit, usually ranging in thickness from a centimeter to several meters and distinguishable from _____s above and below it. _____s can be differentiated in various ways, including rock or mineral type and particle size.
   a. Sequence stratigraphy
   b. Cyclostratigraphy
   c. Biozones
   d. Bed

10. _____ are the preserved remains or traces of animals, plants, and other organisms from the remote past. The totality of _____, both discovered and undiscovered, and their placement in fossiliferous rock formations and sedimentary layers (strata) is known as the fossil record. The study of _____ across geological time, how they were formed, and the evolutionary relationships between taxa (phylogeny) are some of the most important functions of the science of paleontology.
    a. Fossils
    b. 1700 Cascadia earthquake
    c. 1703 Genroku earthquake
    d. 1509 Istanbul earthquake

11. The _____ is the geologic eon before the Archean. It started at Earth's formation about 4.6 billion years ago (4,600 Ma), and ended roughly 3.8 billion years ago, though the latter date varies according to different sources.
    a. 1700 Cascadia earthquake
    b. 1703 Genroku earthquake
    c. 1509 Istanbul earthquake
    d. Hadean

12. The _____, is a geologic eon before the Proterozoic and Paleoproterozoic, before 2.5 Ga (billion years ago, or 2,500 Ma.) Instead of being based on stratigraphy, this date is defined chronometrically. The lower boundary (starting point) has not been officially recognized by the International Commission on Stratigraphy, but it is usually set to 3.8 Ga, at the end of the Hadean eon.
    a. AL 129-1
    b. AASHTO Soil Classification System
    c. AL 333
    d. Archean

13. The _____ is the first geological period of the Phanerozoic eon, lasting from 542 ± 0.3 million years ago to 488.3 ± 1.7 million years ago (ICS, 2004); it is succeeded by the Ordovician. Its subdivisions, and indeed its base, are somewhat in flux. The period was established by Adam Sedgwick, who named it after Cambria, the classical name for Wales, where Britain's _____ rocks are best exposed.

a. 1703 Genroku earthquake
b. 1700 Cascadia earthquake
c. 1509 Istanbul earthquake
d. Cambrian

14. The _____ Era, is the most recent of the three classic geological eras and covers the period from 65.5 million years ago to the present. It is marked by the Cretaceous-Tertiary extinction event at the end of the Cretaceous that saw the demise of the last non-avian dinosaurs and the end of the Mesozoic Era. The _____ era is ongoing.
   a. Cenozoic
   b. 1700 Cascadia earthquake
   c. 1509 Istanbul earthquake
   d. 1703 Genroku earthquake

15. The _____ Era is one of three geologic eras of the Phanerozoic eon. The division of time into eras dates back to Giovanni Arduino, in the 18th century, although his original name for the era now called the '_____' was 'Secondary' (making the modern era the 'Tertiary'.)

The _____ was a time of tectonic, climatic and evolutionary activity. The continents gradually shifted from a state of connectedness into their present configuration; the drifting provided for speciation and other important evolutionary developments.

   a. Mesozoic
   b. 1703 Genroku earthquake
   c. 1509 Istanbul earthquake
   d. 1700 Cascadia earthquake

16. The _____ is the earliest of three geologic eras of the Phanerozoic eon. The _____ spanned from roughly 542 to 251 million years ago (ICS, 2004), and is subdivided into six geologic periods; from oldest to youngest they are: the Cambrian, Ordovician, Silurian, Devonian, Carboniferous, and Permian.

The _____ covers the time from the first appearance of abundant, soft-shelled fossils to the time when the continents were beginning to be dominated by large, relatively sophisticated reptiles and modern plants. The lower (oldest) boundary was classically set at the first appearance of creatures known as trilobites and archeocyathids.

   a. Paleozoic
   b. 1703 Genroku earthquake
   c. 1509 Istanbul earthquake
   d. 1700 Cascadia earthquake

17. The _____ Eon is the current eon in the geologic timescale, and the one during which abundant animal life has existed. It covers roughly 545 million years and goes back to the time when diverse hard-shelled animals first appeared.
   a. Phanerozoic
   b. 1509 Istanbul earthquake
   c. 1703 Genroku earthquake
   d. 1700 Cascadia earthquake

18. The _____ is a geological eon representing a period before the first abundant complex life on Earth. The _____ extended from 2500 Ma to 542.0 >± 1.0 Ma (million years ago), and is the most recent part of the old, informally named 'e;Precambrian'e; time.

Chapter 11. Geologic Time and the Rock Record

The Proterozoic consists of 3 geologic eras, from oldest to youngest:

- Paleoproterozoic
- Mesoproterozoic
- Neoproterozoic

The well-identified events were:

- The transition to an oxygenated atmosphere during the Mesoproterozoic.
- Several glaciations, including the hypothesized Snowball Earth during the Cryogenian period in the late Neoproterozoic.
- The Ediacaran Period (635 to 542 Ma) which is characterized by the evolution of abundant soft-bodied multicellular organisms.

The geoloic record of the Proterozoic is much better than that for the preceding Archean. In contrast to the deep-water deposits of the Archean, the Proterozoic features many strata that were laid down in extensive shallow epicontinental seas; furthermore, many of these rocks are less metamorphosed than Archean-age ones, and plenty are unaltered.

a. 1700 Cascadia earthquake
b. 1703 Genroku earthquake
c. 1509 Istanbul earthquake
d. Proterozoic Eon

19. _____ is the solid-state recrystallization of pre-existing rocks due to changes in physical and chemical conditions, primarily heat, pressure, and the introduction of chemically active fluids. Both mineralogical, chemical and crystallographic changes can occur during this process.

Three types of _____ exist: dynamic, contact and regional.

a. Lake capture
b. Gibraltar Arc
c. Pumice raft
d. Metamorphism

20. _____ is a type of radioactive decay in which an atomic nucleus emits an alpha particle (two protons and two neutrons bound together into a particle identical to a helium nucleus) and transforms (or 'decays') into an atom with a mass number 4 less and atomic number 2 less. For example:

$$^{238}_{92}U \rightarrow\ ^{234}_{90}Th\ +\ ^{4}_{2}He^{2+}$$

although this is typically written as:

$$^{238}U\ \rightarrow\ ^{234}Th\ +\ \alpha$$

(The second form is preferred because the first form appears electrically unbalanced. Fundamentally, the recoiling nucleus is very quickly stripped of the two extra electrons which give it an unbalanced charge.

a. AL 129-1
b. AASHTO Soil Classification System
c. AL 333
d. Alpha decay

21. In nuclear physics, _____ is a type of radioactive decay in which a beta particle (an electron or a positron) is emitted. In the case of electron emission, it is referred to as beta minus (>>β$^-$), while in the case of a positron emission as beta plus (>>β$^+$.) Kinetic energy of beta particles has continuous spectrum ranging from 0 to maximal available energy (Q), which depends on parent and daughter nuclear states participating in the decay.
   a. Decay product
   b. Mass deficiency
   c. Positron emission
   d. Beta decay

22. _____ is a decay mode for isotopes that will occur when there are too many protons in the nucleus of an atom and insufficient energy to emit a positron; however, it continues to be a viable decay mode for radioactive isotopes that can decay by positron emission. If the energy difference between the parent atom and the daughter atom is less than 1.022 MeV, positron emission is forbidden and _____ is the sole decay mode. For example, Rubidium-83 will decay to Krypton-83 solely by _____ (the energy difference is about 0.9 MeV.)
   a. AL 129-1
   b. AASHTO Soil Classification System
   c. AL 333
   d. Electron capture

23. The _____ is the total number of protons and neutrons in an atomic nucleus. Because protons and neutrons both are baryons, the _____ A is identical with the baryon number B as of the nucleus as of the whole atom or ion. The _____ is different for each different isotope of a chemical element.
   a. Mass number
   b. 1509 Istanbul earthquake
   c. 1703 Genroku earthquake
   d. 1700 Cascadia earthquake

24. _____ is a type of beta decay, sometimes referred to as 'beta plus' (>β$^+$.) In beta plus decay, a proton is converted, via the weak force, to a neutron, a positron (also known as the 'beta plus particle', the antimatter counterpart of an electron), and a neutrino.

Isotopes which undergo this decay and thereby emit positrons include carbon-11, potassium-40, nitrogen-13, oxygen-15, fluorine-18, and iodine-121.

   a. Mass excess
   b. Mass deficiency
   c. Decay product
   d. Positron emission

25. _____ is a technique used to date materials, usually based on a comparison between the observed abundance of a naturally occurring radioactive isotope and its decay products, using known decay rates. It is the principal source of information about the absolute age of rocks and other geological features, including the age of the Earth itself, and can be used to date a wide range of natural and man-made materials. Together with stratigraphic principles, _____ methods are used in geochronology to establish the geological time scale.
   a. Stage
   b. Lichenometry
   c. Radiometric dating
   d. Relative dating

26. In nuclear physics, a _____ is a nuclide produced by radioactive decay. Radioactive decay often involves a sequence of steps For example, U-238 decays to Th-234 which decays to Pa-234 which decays, and so on, to Pb-206:

Chapter 11. Geologic Time and the Rock Record

In this example:

- Th-234, Pa-234,…,Pb-206 are the _____s of U-238.
- Th-234 is the daughter of the parent U-238.
- Pa-234 is the granddaughter of U-238.

Note that Th-234, Pa-234,…,Pb-206 might also be referred to as the daughter products of U-238.

_____s are extremely important in understanding radioactive decay and the management of radioactive waste.

a. Mass excess
b. Mass deficiency
c. Positron emission
d. Decay product

27. The _____ of a quantity whose value decreases with time is the interval required for the quantity to decay to half of its initial value. The concept originated in describing how long it takes atoms to undergo radioactive decay but also applies in a wide variety of other situations.

a. 1700 Cascadia earthquake
b. Radionuclide
c. Half-life
d. 1509 Istanbul earthquake

28. _____ is a radiometric dating method used in geochronology and archeology. It is based on measuring the products of the radioactive decay of potassium (K), which is a common element found in materials such as micas, clay minerals, tephra, and evaporites. In the samples of interest, the decay product ^{40}Ar is not trapped by the molten rock, but is trapped and accumulated in the solid. Time since recrystallization is calculated by measuring the ratio of ^{40}Ar accumulated to ^{40}K remaining. The long half-life of ^{40}K allows the method to be used to calculate the absolute age of samples older than a few thousand years.

a. Fission track dating
b. Rubidium-strontium dating
c. Helium dating
d. Potassium-argon dating

29. _____, is a radiometric dating method that uses the naturally occurring radioisotope carbon-14 (^{14}C) to determine the age of carbonaceous materials up to about 60,000 years. Raw, i.e. uncalibrated, radiocarbon ages are usually reported in radiocarbon years 'Before Present' (BP), 'Present' being defined as AD 1950. Such raw ages can be calibrated to give calendar dates.

a. Carbon dating
b. Lichenometry
c. Geologic record
d. Cenomanian

30. In thermodynamics, an _____ or an isocaloric process is a thermodynamic process in which no heat is transferred to or from the working fluid. Conversely, a process that involves heat transfer (addition or loss of heat to the surroundings) is generally called diabatic.

a. AL 129-1
b. AL 333
c. Adiabatic process
d. AASHTO Soil Classification System

31. _____ describes the large scale motions of Earth's lithosphere. The theory encompasses the older concepts of continental drift, developed during the first decades of the 20th century by Alfred Wegener, and seafloor spreading, understood during the 1960s.

The outermost part of the Earth's interior is made up of two layers: the lithosphere and the asthenosphere.

a. Continental crust
c. Mantle convection
b. Plate tectonics
d. Nappe

32. The _____ is a fundamental concept in geology that describes the dynamic transitions through geologic time among the three main rock types: sedimentary, metamorphic, and igneous. Each type of rock is altered or destroyed when it is forced out of its equilibrium conditions. An igneous rock such as basalt may break down and dissolve when exposed to the atmosphere, or melt as it is subducted under a continent.

a. Felsic
c. Metamorphic zone
b. Vesicular texture
d. Rock cycle

33. _____s is a field of study within geology concerned generally with the structures within the lithosphere of the Earth and particularly with the forces and movements that have operated in a region to create these structures.

_____s is concerned with the orogenies and _____ development of cratons and _____ terranes as well as the earthquake and volcanic belts which directly affect much of the global population. _____ studies are also important for understanding erosion patterns in geomorphology and as guides for the economic geologist searching for petroleum and metallic ores.

a. Rivera Plate
c. Fault trace
b. Cocos Plate
d. Tectonic

34. _____ is a field of study within geology concerned generally with the structures within the lithosphere of the Earth and particularly with the forces and movements that have operated in a region to create these structures.

_____ is concerned with the orogenies and tectonic development of cratons and tectonic terranes as well as the earthquake and volcanic belts which directly affect much of the global population. Tectonic studies are also important for understanding erosion patterns in geomorphology and as guides for the economic geologist searching for petroleum and metallic ores.

a. Tectonics
c. Fault trace
b. Cocos Plate
d. Rivera Plate

Chapter 12. The Changing Face of the Land

1. _____ is the process by which the removal of material, through means of erosion and weathering, leads to a reduction of elevation and relief in landforms and landscapes. Exogenic processes, including the action of water, ice, and wind, predominantly involve _____. Denudation can involve the removal of both solid particles and dissolved material.
    a. Denudation
    b. Palustrine
    c. 1509 Istanbul earthquake
    d. Mesa

2. _____ is the scientific study of landforms and the processes that shape them. Geomorphologists seek to understand why landscapes look the way they do: to understand landform history and dynamics, and predict future changes through a combination of field observation, physical experiment, and numerical modeling. _____ is practiced within geology, engineering geology, geodesy, geography, archaeology, and geological engineering.
    a. Musgrave Block
    b. Sahara pump theory
    c. Canadian Shield
    d. Geomorphology

3. _____ refers to natural mountain building, and may be studied as a tectonic structural event, (b) as a geographical event, and (c) a chronological event. Orogenic events (a) cause distinctive structural phenomena and related tectonic activity, (b) affect certain regions of rocks and crust, and (c) happen within a specific period of time.
    a. Alice Springs Orogeny
    b. Orogenesis
    c. Orogeny
    d. Antler orogeny

4. A _____ is a type of arid terrain where softer sedimentary rocks and clay-rich soils have been extensively eroded by wind and water. It can resemble malpa>ís, a terrain of volcanic rocks. Canyons, ravines, gullies, hoodoos and other such geological forms are common in _____.
    a. 1703 Genroku earthquake
    b. 1509 Istanbul earthquake
    c. 1700 Cascadia earthquake
    d. Badlands

5. In geology, petrology is the study of rocks, and the conditions in which they form. _____ once was approximately synonymous with petrography, but in current usage, _____ is a subdivision of petrology focusing on macroscopic hand-sample or outcrop-scale description of rocks, while petrography is the speciality that deals with microscopic details.

    In the oil industry, _____, or more specifically mud logging, is the graphic representation of geological formations being drilled through, and drawn on a log called a mud log.

    a. Metamorphic zone
    b. Serpentinite
    c. Lithology
    d. Volcanic rock

6. A _____ is a drainage divide on a continent such that the drainage basin on one side of the divide feeds into one ocean or sea and the basin on the other side either feeds into a different ocean or sea, or else is endorheic, not connected to the open sea. The endpoints where a _____ meets the coast are not always definite, because the exact border between adjacent bodies of water is usually not clearly defined. The International Hydrographic Organization's publication Limits of Oceans and Seas defines exact boundaries of oceans, but it is not universally recognized.
    a. 1703 Genroku earthquake
    b. Continental divide
    c. 1509 Istanbul earthquake
    d. 1700 Cascadia earthquake

7. A system in a _____ has numerous properties that are unchanging in time. The concept of _____ has relevance in many fields, in particular thermodynamics. _____ is a more general situation than dynamic equilibrium.

Chapter 12. The Changing Face of the Land

   a. 1703 Genroku earthquake
   b. 1509 Istanbul earthquake
   c. Steady state
   d. 1700 Cascadia earthquake

8. In particle physics, the term _____ usually refers to small corrections to rough calculations based on the renormalization group that arise from the detailed behavior near the scale where new physics takes place. In the context of renormalization group, we often 'integrate out' modes of quantum fields with frequencies exceeding a certain energy scale (cutoff.) If the cutoff is very close to the energy scale that we want to study, the _____s become important and contribute small terms to formulae such as those for the beta functions.
   a. 1703 Genroku earthquake
   b. 1700 Cascadia earthquake
   c. 1509 Istanbul earthquake
   d. Threshold effect

9. An _____ is the result of a sudden release of energy in the Earth's crust that creates seismic waves. They are recorded with a seismometer or the related and mostly obsolete Richter magnitude, with a magnitude 3 or lower _____ being mostly imperceptible and magnitude 7 causing serious damage over large areas.
   a. AL 129-1
   b. AL 333
   c. AASHTO Soil Classification System
   d. Earthquake

10. In geology and related fields, a _____ is a layer of rock or soil with internally consistent characteristics that distinguishes it from contiguous layers. Each layer is generally one of a number of parallel layers that lie one upon another, laid down by natural forces. They may extend over hundreds of thousands of square kilometers of the Earth's surface.
   a. Stratum
   b. 1700 Cascadia earthquake
   c. 1703 Genroku earthquake
   d. 1509 Istanbul earthquake

11. In radiometric dating, _____ or blocking temperature refers to the temperature of a system, such as a mineral, at the time given by its radiometric date. In physical terms, the _____ at which a system has cooled so that there is no longer any exchange of parent or daughter isotopes with the external environment. This temperature varies broadly between different minerals and also differs depending on the parent and daughter atoms being considered.
   a. Rubidium-strontium dating
   b. Helium dating
   c. Fission track dating
   d. Closure temperature

12. _____ are rare isotopes created when a high-energy cosmic ray interacts with the nucleus of an in situ atom. These isotopes are produced within earth materials such as rocks or soil, in Earth's atmosphere, and in extraterrestrial items such as meteorites. By measuring _____, scientists are able to gain insight into a range of geological and astronomical processes.
   a. 1509 Istanbul earthquake
   b. Cosmogenic isotopes
   c. Nanogeoscience
   d. Carbonate-silicate geochemical cycle

13. _____ is a technique used to date materials, usually based on a comparison between the observed abundance of a naturally occurring radioactive isotope and its decay products, using known decay rates. It is the principal source of information about the absolute age of rocks and other geological features, including the age of the Earth itself, and can be used to date a wide range of natural and man-made materials. Together with stratigraphic principles, _____ methods are used in geochronology to establish the geological time scale.
   a. Stage
   b. Lichenometry
   c. Radiometric dating
   d. Relative dating

14. _____ is any particulate matter that can be transported by fluid flow, and which eventually is deposited.

Chapter 12. The Changing Face of the Land

They are most often transported by water (fluvial processes) transported by wind (aeolian processes) and glaciers. Beach sands and river channel deposits are examples of fluvial transport and deposition, though _____ also often settles out of slow-moving or standing water in lakes and oceans.

a. Brickearth
b. Salt glacier
c. Sediment
d. Fech fech

15. _____ describes the large scale motions of Earth's lithosphere. The theory encompasses the older concepts of continental drift, developed during the first decades of the 20th century by Alfred Wegener, and seafloor spreading, understood during the 1960s.

The outermost part of the Earth's interior is made up of two layers: the lithosphere and the asthenosphere.

a. Mantle convection
b. Plate tectonics
c. Continental crust
d. Nappe

16. _____s is a field of study within geology concerned generally with the structures within the lithosphere of the Earth and particularly with the forces and movements that have operated in a region to create these structures.

_____s is concerned with the orogenies and _____ development of cratons and _____ terranes as well as the earthquake and volcanic belts which directly affect much of the global population. _____ studies are also important for understanding erosion patterns in geomorphology and as guides for the economic geologist searching for petroleum and metallic ores.

a. Cocos Plate
b. Rivera Plate
c. Fault trace
d. Tectonic

17. _____ is a field of study within geology concerned generally with the structures within the lithosphere of the Earth and particularly with the forces and movements that have operated in a region to create these structures.

_____ is concerned with the orogenies and tectonic development of cratons and tectonic terranes as well as the earthquake and volcanic belts which directly affect much of the global population. Tectonic studies are also important for understanding erosion patterns in geomorphology and as guides for the economic geologist searching for petroleum and metallic ores.

a. Cocos Plate
b. Tectonics
c. Rivera Plate
d. Fault trace

18. The _____ is the biogeochemical cycle by which carbon is exchanged among the biosphere, pedosphere, geosphere, hydrosphere, and atmosphere of the Earth.

Chapter 12. The Changing Face of the Land

The _____ is usually thought of as four major reservoirs of carbon interconnected by pathways of exchange. These reservoirs are:

- The plants
- The terrestrial biosphere, which is usually defined to include fresh water systems and non-living organic material, such as soil carbon.
- The oceans, including dissolved inorganic carbon and living and non-living marine biota,
- The sediments including fossil fuels.

The annual movements of carbon, the carbon exchanges between reservoirs, occur because of various chemical, physical, geological, and biological processes. The ocean contains the largest active pool of carbon near the surface of the Earth, but the deep ocean part of this pool does not rapidly exchange with the atmosphere.

a. Cosmogenic isotopes
c. 1509 Istanbul earthquake
b. Nanogeoscience
d. Carbon cycle

19. The _____ is the rigid outermost shell of a rocky planet.

In the Earth, the _____ includes the crust and the uppermost mantle, which constitute the hard and rigid outer layer of the planet. The _____ is underlain by the asthenosphere, the weaker, hotter, and deeper part of the upper mantle.

a. Mantle convection
c. Subduction
b. Lithosphere
d. Continental crust

20. _____ is typically about 50-100 km thick (but beneath the mid-ocean ridges is no thicker than the crust), while continental lithosphere has a range in thickness from about 40 km to perhaps 200 km; the upper ~30 to ~50 km of typical continental lithosphere is crust. The mantle part of the lithosphere consists largely of peridotite. The crust is distinguished from the upper mantle by the change in chemical composition that takes place at the Moho discontinuity.

_____ consists mainly of mafic crust and ultramafic mantle (peridotite) and is denser than continental lithosphere, for which the mantle is associated with crust made of felsic rocks. _____ thickens as it ages and moves away from the mid-ocean ridge.

a. AL 333
c. AASHTO Soil Classification System
b. AL 129-1
d. Oceanic lithosphere

Chapter 13. Mass Wasting

1. _____ is the geomorphic process by which soil, regolith, and rock move downslope under the force of gravity. Types of _____ include creep, slides, flows, topples, and falls, each with its own characteristic features, and taking place over timescales from seconds to years. _____ occurs on both terrestrial and submarine slopes, and has been observed on Earth, Mars, and Venus.
   - a. 1509 Istanbul earthquake
   - b. Soil liquefaction
   - c. 1700 Cascadia earthquake
   - d. Mass wasting

2. The _____ of any physical feature such as a hill, stream, roof, railroad, or road refers to the amount of inclination of that surface where zero indicates level (with respect to gravity) and larger numbers indicate higher degrees of 'tilt'. Often slope is calculated as a ratio of 'rise over run' in which run is the horizontal distance and rise is the vertical distance.

   There are several systems for expressing slope:

   1. as an angle of inclination from the horizontal of a right triangle. (This is the angle >α opposite the 'rise' side of the triangle.)
   2. as a percentage (also known as the _____), the formula for which is > which could also be expressed as the tangent of the angle of inclination times 100. In the U.S., the _____ is the most commonly used unit for communicating slopes in transportation, surveying, construction, and civil engineering.
   3. as a per mille figure, the formula for which is > which could also be expressed as the tangent of the angle of inclination times 1000. This is commonly used in Europe to denote the incline of a railway.
   4. as a ratio of one part rise per so many parts run. For example, a slope that has a rise of 5 feet for every 100 feet of run would have a slope ratio of 1 in 20.

   Any one of these expressions may be used interchangeably to express the characteristics of a slope. _____ is usually expressed as a percentage, but this may easily be converted to the angle >α from horizontal since that carries the same information.
   - a. Diamond Head
   - b. Heavy metal
   - c. Compaction
   - d. Grade

3. _____ is water located beneath the ground surface in soil pore spaces and in the fractures of lithologic formations. A unit of rock or an unconsolidated deposit is called an aquifer when it can yield a usable quantity of water. The depth at which soil pore spaces or fractures and voids in rock become completely saturated with water is called the water table.
   - a. 1509 Istanbul earthquake
   - b. Depression focused recharge
   - c. 1700 Cascadia earthquake
   - d. Groundwater

4. A _____ is a geological phenomenon which includes a wide range of ground movement, such as rock falls, deep failure of slopes and shallow debris flows, which can occur in offshore, coastal and onshore environments. Although the action of gravity is the primary driving force for a _____ to occur, there are other contributing factors affecting the original slope stability. Typically, pre-conditional factors build up specific sub-surface conditions that make the area/slope prone to failure, whereas the actual _____ often requires a trigger before being released.
   - a. Mass wasting
   - b. Landslide
   - c. 1700 Cascadia earthquake
   - d. 1509 Istanbul earthquake

Chapter 13. Mass Wasting

5. _____ refers to quantities of rock falling freely from a cliff face. A _____ is a fragment of rock (a block) detached by sliding, toppling, or falling, that falls along a vertical or sub-vertical cliff, proceeds down slope by bouncing and flying along ballistic trajectories or by rolling on talus or debris slopes,'e; (Varnes, 1978.) Alternatively, a '_____ is the natural downward motion of a detached block or series of blocks with a small volume involving free falling, bouncing, rolling, and sliding'.

   a. Geohazard
   b. Debris flow
   c. Predator trap
   d. Rockfall

6. _____ is a form of mass wasting event that occurs when loosely consolidated materials or rock layers move a short distance down a slope. The landmass and the surface it _____s upon is called a failure surface. When the movement occurs in soil, there is often a distinctive rotational movement to the mass, that cuts vertically through bedding planes (landslides take place along a bedding plane or fault). This rotational movement moves along a curved slip surface of regolith (the failure surface) which overlies bedrock. This results in internal deformation of the moving mass consisting chiefly of overturned folds called 'sheath folds.'

   a. Soil
   b. Topsoil
   c. 1509 Istanbul earthquake
   d. Slump

7. The _____ is an engineering property of granular materials. The _____ is the maximum angle of a stable slope determined by friction, cohesion and the shapes of the particles.

   When bulk granular materials are poured onto a horizontal surface, a conical pile will form. The internal angle between the surface of the pile and the horizontal surface is known as the _____ and is related to the density, surface area, and coefficient of friction of the material.

   a. AL 129-1
   b. Angle of repose
   c. AASHTO Soil Classification System
   d. AL 333

8. A _____ is a conglomeration of discrete solid, macroscopic particles characterized by a loss of energy whenever the particles interact (the most common example would be friction when grains collide.) The constituents that compose _____ must be large enough such that they are not subject to thermal motion fluctuations. Thus, the lower size limit for grains in _____ is about 1 µm.

   a. 1700 Cascadia earthquake
   b. 1703 Genroku earthquake
   c. 1509 Istanbul earthquake
   d. Granular material

9. _____ is any particulate matter that can be transported by fluid flow, and which eventually is deposited.

   They are most often transported by water (fluvial processes) transported by wind (aeolian processes) and glaciers. Beach sands and river channel deposits are examples of fluvial transport and deposition, though _____ also often settles out of slow-moving or standing water in lakes and oceans.

   a. Brickearth
   b. Salt glacier
   c. Fech fech
   d. Sediment

Chapter 13. Mass Wasting

10. _____ is a term given to an accumulation of broken rock fragments at the base of crags, mountain cliffs, or valley shoulders. Landforms associated with these materials are sometimes called _____ slopes or talus piles. These deposits typically have a concave upwards form, while the maximum inclination of such deposits corresponds to the angle of repose of the mean debris size.
    a. Scree
    b. 1700 Cascadia earthquake
    c. 1703 Genroku earthquake
    d. 1509 Istanbul earthquake

11. A _____ is a fast moving mass of unconsolidated, saturated debris that looks like flowing concrete. They differentiate from a mudflow by terms of the viscosity of the flow. Flows can carry clasts ranging in size from clay particles to boulders, and also often contains a large amount of woody debris.
    a. Cryoseism
    b. Geohazard
    c. Sturzstrom
    d. Debris flow

12. A _____ or mudslide is the most rapid (up to 80 km/h, or 50 mph) and fluid type of downhill mass wasting. It is a rapid movement of a large mass of mud formed from loose earth and water. Similar terms are mudslide (not very liquid), mud stream, debris flow (e.g. in high mountains), j>ökulhlaup, and lahar
    a. 1700 Cascadia earthquake
    b. 1509 Istanbul earthquake
    c. 1703 Genroku earthquake
    d. Mudflow

13. In geology, _____ is a type of mass wasting where waterlogged sediment slowly moves downslope over impermeable material. It can occur in any climate where the ground is saturated by water, though it is most often found in periglacial environments where the ground is permanently frozen, under which conditions the process is often called gelifluction. During warm seasonal periods the surface layer melts and slides over the frozen underlayer, slowly moving downslope due to frost heave that occurs normal to the slope.
    a. Rockfall
    b. Sturzstrom
    c. Geohazard
    d. Solifluction

14. _____ is the name for loose bodies of sediment that have been deposited or built up at the bottom of a low-grade slope or against a barrier on that slope, transported by gravity. The deposits that collect at the foot of a steep slope or cliff are also known by the same name. _____ often outerfingers with alluvium (deposits transported downslope by water).
    a. Subsequent streams
    b. Coastal erosion
    c. Salt pans
    d. Colluvium

15. An _____ is a downslope viscous flow of fine grained materials that have been saturated with water, and moves under the pull of gravity. They are an intermediate type of mass wasting that is between downhill creep and mudflow. The types of materials that are susceptible to _____s are clay, fine sand and silt, and fine-grained pyroclastic material.
    a. Earthflow
    b. AL 129-1
    c. AASHTO Soil Classification System
    d. AL 333

16. An _____ is a rapid flow of snow down a slope, from either natural triggers or human activity. Typically occurring in mountainous terrain, an _____ can mix air and water with the descending snow. Powerful _____s have the capability to entrain ice, rocks, trees, and other material on the slope; however _____s are always initiated in snow, are primarily composed of flowing snow, and are distinct from mudslides, rock slides, rock _____s, and serac collapses from an icefall.

Chapter 13. Mass Wasting

a. AL 333
c. AL 129-1

b. AASHTO Soil Classification System
d. Avalanche

17. _____ is the process by which the freezing of water-saturated soil causes the deformation and upward thrust of the ground surface. This process can damage plant roots through breaking or desiccation, cause cracks in pavement, and damage the foundations of buildings, even below the frost line. Moist, fine-grained soil at certain temperatures is most susceptible to _____.

a. Frost heaving
c. 1509 Istanbul earthquake

b. 1703 Genroku earthquake
d. 1700 Cascadia earthquake

18. _____ are distinctive geomorphological landforms of blocky detritus which may extend outward and downslope from talus cones or from glaciers or the terminal moraines of glaciers. Their growth and formation is subject to some debate, with three main theories in prominence:

- They originated from cirque glaciers and contain a glacial ice core or interstitial ice between the rocks which causes the formation to move downslope;

- A permafrost origin, which implies that the features are related to permafrost action rather than glacial action;

- A mass wasting or landslide origin which does not require the presence of ice and suggests a sudden catastrophic origin with little subsequent movement.

_____ may move or creep at a very slow rate in part dependent on the amount of ice present.

a. Pastonian Stage
c. Pressure melting point

b. Pre-Pastonian Stage
d. Rock glaciers

19. A _____ is a large, slow-moving mass of ice, formed from compacted layers of snow, that slowly deforms and flows in response to gravity and high pressure.

_____ ice is the largest reservoir of fresh water on Earth, and second only to oceans as the largest reservoir of total water.

a. Deforestation
c. Keeling Curve

b. Little Ice Age
d. Glacier

20. A _____ is a mountain rising from the ocean seafloor that does not reach to the water's surface (sea level), and thus is not an island. These are typically formed from extinct volcanoes, that rise abruptly and are usually found rising from a seafloor of 1,000-4,000 meters depth. They are defined by oceanographers as independent features that rise to at least 1,000 meters above the seafloor.

a. 1509 Istanbul earthquake
c. 1700 Cascadia earthquake

b. 1703 Genroku earthquake
d. Seamount

21. A _____ is a marine landslide that transports sediment across the continental shelf and into the deep ocean. A _____ is initiated when the downwards driving stress (gravity and other factors) exceeds the resisting stress of the seafloor slope material causing movements along one or more concave to planer rupture surfaces. _____s take place in a variety of different settings including planes as low as 1>° and can cause significant damage to both life and property.

   a. 1700 Cascadia earthquake   b. 1509 Istanbul earthquake
   c. 1703 Genroku earthquake   d. Submarine landslide

22. _____ describes the large scale motions of Earth's lithosphere. The theory encompasses the older concepts of continental drift, developed during the first decades of the 20th century by Alfred Wegener, and seafloor spreading, understood during the 1960s.

The outermost part of the Earth's interior is made up of two layers: the lithosphere and the asthenosphere.

   a. Continental crust   b. Mantle convection
   c. Nappe   d. Plate tectonics

23. _____s is a field of study within geology concerned generally with the structures within the lithosphere of the Earth and particularly with the forces and movements that have operated in a region to create these structures.

_____s is concerned with the orogenies and _____ development of cratons and _____ terranes as well as the earthquake and volcanic belts which directly affect much of the global population. _____ studies are also important for understanding erosion patterns in geomorphology and as guides for the economic geologist searching for petroleum and metallic ores.

   a. Cocos Plate   b. Fault trace
   c. Rivera Plate   d. Tectonic

24. _____ is a field of study within geology concerned generally with the structures within the lithosphere of the Earth and particularly with the forces and movements that have operated in a region to create these structures.

_____ is concerned with the orogenies and tectonic development of cratons and tectonic terranes as well as the earthquake and volcanic belts which directly affect much of the global population. Tectonic studies are also important for understanding erosion patterns in geomorphology and as guides for the economic geologist searching for petroleum and metallic ores.

   a. Cocos Plate   b. Tectonics
   c. Rivera Plate   d. Fault trace

Chapter 14. Streams and Drainage Systems

1. _____ occurs when the rate of rainfall on a surface exceeds the rate at which water can infiltrate the ground, and any depression storage has already been filled. This is called infiltration excess _____, Hortonian _____, or unsaturated _____. This more commonly occurs in arid and semi-arid regions, where rainfall intensities are high and the soil infiltration capacity is reduced because of surface sealing, or in paved areas.
   a. Overland flow
   b. Upwelling
   c. Intertidal
   d. Eutrophication

2. _____ is the flow of water in streams, rivers, and other channels, and is a major element of the water cycle. It is one component of the runoff of water from the land to waterbodies, the other component being surface runoff. Water flowing in channels comes from surface runoff from adjacent hillslopes, from groundwater flow out of the ground, and from water discharged from pipes.
   a. Streamflow
   b. Vadose zone
   c. Stemflow
   d. Cone of depression

3. A _____ is a stream or river which flows into a mainstem (or parent) river. A _____ does not flow directly into a sea. Tributaries and the mainstem river serve to drain the surrounding drainage basin of its surface water and groundwater by leading the water out into an ocean or some other large body of water.
   a. Sahara pump theory
   b. Tributary
   c. Great Artesian Basin
   d. Gawler craton

4. There are two meanings for _____s both coming from hydro- meaning water, and -graph meaning chart. A _____ plots the discharge of a river as a function of time. This activity can be in response to episodal event such as a flood.
   a. Flownet
   b. Streamflow
   c. Vadose zone
   d. Hydrograph

5. In physics, _____ is the rate at which work is performed or energy is transmitted, or the amount of energy required or expended for a given unit of time. As a rate of change of work done or the energy of a subsystem, _____ is:

$$P = \frac{W}{t}$$

where P is _____, W is work and t is time.

The average _____ (often simply called '_____' when the context makes it clear) is the average amount of work done or energy transferred per unit time.

   a. Turbulent flow
   b. Potentiometric surface
   c. Strong interaction
   d. Power

6. A _____ is one of a number of channel types and has a channel that consists of a network of small channels separated by small and often temporary islands called braid bars or, in British usage, aits or eyots. Braided streams occur in rivers with high slope and/or large sediment load (Schumm and Kahn 1972.) Braided channels are also typical of environments that dramatically decrease channel depth, and consequently channel velocity, such as river deltas, alluvial fans and peneplains.

Chapter 14. Streams and Drainage Systems

_____s, as distinct from meandering rivers, occur when a threshold level of sediment load or slope is reached. Geologically speaking an increase in sediment load will over time increase the slope of the river, so these two conditions can be considered synonymous and consequently a variation of slope can model a variation in sediment load.

- a. Meander
- b. Stream capture
- c. 1509 Istanbul earthquake
- d. Braided river

7. A _____ in general is a bend in a sinuous watercourse. A _____ is formed when the moving water in a river erodes the outer banks and widens its valley. A stream of any volume may assume a meandering course, alternatively eroding sediments from the outside of a bend and depositing them on the inside.
- a. Stream capture
- b. 1509 Istanbul earthquake
- c. Distributary
- d. Meander

8. An _____ is a U-shaped body of water formed when a wide meander from the mainstem of a river is cut off to create a lake. This landform is called an _____ for the distinctive curved shape that results from this process. In Australia, an _____ is called a billabong.
- a. AL 333
- b. AASHTO Soil Classification System
- c. Oxbow lake
- d. AL 129-1

9. A _____ is a depositional feature of streams. _____s are found in abundance in mature or meandering streams. They are crescent-shaped and located on the inside of a stream bend, being very similar to, though often smaller than towheads, or river islands. They are composed of sediment that is well sorted and typically reflects the overall capacity of the stream.
- a. Point bar
- b. 1703 Genroku earthquake
- c. 1509 Istanbul earthquake
- d. 1700 Cascadia earthquake

10. _____ is soil or sediments deposited by a river or other running water. _____ is typically made up of a variety of materials, including fine particles of silt and clay and larger particles of sand and gravel.

Flowing water associated with glaciers may also deposit _____, but deposits directly from ice are not _____.

- a. Alluvium
- b. AL 129-1
- c. AL 333
- d. AASHTO Soil Classification System

11. In geology a _____ is the smallest division of a geologic formation or stratigraphic rock series marked by well-defined divisional planes (bedding planes) separating it from layers above and below. A _____ is the smallest lithostratigraphic unit, usually ranging in thickness from a centimeter to several meters and distinguishable from _____s above and below it. _____s can be differentiated in various ways, including rock or mineral type and particle size.
- a. Sequence stratigraphy
- b. Biozones
- c. Cyclostratigraphy
- d. Bed

Chapter 14. Streams and Drainage Systems

12. The term _____ describes particles in a flowing fluid (usually a river) that are transported along the bed. This is in opposition to suspended load and wash load which are carried entirely in suspension.

_____ moves by a variety of methods, including rolling, sliding, traction, and saltation.

- a. Colluvium
- b. Toreva block
- c. Stream gradient
- d. Bed load

13. _____ is the term for material, especially ions from chemical weathering, that are carried in solution by a stream.
- a. Dissolved load
- b. Teilzone
- c. Subfossil
- d. Lithostatic pressure

14. _____ is the removal of solids (sediment, soil, rock and other particles) in the natural environment. It usually occurs due to transport by wind, water, or ice; by down-slope creep of soil and other material under the force of gravity; or by living organisms, such as burrowing animals, in the case of bioerosion.

_____ is distinguished from weathering, which is the process of chemical or physical breakdown of the minerals in the rocks, although the two processes may occur concurrently.

- a. AASHTO Soil Classification System
- b. AL 333
- c. AL 129-1
- d. Erosion

15. _____, sometimes known as streamline flow, occurs when a fluid flows in parallel layers, with no disruption between the layers. In fluid dynamics, _____ is a flow regime characterized by high momentum diffusion, low momentum convection, pressure and velocity independent from time. It is the opposite of turbulent flow.
- a. 1509 Istanbul earthquake
- b. 1703 Genroku earthquake
- c. 1700 Cascadia earthquake
- d. Laminar flow

16. In geology, a _____ deposit or _____ is an accumulation of valuable minerals formed by deposition of dense mineral phases in a trap site. Types of _____ deposits include alluvium, eluvium, beach _____s, and paleoplacers.

Typical locations for alluvial _____ deposits are on the inside bends of rivers and creeks, in natural hollows, at the break of slope on a stream, the base of an escarpment, waterfall or other barrier, within sand dunes, beach profiles or in gravel beds.

- a. Placer
- b. 1509 Istanbul earthquake
- c. 1703 Genroku earthquake
- d. 1700 Cascadia earthquake

17. In geology, _____ is a specific type of particle transport by fluids such as wind, or the denser fluid water. It occurs when loose material is removed from a bed and carried by the fluid, before being transported back to the surface. Examples include pebble transport by rivers, sand drift over desert surfaces, soil blowing over fields, or even snow drift over smooth surfaces such as those in the Arctic or Canadian Prairies.
- a. Wave pounding
- b. Stoping
- c. Downcutting
- d. Saltation

Chapter 14. Streams and Drainage Systems

18. _____ is the term for the fine particles that are light enough to be carried in a stream without touching the stream bed. These particles are generally of the fine sand, silt and clay size, although they can be larger, especially in cases of high discharge, such as during floods. This is in contrast to bed load which is carried along the bottom of the stream.
   a. Star dunes
   b. Pahoehoe lava
   c. Valley glaciers
   d. Suspended load

19. In fluid dynamics, turbulence or _____ is a fluid regime characterized by chaotic, stochastic property changes. This includes low momentum diffusion, high momentum convection, and rapid variation of pressure and velocity in space and time. Flow that is not turbulent is called laminar flow.
   a. Strong interaction
   b. Potentiometric surface
   c. Power
   d. Turbulent flow

20. _____ is any particulate matter that can be transported by fluid flow, and which eventually is deposited.

They are most often transported by water (fluvial processes) transported by wind (aeolian processes) and glaciers. Beach sands and river channel deposits are examples of fluvial transport and deposition, though _____ also often settles out of slow-moving or standing water in lakes and oceans.

   a. Salt glacier
   b. Brickearth
   c. Fech fech
   d. Sediment

21. A _____ is flat or nearly flat land adjacent to a stream or river that experiences occasional or periodic flooding. It includes the floodway, which consists of the stream channel and adjacent areas that carry flood flows, and the flood fringe, which are areas covered by the flood, but which do not experience a strong current.

They generally contain unconsolidated sediments, often extending below the bed of the stream.

   a. 1509 Istanbul earthquake
   b. 1700 Cascadia earthquake
   c. 1703 Genroku earthquake
   d. Floodplain

22. A _____, dike (or dyke), embankment, floodbank or stopbank is a natural or artificial slope or wall to regulate water levels. It is usually earthen and often parallel to the course of a river or the coast.
   a. 1700 Cascadia earthquake
   b. 1703 Genroku earthquake
   c. Levee
   d. 1509 Istanbul earthquake

23. An _____ is a fan-shaped deposit formed where a fast flowing stream flattens, slows, and spreads typically at the exit of a canyon onto a flatter plain. A convergence of neighboring fans into a single apron of deposits against a slope is called a bajada, or compound _____.
   a. Alluvial fan
   b. AL 333
   c. AASHTO Soil Classification System
   d. AL 129-1

24. A _____ is a stream that branches off and flows away from a main stream channel. They are a common feature of river deltas. The phenomenon is known as river bifurcation.
   a. Meander
   b. Stream capture
   c. Distributary
   d. 1509 Istanbul earthquake

Chapter 14. Streams and Drainage Systems

25. _____ is the natural or artificial removal of surface and sub-surface water from an area. Many agricultural soils need _____ to improve production or to manage water supplies.

The earliest archaeological record of an advanced system of _____ comes from the Indus Valley Civilization from around 3100 BC in what is now Pakistan and North India.

   a. 1703 Genroku earthquake
   c. 1509 Istanbul earthquake
   b. 1700 Cascadia earthquake
   d. Drainage

26. A _____ is an extent of land where water from rain or snow melt drains downhill into a body of water, such as a river, lake, reservoir, estuary, wetland, sea or ocean. The _____ includes both the streams and rivers that convey the water as well as the land surfaces from which water drains into those channels, and is separated from adjacent basins by a drainage divide.

The _____ acts like a funnel, collecting all the water within the area covered by the basin and channelling it into a waterway.

   a. 1509 Istanbul earthquake
   c. 1703 Genroku earthquake
   b. 1700 Cascadia earthquake
   d. Drainage basin

27. In geomorphology, a _____ is the pattern formed by the streams, rivers, and lakes in a particular drainage basin. They are governed by the topography of the land, whether a particular region is dominated by hard or soft rocks, and the gradient of the land.

They can fall into one of several categories, depending on the topography and geology of the land:

Dendritic _____s are the most common form of _____.

   a. Cohesion
   c. Stack
   b. Drainage system
   d. Nodule

28. In mathematics, the Strahler number or Horton-Strahler number of a mathematical tree is a numerical measure of its branching complexity.

These numbers were first developed in hydrology by and ; in this application, they are referred to as the _____ and are used to define stream size based on a hierarchy of tributaries. They also arise in the analysis of hierarchical biological structures such as (biological) trees and animal respiratory and circulatory systems, in register allocation for compilation of high level programming languages and in the analysis of social networks.

   a. Stream capacity
   c. Water cycle
   b. Flownet
   d. Strahler stream order

29. _____ describes the large scale motions of Earth's lithosphere. The theory encompasses the older concepts of continental drift, developed during the first decades of the 20th century by Alfred Wegener, and seafloor spreading, understood during the 1960s.

Chapter 14. Streams and Drainage Systems

The outermost part of the Earth's interior is made up of two layers: the lithosphere and the asthenosphere.

a. Mantle convection
b. Nappe
c. Plate tectonics
d. Continental crust

30. _____, is a geomorphological phenomenon occurring when a stream or river drainage system or watershed is diverted from its own bed, and flows instead down the bed of a neighbouring stream. This can happen for several reasons, including:

- Tectonic earth movements, where the slope of the land changes, and the stream is tipped out of its former course.
- Natural damming, such as by a landslide or ice sheet.
- Erosion

a. Distributary
b. 1509 Istanbul earthquake
c. Meander
d. Stream capture

31. _____s is a field of study within geology concerned generally with the structures within the lithosphere of the Earth and particularly with the forces and movements that have operated in a region to create these structures.

_____s is concerned with the orogenies and _____ development of cratons and _____ terranes as well as the earthquake and volcanic belts which directly affect much of the global population. _____ studies are also important for understanding erosion patterns in geomorphology and as guides for the economic geologist searching for petroleum and metallic ores.

a. Rivera Plate
b. Fault trace
c. Cocos Plate
d. Tectonic

32. _____ is a field of study within geology concerned generally with the structures within the lithosphere of the Earth and particularly with the forces and movements that have operated in a region to create these structures.

_____ is concerned with the orogenies and tectonic development of cratons and tectonic terranes as well as the earthquake and volcanic belts which directly affect much of the global population. Tectonic studies are also important for understanding erosion patterns in geomorphology and as guides for the economic geologist searching for petroleum and metallic ores.

a. Fault trace
b. Rivera Plate
c. Cocos Plate
d. Tectonics

33. _____ are streams whose course is a direct consequence of the original slope of the surface upon which it developed, i.e., streams that follow slope of the land over which they originally formed.
a. Salt pans
b. Consequent streams
c. Coastal erosion
d. Fault scarp

Chapter 14. Streams and Drainage Systems

34. _____, originally Gondwanaland, is the name given to a southern precursor-supercontinent and then as a remnant separated from Laurasia 180-200 million years ago during the breakup of the Pangaea supercontinent that existed about 500 to 200 Ma ago into two large segments. While the corresponding northern hemisphere continent Laurasia moved further north, the nearly equal in area _____ included most of the landmasses in today's southern hemisphere, including Antarctica, South America, Africa, Madagascar, Australia-New Guinea, and New Zealand, as well as Arabia and the Indian subcontinent, which have now moved into the Northern Hemisphere.
   - a. 1509 Istanbul earthquake
   - b. Laurasia
   - c. 1700 Cascadia earthquake
   - d. Gondwana

35. In geology, a _____ is a place where the Earth's crust and lithosphere are being pulled apart and is an example of extensional tectonics.

   Typical _____ features are a central linear downdropped fault segment, called a graben, with parallel normal faulting and _____-flank uplifts on either side forming a _____ valley, where the _____ remains above sea level. The axis of the _____ area commonly contains volcanic rocks and active volcanism is a part of many, but not all active _____ systems.
   - a. 1509 Istanbul earthquake
   - b. 1700 Cascadia earthquake
   - c. 1703 Genroku earthquake
   - d. Rift

36. _____ are streams whose course has been determined by selective headward erosion along weak strata. These streams have generally developed after the original stream. _____ developed independently of the original relief of the land and generally follow paths determined by the weak rock belts.
   - a. Salt pans
   - b. Coastal erosion
   - c. Gravitational erosion
   - d. Subsequent streams

37. In thermodynamics, an _____ or an isocaloric process is a thermodynamic process in which no heat is transferred to or from the working fluid. Conversely, a process that involves heat transfer (addition or loss of heat to the surroundings) is generally called diabatic.
   - a. AL 333
   - b. Adiabatic process
   - c. AL 129-1
   - d. AASHTO Soil Classification System

38. _____ is a measure of the resistance of a fluid which is being deformed by either shear stress or extensional stress. In everyday terms (and for fluids only), _____ is 'thickness'. Thus, water is 'thin', having a lower _____, while honey is 'thick' having a higher _____.
   - a. Thixotropy
   - b. Shear stress
   - c. Tensile stress
   - d. Viscosity

Chapter 15. Groundwater

1. _____ is water located beneath the ground surface in soil pore spaces and in the fractures of lithologic formations. A unit of rock or an unconsolidated deposit is called an aquifer when it can yield a usable quantity of water. The depth at which soil pore spaces or fractures and voids in rock become completely saturated with water is called the water table.
   a. Depression focused recharge
   b. 1509 Istanbul earthquake
   c. 1700 Cascadia earthquake
   d. Groundwater

2. _____ is the geomorphic process by which soil, regolith, and rock move downslope under the force of gravity. Types of _____ include creep, slides, flows, topples, and falls, each with its own characteristic features, and taking place over timescales from seconds to years. _____ occurs on both terrestrial and submarine slopes, and has been observed on Earth, Mars, and Venus.
   a. 1700 Cascadia earthquake
   b. Mass wasting
   c. Soil liquefaction
   d. 1509 Istanbul earthquake

3. The _____, also termed the unsaturated zone, is the portion of Earth between the land surface and the phreatic zone or zone of saturation . It extends from the top of the ground surface to the water table. Water in the _____ has a pressure head less than atmospheric pressure, and is retained by a combination of adhesion , and capillary action (capillary groundwater.)
   a. Strahler stream order
   b. Hydraulic conductivity
   c. Water cycle
   d. Vadose zone

4. The _____ is the level at which the ground water pressure is equal to atmospheric pressure. It may be conveniently visualized as the 'surface' of the ground water in a given vicinity. It usually coincides with the phreatic surface, but can be many feet above it. As water infiltrates through pore spaces in the soil, it first passes through the zone of aeration, where the soil is unsaturated. At increasing depths water fills in more spaces, until the zone of saturation is reached. The relatively horizontal plane atop this zone constitutes the _____.
   a. Shaft construction
   b. Water table
   c. Crosshole sonic logging
   d. Rock bolt

5. _____ is a measure of the void spaces in a material, and is measured as a fraction, between 0-1, or as a percentage between 0-100%. The term is used in multiple fields including ceramics, metallurgy, materials, manufacturing, earth sciences and construction.

Used in geology, hydrogeology, soil science, and building science, the _____ of a porous medium (such as rock or sediment) describes the fraction of void space in the material, where the void may contain, for example, air or water.

   a. Porosity
   b. Saltwater intrusion
   c. Permeability
   d. Phreatic zone

6. _____ in the earth sciences (commonly symbolized as κ a rock or k) is a measure of the ability of a material (typically unconsolidated material) to transmit fluids. It is of great importance in determining the flow characteristics of hydrocarbons in oil and gas reservoirs, and of groundwater in aquifers. It is typically measured in the lab by application of Darcy's law under steady state conditions or, more generally, by application of various solutions to the diffusion equation for unsteady flow conditions.
   a. Phreatic zone
   b. Saltwater intrusion
   c. Porosity
   d. Permeability

Chapter 15. Groundwater

7. In physics, chemistry and materials science, _____ concerns the movement and filtering of fluids through porous materials. Examples include the movement of solvents through filter paper (chromatography) and the movement of petroleum through fractured rock. Electrical analogs include the flow of electricity through random resistor networks.
   a. 1703 Genroku earthquake
   b. 1509 Istanbul earthquake
   c. 1700 Cascadia earthquake
   d. Percolation

8. An _____ is an underground layer of water-bearing permeable rock or unconsolidated materials (gravel, sand, silt, or clay) from which groundwater can be usefully extracted using a water well. The study of water flow in _____s and the characterization of _____s is called hydrogeology. Related terms include: an aquitard, which is an impermeable layer along an _____, and an aquiclude (or aquifuge), which is a solid, impermeable area beneath an _____.
   a. AL 129-1
   b. AL 333
   c. AASHTO Soil Classification System
   d. Aquifer

9. A _____ occurs in an aquifer when groundwater is pumped from a well. In an unconfined (water table) aquifer, this is an actual depression of the water levels. In confined (artesian) aquifers, the _____ is a reduction in the pressure head surrounding the pumped well.
   a. Streamflow
   b. Cone of depression
   c. Flownet
   d. Strahler stream order

10. _____, symbolically represented as K, is a property of vascular plants, soil or rock, that describes the ease with which water can move through pore spaces or fractures. It depends on the intrinsic permeability of the material and on the degree of saturation. Saturated _____, K_{sat}, describes water movement through saturated media.
    a. Surface water
    b. Strahler stream order
    c. Vadose zone
    d. Hydraulic conductivity

11. _____ or piezometric head is a specific measurement of water pressure above a geodetic datum. It is usually measured as a water surface elevation, expressed in units of length, at the entrance (or bottom) of a piezometer. In an aquifer, it can be calculated from the depth to water in a piezometric well (a specialized water well), and given information of the piezometer's elevation and screen depth.
    a. 1509 Istanbul earthquake
    b. Soft water
    c. Water quality
    d. Hydraulic head

12. _____ in geology is a landform sunken or depressed below the surrounding area. _____s may be formed by various mechanisms, and may be referred to by a variety of technical terms.

- A basin may be any large sediment filled _____. In tectonics, it may refer specifically to a circular, syncline-like _____: a geologic basin; while in sedimentology, it may refer to an area thickly filled with sediment: sedimentary basin.

- A blowout is a _____ created by wind erosion typically in either a desert sand or dry soil (such as a post-glacial loess environment.)

- A graben is a down dropped and typically linear _____ or basin created by rifting in a region under tensional tectonic forces.

- An impact crater is a _____ created by an impact such as a meteorite crater.
- A pit crater is a _____ formed by a sinking, or caving in, of the ground surface lying over a void.
- A kettle is left behind when a piece of ice left behind in glacial deposits melts.

- A _____ may be an area of subsidence caused by the collapse of an underlying structure. Examples include sinkholes above caves in karst topography, or calderas.

a. Lingula
c. Depression
b. Cohesion
d. Melange

13. The _____ of any physical feature such as a hill, stream, roof, railroad, or road refers to the amount of inclination of that surface where zero indicates level (with respect to gravity) and larger numbers indicate higher degrees of 'tilt'. Often slope is calculated as a ratio of 'rise over run' in which run is the horizontal distance and rise is the vertical distance.

There are several systems for expressing slope:

1. as an angle of inclination from the horizontal of a right triangle. (This is the angle >α opposite the 'rise' side of the triangle.)

2. as a percentage (also known as the _____), the formula for which is [×]> which could also be expressed as the tangent of the angle of inclination times 100. In the U.S., the _____ is the most commonly used unit for communicating slopes in transportation, surveying, construction, and civil engineering.

3. as a per mille figure, the formula for which is [×]> which could also be expressed as the tangent of the angle of inclination times 1000. This is commonly used in Europe to denote the incline of a railway.

4. as a ratio of one part rise per so many parts run. For example, a slope that has a rise of 5 feet for every 100 feet of run would have a slope ratio of 1 in 20.

Any one of these expressions may be used interchangeably to express the characteristics of a slope. _____ is usually expressed as a percentage, but this may easily be converted to the angle >α from horizontal since that carries the same information.

a. Diamond Head
b. Heavy metal
c. Compaction
d. Grade

14. The _____ is a vast yet shallow underground water table aquifer located beneath the Great Plains in the United States. One of the world's largest aquifers, it covers an area of approximately 174,000 mi^2 in portions of the eight states of South Dakota, Nebraska, Wyoming, Colorado, Kansas, Oklahoma, New Mexico, and Texas. It was named in 1898 by N.H. Darton from its type locality near the town of Ogallala, Nebraska.

a. AL 333
b. AASHTO Soil Classification System
c. Ogallala Aquifer
d. AL 129-1

15. There are two end members in the spectrum of types of aquifers; confined and _____. Unconfined aquifers are sometimes also called water table or phreatic aquifers, because their upper boundary is the water table or phreatic surface. Typically (but not always) the shallowest aquifer at a given location is _____, meaning it does not have a confining layer (an aquitard or aquiclude) between it and the surface.

a. AL 129-1
b. AASHTO Soil Classification System
c. AL 333
d. Unconfined

16. An _____ is a confined aquifer containing groundwater that will flow upward through a well without the need for pumping. Water may even reach the ground surface if the natural pressure is high enough, in which case the well is called a flowing artesian well. An aquifer provides the water for an artesian well.

a. AL 333
b. AASHTO Soil Classification System
c. Artesian aquifer
d. AL 129-1

17. In geology, engineering, and surveying, _____ is the motion of a surface (usually, the Earth's surface) as it shifts downward relative to a datum such as sea-level. The opposite of _____ is uplift, which results in an increase in elevation. There are several types of _____.

a. Subsidence
b. 1509 Istanbul earthquake
c. Pothole
d. 1700 Cascadia earthquake

18. _____ is water that has high mineral content (mainly calcium and magnesium ions) (in contrast with soft water.) _____ minerals primarily consist of calcium (Ca^{2+}), and magnesium (Mg^{2+}) metal cations, and sometimes other dissolved compounds such as bicarbonates and sulfates. Calcium usually enters the water as either calcium carbonate ($CaCO_3$), in the form of limestone and chalk, or calcium sulfate ($CaSO_4$), in the form of other mineral deposits.

a. Soft water
b. Hard water
c. 1509 Istanbul earthquake
d. Hydraulic head

19. _____ the term used to describe types of water that contain few or no calcium or magnesium metal cations. The term is usually related to hard water, which does contain significant amounts of these ions.

_____ usually comes from peat or igneous rock sources, such as granite but may also derive from sandstone sources, since such sedimentary rocks are usually low in calcium and magnesium.

a. Hydraulic head
b. Water quality
c. 1509 Istanbul earthquake
d. Soft water

Chapter 15. Groundwater

20. A _____ is a mountain rising from the ocean seafloor that does not reach to the water's surface (sea level), and thus is not an island. These are typically formed from extinct volcanoes, that rise abruptly and are usually found rising from a seafloor of 1,000-4,000 meters depth. They are defined by oceanographers as independent features that rise to at least 1,000 meters above the seafloor.
    a. 1509 Istanbul earthquake
    b. 1703 Genroku earthquake
    c. Seamount
    d. 1700 Cascadia earthquake

21. In chemistry, a _____ is a salt or ester of carbonic acid.

To test for the presence of the _____ anion in a salt, the addition of dilute mineral acid (e.g. hydrochloric acid) will yield carbon dioxide gas.

_____-containing salts are industrially and mineralogically ubiquitous.

    a. 1509 Istanbul earthquake
    b. Carbonate
    c. 1703 Genroku earthquake
    d. 1700 Cascadia earthquake

22. _____ is a type of fossil: it consists of fossil wood where all the organic materials have been replaced with minerals, while retaining the original structure of the wood. The petrifaction process occurs underground, when wood becomes buried under sediment and is initially preserved due to a lack of oxygen. Mineral-rich water flowing through the sediment deposits minerals in the plant's cells and as the plant's lignin and cellulose decay away, a stone mould forms in its place.
    a. Pteridospermatophyta
    b. 1509 Istanbul earthquake
    c. Glossopteris
    d. Petrified wood

23. A _____ is a type of speleothem (secondary mineral) that hangs from the ceiling or wall of limestone caves. It is sometimes referred to as dripstone.

They are formed by the deposition of calcium carbonate and other minerals, which is precipitated from mineralized water solutions.

    a. 1703 Genroku earthquake
    b. 1700 Cascadia earthquake
    c. 1509 Istanbul earthquake
    d. Stalactite

24. _____ are composed of sheetlike deposits of calcite formed where water flows down the walls or along the floors of a cave. They are typically found in 'solution', or limestone caves, where they are the most common speleothem. However, they may form in any type of cave where water enters that has picked up dissolved minerals.
    a. 1703 Genroku earthquake
    b. Flowstones
    c. 1700 Cascadia earthquake
    d. 1509 Istanbul earthquake

25. A _____ is a type of speleothem that rises from the floor of a limestone cave due to the dripping of mineralized solutions and the deposition of calcium carbonate.

The corresponding formation on the ceiling of a cave is known as a stalactite. If these formations grow together, the result is known as a column.

Chapter 15. Groundwater

a. 1700 Cascadia earthquake
b. 1703 Genroku earthquake
c. Stalagmite
d. 1509 Istanbul earthquake

26. A _____ is a natural depression or hole in the surface topography caused by the removal of soil or bedrock, often both, by water. They may vary in size from less than a meter to several hundred meters both in diameter and depth, and vary in form from soil-lined bowls to bedrock-edged chasms. They may be formed gradually or suddenly, and are found worldwide.
a. 1509 Istanbul earthquake
b. 1700 Cascadia earthquake
c. 1703 Genroku earthquake
d. Sinkhole

27. _____ is a landscape shaped by the dissolution of a layer or layers of soluble bedrock, usually carbonate rock such as limestone or dolomite.

Due to subterranean drainage, there may be very limited surface water, even to the absence of all rivers and lakes. Many karst regions display distinctive surface features, with sinkholes or dolines being the most common.

a. Amblypoda
b. Andrija Mohorović iÄ‡
c. Ambulocetus
d. Karst topography

28. _____ is a radiometric dating method used in geochronology and archeology. It is based on measuring the products of the radioactive decay of potassium (K), which is a common element found in materials such as micas, clay minerals, tephra, and evaporites. In the samples of interest, the decay product ^{40}Ar is not trapped by the molten rock, but is trapped and accumulated in the solid. Time since recrystallization is calculated by measuring the ratio of ^{40}Ar accumulated to ^{40}K remaining. The long half-life of ^{40}K allows the method to be used to calculate the absolute age of samples older than a few thousand years.
a. Helium dating
b. Fission track dating
c. Rubidium-strontium dating
d. Potassium-argon dating

29. _____ describes the large scale motions of Earth's lithosphere. The theory encompasses the older concepts of continental drift, developed during the first decades of the 20th century by Alfred Wegener, and seafloor spreading, understood during the 1960s.

The outermost part of the Earth's interior is made up of two layers: the lithosphere and the asthenosphere.

a. Plate tectonics
b. Continental crust
c. Nappe
d. Mantle convection

30. _____s is a field of study within geology concerned generally with the structures within the lithosphere of the Earth and particularly with the forces and movements that have operated in a region to create these structures.

_____s is concerned with the orogenies and _____ development of cratons and _____ terranes as well as the earthquake and volcanic belts which directly affect much of the global population. _____ studies are also important for understanding erosion patterns in geomorphology and as guides for the economic geologist searching for petroleum and metallic ores.

a. Fault trace
c. Cocos Plate
b. Rivera Plate
d. Tectonic

31. _____ is a field of study within geology concerned generally with the structures within the lithosphere of the Earth and particularly with the forces and movements that have operated in a region to create these structures.

_____ is concerned with the orogenies and tectonic development of cratons and tectonic terranes as well as the earthquake and volcanic belts which directly affect much of the global population. Tectonic studies are also important for understanding erosion patterns in geomorphology and as guides for the economic geologist searching for petroleum and metallic ores.

a. Fault trace
c. Tectonics
b. Rivera Plate
d. Cocos Plate

Chapter 16. Glaciers and Glaciation

1. A _____ is a large, slow-moving mass of ice, formed from compacted layers of snow, that slowly deforms and flows in response to gravity and high pressure.

_____ ice is the largest reservoir of fresh water on Earth, and second only to oceans as the largest reservoir of total water.

a. Glacier
b. Little Ice Age
c. Keeling Curve
d. Deforestation

2. _____ are the largest glaciers, enormous masses of ice that are not visibly affected by the landscape and that cover the entire surface beneath them, except possibly on the margins where they are thinnest. Antarctica and Greenland are the only places where continental _____ currently exist. These regions contain vast quantities of fresh water.
a. AASHTO Soil Classification System
b. AL 333
c. AL 129-1
d. Ice sheets

3. An _____ is a thick, floating platform of ice that forms where a glacier or ice sheet flows down to a coastline and onto the ocean surface. They are found in Antarctica, Greenland and Canada only. The boundary between the floating _____ and the grounded (resting on bedrock) ice that feeds it is called the grounding line.
a. AL 333
b. AASHTO Soil Classification System
c. AL 129-1
d. Ice shelf

4. A _____ is an amphitheatre-like valley formed at the head of a glacier by erosion. A _____ is also known as a coombe or coomb in England, a combe or comb in America, a corrie in Scotland and Ireland, and a cwm in Wales, although these terms apply to a specific feature of which several may be found in a _____. The term 'comb' is often found at the end of placenames such as Newcomb and Maycomb, where it is pronounced /kÉ™m/.
a. 1703 Genroku earthquake
b. 1509 Istanbul earthquake
c. 1700 Cascadia earthquake
d. Cirque

5. Geologically, a _____ is a long, narrow inlet with steep sides, created in a valley carved by glacial activity.

The seeds of a _____ are laid when a glacier cuts a U-shaped valley through abrasion of the surrounding bedrock by the sediment it carries. Many such valleys were formed during the recent ice age.

a. 1700 Cascadia earthquake
b. 1703 Genroku earthquake
c. 1509 Istanbul earthquake
d. Fjord

6. An _____ is an ice mass that covers less than 50 000 km^2 of land area (usually covering a highland area.) Masses of ice covering more than 50 000 km^2 are termed an ice sheet.

They are not constrained by topographical features (i.e., they will lie over the top of mountains) but their dome is usually centred on the highest point of a massif.

a. AL 333
b. AL 129-1
c. AASHTO Soil Classification System
d. Ice cap

7. A _____ is formed in a cirque, bowl-shaped depressions on the side of mountains. Snow and ice accumulation in corries often occurs as the result of avalanching from higher surrounding slopes.

Chapter 16. Glaciers and Glaciation

In these depressions, snow persists through summer months, and becomes glacier ice.

a. Cirque glacier
b. Wolstonian Stage
c. Pressure melting point
d. Drumlin field

8. Alpine glaciers form high on the mountain slopes and are niche, slope or cirque glaciers. As a mountain glacier increases in size it can begin to flow down valley, and are referred to as _____.
a. Historical geology
b. Star dunes
c. Suspended load
d. Valley glaciers

9. The _____ is a vast body of ice covering 1.71 million km^2, roughly 80% of the surface of Greenland. It is the second largest ice body in the World, after the Antarctic Ice Sheet. The ice sheet is almost 2,400 kilometers long in a north-south direction, and its greatest width is 1,100 kilometers at a latitude of 77>°N, near its northern margin.
a. 1700 Cascadia earthquake
b. 1509 Istanbul earthquake
c. 1703 Genroku earthquake
d. Greenland Ice Sheet

10. _____ used in the glaciological literature to refer to the melting point of ice under pressure. As the pressure increases in the downward direction, the melting temperature of ice decreases. This _____ can reach values many degrees below 0>°C.
a. Rock glaciers
b. Bergschrund
c. Cirque glacier
d. Pressure melting point

11. _____ is defined as the removal of material from the surface of an object by vaporization, chipping, or other erosive processes.

In glaciology, _____ is used to define the removal of ice or snow from the surface of a glacier. It is primarily driven by solar insolation. _____ may refer to melting and runoff or evaporation and sublimation of the ice, resulting in a thinning of the ice if it is not replenished by some other process. _____ deposits are the masses of detritus left after surface melting of glacial ice.

a. AL 333
b. Ablation
c. AASHTO Soil Classification System
d. AL 129-1

12. A _____ is an application of conservation of mass to the analysis of physical systems. By accounting for material entering and leaving a system, mass flows can be identified which might have been unknown, or difficult to measure without this technique. The exact Conservation law used in the analysis of the system depends on the context of the problem but all revolve around mass conservation, i.e. that matter cannot disappear or be created spontaneously.
a. 1700 Cascadia earthquake
b. Mass balance
c. 1509 Istanbul earthquake
d. 1703 Genroku earthquake

13. On a glacier, the _____, zone of ablation or zone of wastage is the area in which annual loss of snow through melting, evaporation, iceberg calving and sublimation exceeds annual gain of snow and ice on the surface. Of these, melting is most important in most glaciers, but the others, especially iceberg calving, can be significant. Spatially, the zone of ablation can be identified as the part of the glacier below the snowline.

Chapter 16. Glaciers and Glaciation

  a. AL 129-1
  c. AL 333
  b. Ablation zone
  d. AASHTO Soil Classification System

14. On a glacier, the _____ is the area above the firn line, where snowfall accumulates and exceeds the losses from ablation, (melting, evaporation, and sublimation.) The annual Glacier equilibrium line separates the accumulation and ablation zone annually. The _____ is also defined as the part of a glacier'e;s surface, usually at higher elevations, on which there is net accumulation of snow, which subsequently turns into firn and then glacier ice.
  a. Accumulation zone
  c. AL 333
  b. AASHTO Soil Classification System
  d. AL 129-1

15. A _____ is a huge crack formed by two glaciers colliding. Accelerations in glacier speed cause extension and can initiate a _____. Crevasses often have vertical or near-vertical walls, which can then melt and create seracs, arches, etc.; these walls sometimes expose layers that represent the glacier's stratigraphy.
  a. Geohazard
  c. Debris flow
  b. Crevasse
  d. Cryoseism

16. In fluid mechanics, _____ is a flow for which the fluid is confined by a surface. Hence the boundary layer is unable to develop without eventually being constrained. The _____ configuration represents a convenient geometry for heating and cooling fluids used in chemical processing. environmental control, and energy conversion technologies.
  a. Internal flow
  c. AL 129-1
  b. AASHTO Soil Classification System
  d. AL 333

17. _____ is the act of a glacier sliding over the bed before it due to meltwater under the ice acting as a lubricant. This movement very much depends on the temperature of the area, the slope of the glacier, the bed's sediment size, the amount of meltwater from the glacier, and the glacier's size.

The movement that happens to these glaciers as they slide is that of a jerky motion where any seismic events, especially at the base of glacier, can cause movement.

  a. Glacial plucking
  c. Glacial polish
  b. Glacial striations
  d. Basal sliding

18. _____ is the removal of solids (sediment, soil, rock and other particles) in the natural environment. It usually occurs due to transport by wind, water, or ice; by down-slope creep of soil and other material under the force of gravity; or by living organisms, such as burrowing animals, in the case of bioerosion.

_____ is distinguished from weathering, which is the process of chemical or physical breakdown of the minerals in the rocks, although the two processes may occur concurrently.

  a. AL 333
  c. Erosion
  b. AL 129-1
  d. AASHTO Soil Classification System

19. _____ or glacial grooves are scratches or gouges cut into bedrock by process of glacial abrasion. _____ usually occur as multiple straight, parallel grooves representing the movement of the sediment-loaded base of the glacier. Large amounts of coarse gravel and boulders carried along underneath the glacier provide the abrasive power to cut the grooves, and finer sediments also in the base of the moving glacier further scour and polish the bedrock.

Chapter 16. Glaciers and Glaciation

a. Terminal moraine
b. Firn
c. Glacial polish
d. Glacial striations

20. In geology, _____ is transported rock debris overlying the solid bedrock. The term is also sometimes refers to organic debris so-transported. In the largest sense, it refers to the material left behind by retreating continental glaciers.
   a. Metamorphic reaction
   b. Riegel
   c. Geomechanics
   d. Drift

21. _____ is caused by movement of ice, typically as glaciers. Glaciers erode predominantly by three different processes: abrasion/scouring, plucking, and ice thrusting. In an abrasion process, debris in the basal ice scrapes along the bed, polishing and gouging the underlying rocks, similar to sandpaper on wood. Glaciers can also cause pieces of bedrock to crack off in the process of plucking. In ice thrusting, the glacier freezes to its bed, then as it surges forward, it moves large sheets of frozen sediment at the base along with the glacier. This method produced some of the many thousands of lake basins that dot the edge of the Canadian Shield. These processes, combined with erosion and transport by the water network beneath the glacier, leave moraines, drumlins, eskers, ground moraine (till), kames, kame deltas, moulins, and glacial erratics in their wake, typically at the terminus or during glacier retreat.
   a. AL 129-1
   b. AL 333
   c. AASHTO Soil Classification System
   d. Ice erosion

22. A _____ is a mountain lake or pool, formed in a cirque excavated by a glacier. A moraine may form a natural dam below a _____. A corrie may be called a cirque.
   a. Tarn
   b. Platform
   c. Grade
   d. Heavy metal

23. A _____ is an elongated whale-shaped hill formed by glacial action. Its long axis is parallel with the movement of the ice, with the blunter end facing into the glacial movement. They may be more than 45 m (150 ft) high and more than 0.8 km (1/2 mile) long, and are often in _____ fields of similarly shaped, sized and oriented hills. They usually have layers indicating that the material was repeatedly added to a core, which may be of rock or glacial till.
   a. Sandur
   b. Drumlin
   c. 1509 Istanbul earthquake
   d. Monadnock

24. _____ is any particulate matter that can be transported by fluid flow, and which eventually is deposited.

They are most often transported by water (fluvial processes) transported by wind (aeolian processes) and glaciers. Beach sands and river channel deposits are examples of fluvial transport and deposition, though _____ also often settles out of slow-moving or standing water in lakes and oceans.

   a. Fech fech
   b. Salt glacier
   c. Sediment
   d. Brickearth

25. _____ are isolated fragments of rock found within finer-grained water-deposited sedimentary rocks. They range in size from small pebbles to boulders. The critical distinguishing feature is that there is evidence that they were not transported by normal water currents, but rather dropped in vertically through the water column.
   a. 1700 Cascadia earthquake
   b. 1703 Genroku earthquake
   c. Dropstones
   d. 1509 Istanbul earthquake

Chapter 16. Glaciers and Glaciation

26. A _____ is a piece of rock that differs from the size and type of rock native to the area in which it rests. They are carried by glacial ice, often over distances of hundreds of kilometres and can range in size from pebbles to large boulders such as Big Rock (16,500 tons) in Alberta.

    a. 1509 Istanbul earthquake
    b. 1700 Cascadia earthquake
    c. 1703 Genroku earthquake
    d. Glacial erratic

27. A _____ is any glacially formed accumulation of unconsolidated glacial debris (soil and rock) which can occur in currently glaciated and formerly glaciated regions, such as those areas acted upon by a past ice age. This debris may have been plucked off the valley floor as a glacier advanced or it may have fallen off the valley walls as a result of frost wedging. _____s may be composed of silt like glacial flour to large boulders.

    a. 1509 Istanbul earthquake
    b. 1700 Cascadia earthquake
    c. 1703 Genroku earthquake
    d. Moraine

28. _____ consists of clay-sized particles of rock, generated by glacial erosion or by artificial grinding to a similar size. Because the material is very small, it becomes suspended in river water making the water appear cloudy.

If the river flows into a glacial lake, the lake may appear turquoise in color as a result.

    a. Post-glacial rebound
    b. Snowball Earth
    c. Pastonian Stage
    d. Rock flour

29. _____ is unsorted glacial sediment. Glacial drift is a general term for the coarsely graded and extremely heterogeneous sediments of glacial origin. Glacial _____ is that part of glacial drift which was deposited directly by the glacier. In cases where _____ has been indurated or lithified by subsequent burial into solid rock, it is known as the sedimentary rock tillite.

    a. 1703 Genroku earthquake
    b. 1700 Cascadia earthquake
    c. 1509 Istanbul earthquake
    d. Till

30. A _____ is a moraine that forms at the end of the glacier called the snout.

They mark the maximum advance of the glacier. An end moraine is at the present boundary of the glacier. They are one of the most prominent types of moraines in the Arctic. One famous _____ is the Giant's Wall in Norway.

    a. Firn
    b. Glacial plucking
    c. Bull Lake glaciation
    d. Terminal moraine

31. A _____ is a glacial outwash plain formed of sediments deposited by meltwater at the terminus of a glacier.

_____ are found in glaciated areas, such as Svalbard, Kerguelen Islands, and Iceland. Glaciers and icecaps contain large amounts of silt and sediment, picked up as they erode the underlying rocks when they move slowly downhill, and at the snout of the glacier, meltwater can carry this sediment away from the glacier and deposit it on a broad plain.

a. Monadnock
b. Sandur
c. 1509 Istanbul earthquake
d. Rogen moraine

32. In geology and related fields, a _____ is a layer of rock or soil with internally consistent characteristics that distinguishes it from contiguous layers. Each layer is generally one of a number of parallel layers that lie one upon another, laid down by natural forces. They may extend over hundreds of thousands of square kilometers of the Earth's surface.
 a. 1700 Cascadia earthquake
 b. 1703 Genroku earthquake
 c. Stratum
 d. 1509 Istanbul earthquake

33. In geology, _____ or _____ soil is soil at or below the freezing point of water (0 >°C or 32 >°F) for two or more years. Ice is not always present, as may be in the case of nonporous bedrock, but it frequently occurs and it may be in amounts exceeding the potential hydraulic saturation of the ground material. Most _____ is located in high latitudes (i.e. land in close proximity to the North and South poles), but alpine _____ may exist at high altitudes in much lower latitudes.
 a. 1700 Cascadia earthquake
 b. 1703 Genroku earthquake
 c. 1509 Istanbul earthquake
 d. Permafrost

34. The general term '_____' or, more precisely, 'glacial age' denotes a geological period of long-term reduction in the temperature of the Earth's surface and atmosphere, resulting in an expansion of continental ice sheets, polar ice sheets and alpine glaciers. Within a long-term _____, individual pulses of extra cold climate are termed 'glaciations'. Glaciologically, _____ implies the presence of extensive ice sheets in the northern and southern hemispheres; by this definition we are still in an _____
 a. Ice age
 b. AL 333
 c. AASHTO Soil Classification System
 d. AL 129-1

35. In materials science, _____ is a change in the shape or size of an object due to an applied force. This can be a result of tensile (pulling) forces, compressive (pushing) forces, shear, bending or torsion (twisting.) _____ is often described as strain.
 a. Stack
 b. Submersion
 c. Lingula
 d. Deformation

36. The _____ was a period of cooling occurring after a warmer North Atlantic era known as the Medieval Warm Period. While not a true ice age, the term was introduced into scientific literature by Fran>çois E. Matthes in 1939. Climatologists and historians working with local records no longer expect to agree on either the start or end dates of this period, which varied according to local conditions.
 a. Deforestation
 b. Pacific Decadal Oscillation
 c. Glacier
 d. Little Ice Age

37. In chemistry, the _____ of a chemical compound is a simple expression of the relative numbers of each type of atom in it, or the simplest whole number ratio of atoms of each element present in a compound. An _____ makes no reference to isomerism, structure, or absolute number of atoms. The _____ is used as standard for most ionic compounds, such as $CaCl_2$, and for macromolecules, such as SiO_2.
 a. AASHTO Soil Classification System
 b. Empirical formula
 c. AL 333
 d. AL 129-1

38. _____, originally Gondwanaland, is the name given to a southern precursor-supercontinent and then as a remnant separated from Laurasia 180-200 million years ago during the breakup of the Pangaea supercontinent that existed about 500 to 200 Ma ago into two large segments. While the corresponding northern hemisphere continent Laurasia moved further north, the nearly equal in area _____ included most of the landmasses in today's southern hemisphere, including Antarctica, South America, Africa, Madagascar, Australia-New Guinea, and New Zealand, as well as Arabia and the Indian subcontinent, which have now moved into the Northern Hemisphere.

a. Gondwana
b. 1700 Cascadia earthquake
c. 1509 Istanbul earthquake
d. Laurasia

Chapter 17. Atmosphere, Winds and Deserts

1. In physics, the _____ is an apparent deflection of moving objects when they are viewed from a rotating reference frame.

Newton's laws of motion govern the motion of an object in an inertial frame of reference. When transforming Newton's laws to a rotating frame of reference, the Coriolis force appears, along with the centrifugal force.

  a. Coriolis effect
  c. Strain rate
  b. 1700 Cascadia earthquake
  d. 1509 Istanbul earthquake

2. A _____ or sandstorm is a meteorological phenomenon common in arid and semi-arid regions and arises when a gust front passes or when the wind force exceeds the threshold value where loose sand and dust are removed from the dry surface. Particles are transported by saltation and suspension, causing soil erosion from one place and deposition in another. The Sahara and drylands around the Arabian peninsula are the main source of airborne dust, with some contributions from Iran, Pakistan and India into the Arabian Sea, and China's storms deposit dust in the Pacific.

  a. 1700 Cascadia earthquake
  c. 1703 Genroku earthquake
  b. Dust storm
  d. 1509 Istanbul earthquake

3. In chemistry, the _____ of a chemical compound is a simple expression of the relative numbers of each type of atom in it, or the simplest whole number ratio of atoms of each element present in a compound. An _____ makes no reference to isomerism, structure, or absolute number of atoms. The _____ is used as standard for most ionic compounds, such as $CaCl_2$, and for macromolecules, such as SiO_2.

  a. AL 333
  c. AASHTO Soil Classification System
  b. AL 129-1
  d. Empirical formula

4. The _____ is a circulation pattern that dominates the tropical atmosphere, with rising motion near the equator, poleward flow 10-15 kilometers above the surface, descending motion in the subtropics, and equatorward flow near the surface. This circulation is intimately related to the trade winds, tropical rainbelts, subtropical deserts and the jet streams.

The major driving force of atmospheric circulation is solar heating, which on average is largest near the equator and smallest at the poles.

  a. 1700 Cascadia earthquake
  c. 1509 Istanbul earthquake
  b. 1703 Genroku earthquake
  d. Hadley cell

5. The _____, theorized by William Ferrel (1817-1891), is a secondary circulation feature, dependent for its existence upon the Hadley cell and the Polar cell. It behaves much as an atmospheric ball bearing between the Hadley cell and the Polar cell, and comes about as a result of the eddy circulations (the high and low pressure areas) of the midlatitudes. For this reason it is sometimes known as the 'zone of mixing.' At its southern extent (in the Northern hemisphere), it overrides the Hadley cell, and at its northern extent, it overrides the Polar cell.

  a. 1700 Cascadia earthquake
  c. Ferrel cell
  b. 1509 Istanbul earthquake
  d. 1703 Genroku earthquake

6. In meteorology, the _____ is the boundary between the polar cell and the Ferrel cell in each hemisphere. At this boundary a sharp gradient in temperature occurs between these two air masses, each at very different temperatures.

The _____ arises as a result of cold polar air meeting warm tropical air.

Chapter 17. Atmosphere, Winds and Deserts

a. Mesosphere
b. 1509 Istanbul earthquake
c. Pluvial
d. Polar front

7. In geology, _____ is a specific type of particle transport by fluids such as wind, or the denser fluid water. It occurs when loose material is removed from a bed and carried by the fluid, before being transported back to the surface. Examples include pebble transport by rivers, sand drift over desert surfaces, soil blowing over fields, or even snow drift over smooth surfaces such as those in the Arctic or Canadian Prairies.
   a. Wave pounding
   b. Saltation
   c. Downcutting
   d. Stoping

8. _____ is a naturally occurring granular material composed of finely divided rock and mineral particles.

As the term is used by geologists, _____ particles range in diameter from 0.0625 (or >$^1\!/_{16}$ mm, or 62.5 micrometers) to 2 millimeters. An individual particle in this range size is termed a _____ grain.

   a. 1703 Genroku earthquake
   b. 1509 Istanbul earthquake
   c. 1700 Cascadia earthquake
   d. Sand

9. _____ is any particulate matter that can be transported by fluid flow, and which eventually is deposited.

They are most often transported by water (fluvial processes) transported by wind (aeolian processes) and glaciers. Beach sands and river channel deposits are examples of fluvial transport and deposition, though _____ also often settles out of slow-moving or standing water in lakes and oceans.

   a. Fech fech
   b. Brickearth
   c. Salt glacier
   d. Sediment

10. The _____ are the prevailing pattern of easterly surface winds found in the tropics near the Earth's equator. The _____ blow predominantly from the northeast in the Northern Hemisphere and from the southeast in the Southern Hemisphere. The _____ act as the steering flow for tropical storms that form over the Atlantic, Pacific, and Indian Oceans that make landfall in North America, Southeast Asia, and India, respectively.
   a. Trade winds
   b. 1703 Genroku earthquake
   c. 1509 Istanbul earthquake
   d. 1700 Cascadia earthquake

11. _____ is the process by which the removal of material, through means of erosion and weathering, leads to a reduction of elevation and relief in landforms and landscapes. Exogenic processes, including the action of water, ice, and wind, predominantly involve _____. Denudation can involve the removal of both solid particles and dissolved material.
   a. Palustrine
   b. Mesa
   c. 1509 Istanbul earthquake
   d. Denudation

12. _____, sometimes known as streamline flow, occurs when a fluid flows in parallel layers, with no disruption between the layers. In fluid dynamics, _____ is a flow regime characterized by high momentum diffusion, low momentum convection, pressure and velocity independent from time. It is the opposite of turbulent flow.

Chapter 17. Atmosphere, Winds and Deserts

    a. 1700 Cascadia earthquake
    c. 1703 Genroku earthquake
    b. 1509 Istanbul earthquake
    d. Laminar flow

13. In fluid dynamics, turbulence or _____ is a fluid regime characterized by chaotic, stochastic property changes. This includes low momentum diffusion, high momentum convection, and rapid variation of pressure and velocity in space and time. Flow that is not turbulent is called laminar flow.
    a. Strong interaction
    c. Power
    b. Potentiometric surface
    d. Turbulent flow

14. _____ is mechanical scraping of a rock surface by friction between rocks and moving particles during their transport in wind, glacier, waves, gravity or running water, after friction, the moving particles dislodge loose and weak debris from the side of the rock, these particles can be dissolved in the water source.

The intensity of _____ depends on the hardness, concentration, velocity and mass of moving particles.

A virtually smooth marine platform cut by the ocean waves at a coastline.

    a. AASHTO Soil Classification System
    c. AL 333
    b. Abrasion
    d. AL 129-1

15. _____ is the removal of solids (sediment, soil, rock and other particles) in the natural environment. It usually occurs due to transport by wind, water, or ice; by down-slope creep of soil and other material under the force of gravity; or by living organisms, such as burrowing animals, in the case of bioerosion.

_____ is distinguished from weathering, which is the process of chemical or physical breakdown of the minerals in the rocks, although the two processes may occur concurrently.

    a. AL 129-1
    c. AASHTO Soil Classification System
    b. Erosion
    d. AL 333

16. _____ is caused by movement of ice, typically as glaciers. Glaciers erode predominantly by three different processes: abrasion/scouring, plucking, and ice thrusting. In an abrasion process, debris in the basal ice scrapes along the bed, polishing and gouging the underlying rocks, similar to sandpaper on wood. Glaciers can also cause pieces of bedrock to crack off in the process of plucking. In ice thrusting, the glacier freezes to its bed, then as it surges forward, it moves large sheets of frozen sediment at the base along with the glacier. This method produced some of the many thousands of lake basins that dot the edge of the Canadian Shield. These processes, combined with erosion and transport by the water network beneath the glacier, leave moraines, drumlins, eskers, ground moraine (till), kames, kame deltas, moulins, and glacial erratics in their wake, typically at the terminus or during glacier retreat.
    a. AASHTO Soil Classification System
    c. AL 129-1
    b. AL 333
    d. Ice erosion

17. A _____ is a desert surface that is covered with closely packed, interlocking angular or rounded rock fragments of pebble and cobble size.

Several theories have been proposed for their formation. The more common theory is that they form by the gradual removal of the sand, dust and other fine grained material by the wind and intermittent rain leaving only the larger fragments behind.

- a. 1703 Genroku earthquake
- b. 1700 Cascadia earthquake
- c. 1509 Istanbul earthquake
- d. Desert pavement

18. _____ are rocks that have been abraded, pitted, etched, grooved, or polished by wind-driven sand or ice crystals. These geomorphic features are most typically found in arid environments where there is little vegetation to interfere with aeolian particle transport, where there are frequently strong winds, and where there is a steady but not overwhelming supply of sand.

_____ can be abraded to eye-catching natural sculptures.

- a. Coprolite
- b. 1509 Istanbul earthquake
- c. Fault breccia
- d. Ventifacts

19. A _____ is a wind-abraded ridge found in a desert environment. They are elongate features typically three or more times longer than they are wide, and when viewed from above, resemble the hull of a boat. Facing the wind is a steep, blunt face that gradually gets lower and narrower toward the lee end.

- a. 1703 Genroku earthquake
- b. 1700 Cascadia earthquake
- c. 1509 Istanbul earthquake
- d. Yardang

20. A _____ dune is an arc-shaped sand ridge, comprising well-sorted sand. This type of dune possesses two 'horns' that face downwind, with the slip face (the downwind slope) at the angle of repose, or approximately 32 degrees. The upwind side is packed by the wind, and stands at about 15 degrees. Simple _____ dunes may stretch from meters to a hundred meters or so between the tips of the horns.

- a. 1703 Genroku earthquake
- b. 1700 Cascadia earthquake
- c. Barchan
- d. 1509 Istanbul earthquake

21. Radially symmetrical, _____ are pyramidal sand mounds with slipfaces on three or more arms that radiate from the high center of the mound. They tend to accumulate in areas with multidirectional wind regimes. _____ grow upward rather than laterally. They dominate the Grand Erg Oriental of the Sahara. In other deserts, they occur around the margins of the sand seas, particularly near topographic barriers. In the southeast Badain Jaran Desert of China, the _____ are up to 500 meters tall and may be the tallest dunes on Earth.

- a. Star dunes
- b. Loihi Seamount
- c. Historical geology
- d. Pahoehoe lava

22. An _____ is a large, relatively flat area of desert covered with wind-swept sand with little or no vegetative cover. The term takes its name from the Arabic word _____ , meaning 'dune field'. Strictly speaking, an _____ is defined as a desert area that contains more than 125 square kilometers of aeolian or wind-blown sand and where sand covers more than 20% of the surface.

- a. AL 333
- b. AASHTO Soil Classification System
- c. AL 129-1
- d. Erg

Chapter 17. Atmosphere, Winds and Deserts

23. _____ is a homogeneous, typically nonstratified, porous, friable, slightly coherent, often calcareous, fine-grained, silty, pale yellow or buff, windblown (aeolian) sediment. It generally occurs as a widespread blanket deposit that covers areas of hundreds of square kilometers and tens of meters thick. _____ often stands in either steep or vertical faces.
   a. 1509 Istanbul earthquake
   b. 1700 Cascadia earthquake
   c. 1703 Genroku earthquake
   d. Loess

24. _____ consists of small tephra, which are bits of pulverized rock and glass created by volcanic eruptions, less than 2 millimetres (0.079 in) in diameter. There are three mechanisms of _____ formation: gas release under decompression causing magmatic eruptions; thermal contraction from chilling on contact with water causing phreatomagmatic eruptions and ejection of entrained particles during steam eruptions causing phreatic eruptions. The violent nature of volcanic eruptions involving steam results in the magma and solid rock surrounding the vent being torn into particles of clay to sand size.
   a. Supervolcano
   b. Cinder
   c. Volcanic ash
   d. Wadati-Benioff zone

25. A _____ is a large, slow-moving mass of ice, formed from compacted layers of snow, that slowly deforms and flows in response to gravity and high pressure.

   _____ ice is the largest reservoir of fresh water on Earth, and second only to oceans as the largest reservoir of total water.

   a. Glacier
   b. Little Ice Age
   c. Keeling Curve
   d. Deforestation

26. In materials science, _____ is a change in the shape or size of an object due to an applied force. This can be a result of tensile (pulling) forces, compressive (pushing) forces, shear, bending or torsion (twisting.) _____ is often described as strain.
   a. Lingula
   b. Submersion
   c. Stack
   d. Deformation

27. _____ are areas with annual precipitation less than 250 millimetres and a mean temperature during the warmest month of less than 10>° C. _____ on Earth cover nearly 5 million square kilometres and are mostly bedrock or gravel plains. Sand dunes are not prominent features in these deserts, but snow dunes occur commonly in areas where precipitation is locally more abundant.
   a. Landform
   b. 1509 Istanbul earthquake
   c. 1700 Cascadia earthquake
   d. Polar deserts

28. _____ is a dark coating found on exposed rock surfaces in arid environments.

   _____ forms only on physically stable rock surfaces that are no longer subject to frequent precipitation, fracturing or wind abrasion. The varnish is primarily composed of particles of clay along with iron and manganese oxides. There is also a host of trace elements and almost always some organic matter. The color of the varnish varies from shades of brown to black.

Chapter 17. Atmosphere, Winds and Deserts

a. 1509 Istanbul earthquake
c. 1703 Genroku earthquake
b. 1700 Cascadia earthquake
d. Desert varnish

29. _____ is the geomorphic process by which soil, regolith, and rock move downslope under the force of gravity. Types of _____ include creep, slides, flows, topples, and falls, each with its own characteristic features, and taking place over timescales from seconds to years. _____ occurs on both terrestrial and submarine slopes, and has been observed on Earth, Mars, and Venus.

a. Soil liquefaction
c. 1700 Cascadia earthquake
b. 1509 Istanbul earthquake
d. Mass wasting

30. A _____ is an elevated area of land with a flat top and sides that are usually steep cliffs. It takes its name from its characteristic table-top shape. It is a characteristic landform of arid environments, particularly the southwestern United States.

_____s form usually in areas where horizontally layered rocks are uplifted by tectonic activity, but may form also in its absence.

_____s are formed by weathering and erosion. Variations in the ability of different types of rock to resist weathering and erosion cause the weaker types of rocks to be eroded away, leaving the more resistant types of rocks topographically higher relative to their surroundings. This process is called differential erosion.

a. Truncated spur
c. 1509 Istanbul earthquake
b. Mesa
d. Palustrine

31. _____ is the decomposition of Earth rocks, soils and their minerals through direct contact with the planet's atmosphere. _____ occurs in situ, or 'with no movement', and thus should not be confused with erosion, which involves the movement of rocks and minerals by agents such as water, ice, wind and gravity.

Two important classifications of _____ processes exist -- physical and chemical _____.

a. 1700 Cascadia earthquake
c. Physical weathering
b. 1509 Istanbul earthquake
d. Weathering

32. A _____ is a rapid flooding of geomorphic low-lying areas - washes, rivers and streams. It is caused by heavy rain associated with a thunderstorm, hurricane, or tropical storm. _____s can also occur after the collapse of an ice dam, or a human structure, such as a dam, for example, the Johnstown Flood of 1889.

a. 1700 Cascadia earthquake
c. Lake breakout
b. Flash flood
d. 1509 Istanbul earthquake

33. In the earth sciences and geology sub-fields, a _____ or physical feature comprises a geomorphological unit, and is largely defined by its surface form and location in the landscape, as part of the terrain, and as such, is typically an element of topography. _____ elements also include seascape and oceanic waterbody interface features such as bays, peninsulas, seas and so forth, including sub-surface terrain features such as submersed mountain ranges, volcanoes, and the great ocean basins under the thin skin of water, for the whole earth is the province and domain of geology. This panorama in Great Smoky Mountains National Park has the readily identifiable physical features of a rolling plain, actually part of a broad valley, distant foothills, and a backdrop of the old much weathered Appalachian mountain range.

Chapter 17. Atmosphere, Winds and Deserts

_____s are categorised by characteristic physical attributes such as elevation, slope, orientation, stratification, rock exposure, and soil type.

a. 1509 Istanbul earthquake
b. Polar deserts
c. 1700 Cascadia earthquake
d. Landform

34. An _____ is a fan-shaped deposit formed where a fast flowing stream flattens, slows, and spreads typically at the exit of a canyon onto a flatter plain. A convergence of neighboring fans into a single apron of deposits against a slope is called a bajada, or compound _____.

a. AL 129-1
b. AL 333
c. AASHTO Soil Classification System
d. Alluvial fan

35. A _____ is a gently inclined erosional surface carved into bedrock. It is thinly covered with Fluvial gravel that has developed at the foot of mountains. It develops when running water erodes most of the mass of the mountain. It is typically a concave surface gently sloping away from mountainous desert areas.

a. Patterned ground
b. Gradualism
c. Pediment
d. Stream Load

36. A _____ is a dry or ephemeral lakebed, generally extending to the shore, or remnant of, an endorheic lake. Such flats consist of fine-grained sediments infused with alkali salts. _____s are also known as alkali flats, sabkhas, dry lakes or mud flats.

a. Playa
b. 1700 Cascadia earthquake
c. 1509 Istanbul earthquake
d. 1703 Genroku earthquake

37. A _____ or inselberg is an isolated rock hill, knob, ridge, or small mountain that rises abruptly from a gently sloping or virtually level surrounding plain. The term '_____' is usually used in the United States, whereas 'inselberg' is the more common international term. In southern and southern-central Africa, a similar formation of granite is known as a kopje (in fact a Dutch word) from the Afrikaans word: koppie.

_____ is an originally Native American term for an isolated hill or a lone mountain that has risen above the surrounding area, typically by surviving erosion.

a. 1509 Istanbul earthquake
b. Rogen moraine
c. Sandur
d. Monadnock

38. _____ describes the large scale motions of Earth's lithosphere. The theory encompasses the older concepts of continental drift, developed during the first decades of the 20th century by Alfred Wegener, and seafloor spreading, understood during the 1960s.

The outermost part of the Earth's interior is made up of two layers: the lithosphere and the asthenosphere.

a. Nappe
b. Continental crust
c. Mantle convection
d. Plate tectonics

39. _____s is a field of study within geology concerned generally with the structures within the lithosphere of the Earth and particularly with the forces and movements that have operated in a region to create these structures.

_____s is concerned with the orogenies and _____ development of cratons and _____ terranes as well as the earthquake and volcanic belts which directly affect much of the global population. _____ studies are also important for understanding erosion patterns in geomorphology and as guides for the economic geologist searching for petroleum and metallic ores.

    a. Rivera Plate
    c. Cocos Plate
    b. Tectonic
    d. Fault trace

40. _____ is a field of study within geology concerned generally with the structures within the lithosphere of the Earth and particularly with the forces and movements that have operated in a region to create these structures.

_____ is concerned with the orogenies and tectonic development of cratons and tectonic terranes as well as the earthquake and volcanic belts which directly affect much of the global population. Tectonic studies are also important for understanding erosion patterns in geomorphology and as guides for the economic geologist searching for petroleum and metallic ores.

    a. Rivera Plate
    c. Tectonics
    b. Cocos Plate
    d. Fault trace

41. _____ is a phenomenon of the plate tectonics of Earth that occurs at convergent boundaries. _____ is a variation on the fundamental process of subduction, whereby the subduction zone is destroyed, mountains produced, and two continents sutured together. _____ is known only from this planet and is an interesting example of how our different crusts, oceanic and continental, behave during subduction.

    a. Supercontinent cycle
    c. Continental collision
    b. Mirovia
    d. Copperbelt Province

Chapter 18. The Oceans and Their Margins

1. _____ is the saltiness or dissolved salt content of a body of water. It is a general term used to describe the levels of different salts such as sodium chloride, magnesium and calcium sulfates and bicarbonates. _____ in Australian English and North American English may also refer to the salt content of soil .
   a. 1700 Cascadia earthquake
   b. 1703 Genroku earthquake
   c. 1509 Istanbul earthquake
   d. Salinity

2. _____ is the naturally occurring, unconsolidated or loose covering on the Earth's surface. _____ is composed of particles of broken rock that have been altered by chemical, biological and environmental processes including weathering and erosion. _____ is different from its parent rock(s) source(s), altered by interactions between the lithosphere, hydrosphere, atmosphere, and the biosphere.
   a. Soil
   b. Topsoil
   c. Slump
   d. 1509 Istanbul earthquake

3. In physics, the _____ is an apparent deflection of moving objects when they are viewed from a rotating reference frame.

Newton's laws of motion govern the motion of an object in an inertial frame of reference. When transforming Newton's laws to a rotating frame of reference, the Coriolis force appears, along with the centrifugal force.

   a. 1509 Istanbul earthquake
   b. Strain rate
   c. 1700 Cascadia earthquake
   d. Coriolis effect

4. _____ is a paramount and base concept in archaeology, especially in the course of excavation. It is largely based on the Law of Superposition. When archaeological finds are below the surface of the ground (as is most commonly the case), the identification of the context of each find is vital in enabling the archaeologist to draw conclusions about the site and about the nature and date of its occupation.
   a. Streak
   b. Stratification
   c. Submersion
   d. Fractional crystallization

5. A _____ is any manner of particularly large-scale wind, swirling vortex and ocean currents. _____s are caused by the Coriolis effect; planetary vorticity along with horizontal and vertical friction, which determine the circulation patterns from the wind curl (torque.)

The Earth's oceans have the following major _____s:

- North Atlantic Subpolar _____
- North Pacific Subpolar _____
    - Contains the smaller Alaska _____
- North Atlantic Subtropical _____
    - Gulf Stream, Labrador Current, East Greenland Current, North Atlantic Current, North Atlantic Equatorial Current. Contains the Sargasso Sea.

   a. 1703 Genroku earthquake
   b. 1700 Cascadia earthquake
   c. Gyre
   d. 1509 Istanbul earthquake

6. The _____ is a type of water mass in the seas surrounding Antarctica with temperatures ranging from 0 to -0.8â—¦ C, salinities from 34.6 to 34.7 psu, and a density near 27.88.

Chapter 18. The Oceans and Their Margins

_____ is formed in the Weddell and Ross Seas from surface water cooling in polynyas and below the ice shelf. Surface water is enriched in salt from sea ice formation.

  a. AASHTO Soil Classification System
  b. AL 129-1
  c. AL 333
  d. Antarctic Bottom Water

7. The _____ is an ocean current that flows from west to east around Antarctica. An alternate name for the _____ is the West Wind Drift. The _____ is the dominant circulation feature of the Southern Ocean and, at approximately 125 Sverdrups, the largest ocean current .

  a. AL 129-1
  b. AL 333
  c. AASHTO Soil Classification System
  d. Antarctic Circumpolar Current

8. _____ is a water mass that forms in the North Atlantic Ocean. It is largely formed in the Labrador Sea and in the Greenland Sea by the sinking of highly saline, dense overflow water from the Greenland Sea. The watermass can be traced around the southern end of Greenland and then, at a depth of 2000-4000 meters, down the coast of Canada and the United States where it turns slightly east.

  a. North Atlantic Deep Water
  b. 1700 Cascadia earthquake
  c. 1703 Genroku earthquake
  d. 1509 Istanbul earthquake

9. The term _____ refers to the part of the large-scale ocean circulation that is driven by global density gradients created by surface heat and freshwater fluxes. The adjective thermohaline derives from thermo- referring to temperature and -haline referring to salt content, factors which together determine the density of sea water. Wind-driven surface currents (such as the Gulf Stream) head polewards from the equatorial Atlantic Ocean, cooling all the while and eventually sinking at high latitudes (forming North Atlantic Deep Water.)

  a. 1703 Genroku earthquake
  b. 1509 Istanbul earthquake
  c. 1700 Cascadia earthquake
  d. Thermohaline circulation

10. A _____ is a tidal phenomenon in which the leading edge of the incoming tide forms a wave (or waves) of water that travel up a river or narrow bay against the direction of the current. As such, it is a true tidal wave (not to be confused with a tsunami).

Bores occur in relatively few locations worldwide, usually in areas with a large tidal range (typically more than 20 feet (6.1 m) between high and low water), and where incoming tides are funneled into a shallow, narrowing river via a broad bay.

  a. 1700 Cascadia earthquake
  b. 1509 Istanbul earthquake
  c. Tidal bore
  d. 1703 Genroku earthquake

11. The _____ is the vertical difference between the highest high tide and the lowest low tide. In other words, it is the difference in height between high and low tides. The most extreme _____ will occur around the time of the full or new moons, when gravity of both the Sun and Moon are pulling the same way (new moon), or exact opposite way (full.)

  a. 1703 Genroku earthquake
  b. Tidal range
  c. 1509 Istanbul earthquake
  d. 1700 Cascadia earthquake

12. In physics, _____ is the rate at which work is performed or energy is transmitted, or the amount of energy required or expended for a given unit of time. As a rate of change of work done or the energy of a subsystem, _____ is:

$$P = \frac{W}{t}$$

where P is _____, W is work and t is time.

The average _____ (often simply called '_____' when the context makes it clear) is the average amount of work done or energy transferred per unit time.

    a. Strong interaction
    c. Potentiometric surface
    b. Turbulent flow
    d. Power

13. As ocean surface waves come closer to shore they break, forming the foamy, bubbly surface we call surf. The region of breaking waves defines the _____. After breaking in the _____, the waves (now reduced in height) continue to move in, and they run up onto the sloping front of the beach, forming an uprush of water called swash.

    a. 1703 Genroku earthquake
    c. 1509 Istanbul earthquake
    b. Surf zone
    d. 1700 Cascadia earthquake

14. The _____ is the maximum depth at which a water wave's passage causes significant water motion. For water depths larger than the _____, bottom sediments are no longer stirred by the wave motion above.

In deep water, the water particles are moved in a circular orbital motion when a wave passes.

    a. Wave height
    c. 1700 Cascadia earthquake
    b. Wave base
    d. 1509 Istanbul earthquake

15. _____ is the removal of solids (sediment, soil, rock and other particles) in the natural environment. It usually occurs due to transport by wind, water, or ice; by down-slope creep of soil and other material under the force of gravity; or by living organisms, such as burrowing animals, in the case of bioerosion.

_____ is distinguished from weathering, which is the process of chemical or physical breakdown of the minerals in the rocks, although the two processes may occur concurrently.

    a. AL 129-1
    c. AL 333
    b. AASHTO Soil Classification System
    d. Erosion

16. _____ is mechanical scraping of a rock surface by friction between rocks and moving particles during their transport in wind, glacier, waves, gravity or running water, after friction, the moving particles dislodge loose and weak debris from the side of the rock, these particles can be dissolved in the water source.

The intensity of _____ depends on the hardness, concentration, velocity and mass of moving particles.

A virtually smooth marine platform cut by the ocean waves at a coastline.

Chapter 18. The Oceans and Their Margins

a. AL 333
b. AASHTO Soil Classification System
c. AL 129-1
d. Abrasion

17. _____, sometimes known as shore drift, is a geological process by which sediments such as sand or other materials, move along a beach shore. It uses the process of swash to push the material up the beach and backwash down the beach; until it reaches a groyne or another obstacle.

Where waves approach the coastline at an angle, when they break their swash pushes beach material up the beach at the same angle.

a. Swash
b. 1509 Istanbul earthquake
c. Cuspate forelands
d. Longshore drift

18. _____ is any particulate matter that can be transported by fluid flow, and which eventually is deposited.

They are most often transported by water (fluvial processes) transported by wind (aeolian processes) and glaciers. Beach sands and river channel deposits are examples of fluvial transport and deposition, though _____ also often settles out of slow-moving or standing water in lakes and oceans.

a. Fech fech
b. Brickearth
c. Salt glacier
d. Sediment

19. The term _____ refers to the elevation (on the ground) or altitude (in the air) of any object, relative to the average sea level datum. _____ is used extensively in radio (both in broadcasting and other telecommunications uses) by engineers to determine the coverage area a station will be able to reach. It is also used in aviation, where all heights are recorded and reported with respect to _____ , and in the atmospheric sciences.

a. AASHTO Soil Classification System
b. AL 129-1
c. AL 333
d. Above mean sea level

20. In geology, _____ is transported rock debris overlying the solid bedrock. The term is also sometimes refers to organic debris so-transported. In the largest sense, it refers to the material left behind by retreating continental glaciers.

a. Riegel
b. Drift
c. Metamorphic reaction
d. Geomechanics

21. In geology, a _____ deposit or _____ is an accumulation of valuable minerals formed by deposition of dense mineral phases in a trap site. Types of _____ deposits include alluvium, eluvium, beach _____ s, and paleoplacers.

Typical locations for alluvial _____ deposits are on the inside bends of rivers and creeks, in natural hollows, at the break of slope on a stream, the base of an escarpment, waterfall or other barrier, within sand dunes, beach profiles or in gravel beds.

a. 1703 Genroku earthquake
b. 1509 Istanbul earthquake
c. Placer
d. 1700 Cascadia earthquake

Chapter 18. The Oceans and Their Margins

22. The _____ zone is the area that is exposed to the air at low tide and submerged at high tide, for example, the area between tide marks. This area can include many different types of habitats, including steep rocky cliffs, sandy beaches, or wetlands The area can be a narrow strip, as in Pacific islands that have only a narrow tidal range, or can include many meters of shoreline where shallow beach slope interacts with high tidal excursion.
   a. Intertidal
   b. Overland flow
   c. Eutrophication
   d. Upwelling

23. In geography and geology, a _____ is a significant vertical, or near vertical, rock exposure. _____s are formed as erosion landforms due to the processes of erosion and weathering that produce them. _____s are common on coasts, in mountainous areas, escarpments and along rivers. _____s are usually formed by rock that is resistant to erosion and weathering. Sedimentary rocks are most likely to form sandstone, limestone, chalk, and dolomite. Igneous rocks, such as granite and basalt also often form _____s.
   a. 1700 Cascadia earthquake
   b. Cliff
   c. 1509 Istanbul earthquake
   d. 1703 Genroku earthquake

24. A _____ is a natural formation (or landform) where a rock arch forms, with a natural passageway through underneath. Most _____es form as a narrow ridge, walled by cliffs, become narrower from erosion, with a softer rock stratum under the cliff-forming stratum gradually eroding out until the rock shelters thus formed meet underneath the ridge, thus forming the arch. They commonly form where cliffs are subject to erosion from the sea, rivers or weathering (sub-aerial processes); the processes 'find' weaknesses in rocks and work on them, making them bigger until they break through.
   a. 1703 Genroku earthquake
   b. 1700 Cascadia earthquake
   c. Natural arch
   d. 1509 Istanbul earthquake

25. A _____ is a type of cave formed primarily by the wave action of the sea. The primary process involved is erosion. _____s are found throughout the world, actively forming along present coastlines and as relict _____s on former coastlines.
   a. 1700 Cascadia earthquake
   b. Sea cave
   c. 1703 Genroku earthquake
   d. 1509 Istanbul earthquake

26. A _____ is a geological landform consisting of a steep and often vertical column or columns of rock in the sea near a coast. They are formed when part of a headland is eroded by hydraulic action, which is the force of the sea or water crashing against the rock. The force of the water weakens cracks in the headland, causing them to later collapse, forming free-standing _____s and even a small island.
   a. Leaching
   b. Submersion
   c. Lingula
   d. Stack

27. A _____ or sometimes ayre is a deposition landform in which an island is attached to the mainland by a narrow piece of land such as a spit or bar. They usually form because the island causes wave refraction, depositing sand and shingle moved by longshore drift in each direction around the island where the waves meet. Eustatic sea level rise may also contribute to accretion as material is pushed up with rising sea levels.
   a. Ria
   b. 1700 Cascadia earthquake
   c. Tombolo
   d. 1509 Istanbul earthquake

Chapter 18. The Oceans and Their Margins

28. A _____ or sandbar is a somewhat linear landform within or extending into a body of water, typically composed of sand, silt or small pebbles. A bar is characteristically long and narrow and develops where a stream or ocean current promotes deposition of granular material, resulting in localized shallowing of the water. Bars can appear in the sea, in a lake, or in a river.

The term _____ can be applied to larger geological units that form off a coastline as part of the process of coastal erosion. These include spits and baymouth bars that form across the front of embayments and rias. A tombolo is a bar that forms an isthmus between an island or offshore rock and a mainland shore.

   a. 1703 Genroku earthquake   b. Shoal
   c. 1509 Istanbul earthquake   d. 1700 Cascadia earthquake

29. A _____ is a wave-swept or wave-deposited ridge running parallel to a shoreline. It is commonly composed of sand as well as sediment worked from underlying beach material. The movement of sediment by wave action is called littoral transport.

   a. Beach ridge   b. Ria
   c. 1700 Cascadia earthquake   d. 1509 Istanbul earthquake

30. A _____ is a mountain rising from the ocean seafloor that does not reach to the water's surface (sea level), and thus is not an island. These are typically formed from extinct volcanoes, that rise abruptly and are usually found rising from a seafloor of 1,000-4,000 meters depth. They are defined by oceanographers as independent features that rise to at least 1,000 meters above the seafloor.

   a. 1703 Genroku earthquake   b. 1700 Cascadia earthquake
   c. 1509 Istanbul earthquake   d. Seamount

31. A _____ is a kind of coral reef, that is located in the tropics generally directly off the shoreline. This type of coral reef is the most common type of reef that is found. This type of reef grows the best on some kind of hard surface, so it preferentially grows on areas with rocky bottoms.

   a. 1703 Genroku earthquake   b. 1509 Istanbul earthquake
   c. 1700 Cascadia earthquake   d. Fringing reef

32. An _____ is a semi-enclosed coastal body of water with one or more rivers or streams flowing into it, and with a free connection to the open sea. They are affected by both marine influences, such as tides, waves, and the influx of saline water; and riverine influences, such as flows of fresh water and sediment. As a result they may contain many biological niches within a small area, and so are associated with high biological diversity.

   a. AASHTO Soil Classification System   b. Estuary
   c. AL 333   d. AL 129-1

33. A _____ is a geological phenomenon which includes a wide range of ground movement, such as rock falls, deep failure of slopes and shallow debris flows, which can occur in offshore, coastal and onshore environments. Although the action of gravity is the primary driving force for a _____ to occur, there are other contributing factors affecting the original slope stability. Typically, pre-conditional factors build up specific sub-surface conditions that make the area/slope prone to failure, whereas the actual _____ often requires a trigger before being released.

   a. 1700 Cascadia earthquake   b. Mass wasting
   c. 1509 Istanbul earthquake   d. Landslide

Chapter 18. The Oceans and Their Margins

34. _____ are structures constructed on coasts as part of coastal defence or to protect an anchorage from the effects of weather and longshore drift.

Offshore _____, also called bulkheads, reduce the intensity of wave action in inshore waters and thereby reduce coastal erosion. They are constructed some distance away from the coast or built with one end linked to the coast.

a. 1700 Cascadia earthquake
b. 1509 Istanbul earthquake
c. Breakwaters
d. 1703 Genroku earthquake

35. In the earth sciences and geology sub-fields, a _____ or physical feature comprises a geomorphological unit, and is largely defined by its surface form and location in the landscape, as part of the terrain, and as such, is typically an element of topography. _____ elements also include seascape and oceanic waterbody interface features such as bays, peninsulas, seas and so forth, including sub-surface terrain features such as submersed mountain ranges, volcanoes, and the great ocean basins under the thin skin of water, for the whole earth is the province and domain of geology. This panorama in Great Smoky Mountains National Park has the readily identifiable physical features of a rolling plain, actually part of a broad valley, distant foothills, and a backdrop of the old much weathered Appalachian mountain range.

_____s are categorised by characteristic physical attributes such as elevation, slope, orientation, stratification, rock exposure, and soil type.

a. Polar deserts
b. 1509 Istanbul earthquake
c. 1700 Cascadia earthquake
d. Landform

36. The _____ is the biogeochemical cycle by which carbon is exchanged among the biosphere, pedosphere, geosphere, hydrosphere, and atmosphere of the Earth.

The _____ is usually thought of as four major reservoirs of carbon interconnected by pathways of exchange. These reservoirs are:

- The plants
- The terrestrial biosphere, which is usually defined to include fresh water systems and non-living organic material, such as soil carbon.
- The oceans, including dissolved inorganic carbon and living and non-living marine biota,
- The sediments including fossil fuels.

The annual movements of carbon, the carbon exchanges between reservoirs, occur because of various chemical, physical, geological, and biological processes. The ocean contains the largest active pool of carbon near the surface of the Earth, but the deep ocean part of this pool does not rapidly exchange with the atmosphere.

a. Carbon cycle
b. Cosmogenic isotopes
c. 1509 Istanbul earthquake
d. Nanogeoscience

Chapter 18. The Oceans and Their Margins

37. _____ describes the large scale motions of Earth's lithosphere. The theory encompasses the older concepts of continental drift, developed during the first decades of the 20th century by Alfred Wegener, and seafloor spreading, understood during the 1960s.

The outermost part of the Earth's interior is made up of two layers: the lithosphere and the asthenosphere.

a. Nappe
b. Mantle convection
c. Plate tectonics
d. Continental crust

38. An _____ is a continuous, directed movement of ocean water generated by the forces acting upon the water, such as the Earth's rotation, wind, temperature, salinity differences and tides caused by the gravitational pull of the Moon and the Sun. Depth contours, shoreline configurations and interaction with other currents influence a current's direction and strength.

_____ s can flow for thousands of kilometers, and together they create the great flow of the global conveyor belt which plays a dominant part in determining the climate of many of the Earth's regions.

a. AL 333
b. AASHTO Soil Classification System
c. AL 129-1
d. Ocean current

39. _____ s is a field of study within geology concerned generally with the structures within the lithosphere of the Earth and particularly with the forces and movements that have operated in a region to create these structures.

_____ s is concerned with the orogenies and _____ development of cratons and _____ terranes as well as the earthquake and volcanic belts which directly affect much of the global population. _____ studies are also important for understanding erosion patterns in geomorphology and as guides for the economic geologist searching for petroleum and metallic ores.

a. Rivera Plate
b. Cocos Plate
c. Tectonic
d. Fault trace

40. _____ is a field of study within geology concerned generally with the structures within the lithosphere of the Earth and particularly with the forces and movements that have operated in a region to create these structures.

_____ is concerned with the orogenies and tectonic development of cratons and tectonic terranes as well as the earthquake and volcanic belts which directly affect much of the global population. Tectonic studies are also important for understanding erosion patterns in geomorphology and as guides for the economic geologist searching for petroleum and metallic ores.

a. Cocos Plate
b. Fault trace
c. Rivera Plate
d. Tectonics

Chapter 19. Climate and Our Changing Planet

1. An _____ is a thick, floating platform of ice that forms where a glacier or ice sheet flows down to a coastline and onto the ocean surface. They are found in Antarctica, Greenland and Canada only. The boundary between the floating _____ and the grounded (resting on bedrock) ice that feeds it is called the grounding line.
   a. AASHTO Soil Classification System
   b. AL 129-1
   c. AL 333
   d. Ice shelf

2. _____ or _____ stone is a calcium carbonate or lime-rich mud or mudstone which contains variable amounts of clays and aragonite. _____ is originally an old term loosely applied to a variety of materials, most of which occur as loose, earthy deposits consisting chiefly of an intimate mixture of clay and calcium carbonate, formed under freshwater conditions; specifically an earthy substance containing 35-65% clay and 65-35% carbonate. The term is today often used to describe indurated marine deposits and lacustrine (lake) sediments which more accurately should be named _____ stones.
   a. 1703 Genroku earthquake
   b. 1700 Cascadia earthquake
   c. 1509 Istanbul earthquake
   d. Marl

3. The _____ is the biogeochemical cycle by which carbon is exchanged among the biosphere, pedosphere, geosphere, hydrosphere, and atmosphere of the Earth.

   The _____ is usually thought of as four major reservoirs of carbon interconnected by pathways of exchange. These reservoirs are:

   - The plants
   - The terrestrial biosphere, which is usually defined to include fresh water systems and non-living organic material, such as soil carbon.
   - The oceans, including dissolved inorganic carbon and living and non-living marine biota,
   - The sediments including fossil fuels.

   The annual movements of carbon, the carbon exchanges between reservoirs, occur because of various chemical, physical, geological, and biological processes. The ocean contains the largest active pool of carbon near the surface of the Earth, but the deep ocean part of this pool does not rapidly exchange with the atmosphere.
   a. 1509 Istanbul earthquake
   b. Cosmogenic isotopes
   c. Nanogeoscience
   d. Carbon cycle

4. The terms _____ and icehouse Earth refer to the prevailing global climate on a timescale of millions of years.

   During a _____ Earth period, the planet's atmosphere contains sufficient _____ gases such as carbon dioxide and methane for ice to be entirely absent from the planet's surface.

   During icehouse periods, glaciers are present in fluctuating amounts; variations in the Earth's orbit may result in many ice ages, glacials, and interglacials.
   a. 1509 Istanbul earthquake
   b. 1703 Genroku earthquake
   c. 1700 Cascadia earthquake
   d. Greenhouse

Chapter 19. Climate and Our Changing Planet

5. _____ are gases in an atmosphere that absorb and emit radiation within the thermal infrared range. This process is the fundamental cause of the greenhouse effect. Common _____ in the Earth's atmosphere include water vapor, carbon dioxide, methane, nitrous oxide, ozone, and chlorofluorocarbons.
   a. Greenhouse gases
   b. Glacier
   c. Climate models
   d. Deforestation

6. In chemistry, the _____ of a chemical compound is a simple expression of the relative numbers of each type of atom in it, or the simplest whole number ratio of atoms of each element present in a compound. An _____ makes no reference to isomerism, structure, or absolute number of atoms. The _____ is used as standard for most ionic compounds, such as $CaCl_2$, and for macromolecules, such as SiO_2.
   a. AL 129-1
   b. AL 333
   c. AASHTO Soil Classification System
   d. Empirical formula

7. A _____ or sandstorm is a meteorological phenomenon common in arid and semi-arid regions and arises when a gust front passes or when the wind force exceeds the threshold value where loose sand and dust are removed from the dry surface. Particles are transported by saltation and suspension, causing soil erosion from one place and deposition in another. The Sahara and drylands around the Arabian peninsula are the main source of airborne dust, with some contributions from Iran, Pakistan and India into the Arabian Sea, and China's storms deposit dust in the Pacific.
   a. 1509 Istanbul earthquake
   b. 1700 Cascadia earthquake
   c. 1703 Genroku earthquake
   d. Dust storm

8. _____ are the preserved remains or traces of animals, plants, and other organisms from the remote past. The totality of _____, both discovered and undiscovered, and their placement in fossiliferous rock formations and sedimentary layers (strata) is known as the fossil record. The study of _____ across geological time, how they were formed, and the evolutionary relationships between taxa (phylogeny) are some of the most important functions of the science of paleontology.
   a. 1509 Istanbul earthquake
   b. 1703 Genroku earthquake
   c. 1700 Cascadia earthquake
   d. Fossils

9. _____ is the naturally occurring, unconsolidated or loose covering on the Earth's surface. _____ is composed of particles of broken rock that have been altered by chemical, biological and environmental processes including weathering and erosion. _____ is different from its parent rock(s) source(s), altered by interactions between the lithosphere, hydrosphere, atmosphere, and the biosphere.
   a. Soil
   b. 1509 Istanbul earthquake
   c. Topsoil
   d. Slump

10. A _____ or gem is a piece of attractive mineral, which -- when cut and polished -- is used to make jewelry or other adornments. However certain rocks, and organic materials are not minerals, but are still used for jewelry, and are therefore often considered to be _____s as well. Most _____s are hard, but some soft minerals are used in jewelry because of their lustre or other physical properties that have aesthetic value.
    a. 1509 Istanbul earthquake
    b. 1703 Genroku earthquake
    c. 1700 Cascadia earthquake
    d. Gemstone

11. _____ use quantitative methods to simulate the interactions of the atmosphere, oceans, land surface, and ice. They are used for a variety of purposes from study of the dynamics of the climate system to projections of future climate.

Chapter 19. Climate and Our Changing Planet

All _____ take account of incoming energy as short wave electromagnetic radiation (which in this context means visible and ultraviolet, not to be confused with shortwave) to the earth as well as outgoing energy as long wave (infrared) electromagnetic radiation from the earth.

   a. Pacific Decadal Oscillation
   b. Deforestation
   c. Climate models
   d. Greenhouse gases

12. _____ are crystalline water-based solids physically resembling ice, in which small non polar molecules (typically gases) are trapped inside 'cages' of hydrogen bonded water molecules. In other words, _____ are clathrate compounds in which the host molecule is water and the guest molecule is typically a gas.
   a. 1509 Istanbul earthquake
   b. Clathrate hydrates
   c. 1703 Genroku earthquake
   d. 1700 Cascadia earthquake

13. The _____ describes the continuous movement of water on, above, and below the surface of the Earth. Since the _____ is truly a 'cycle,' there is no beginning or end. Water can change states among liquid, vapor, and ice at various places in the _____.
   a. Streamflow
   b. Hydraulic conductivity
   c. Flownet
   d. Water cycle

14. _____ is a term used in inorganic chemistry and organic chemistry to indicate that a substance contains water. The chemical state of the water varies widely between _____s, some of which were so labeled before their chemical structure was understood.

In organic chemistry, a _____ is a compound formed by the addition of water or its elements to a host molecule.

   a. 1703 Genroku earthquake
   b. 1700 Cascadia earthquake
   c. 1509 Istanbul earthquake
   d. Hydrate

15. _____ are the largest glaciers, enormous masses of ice that are not visibly affected by the landscape and that cover the entire surface beneath them, except possibly on the margins where they are thinnest. Antarctica and Greenland are the only places where continental _____ currently exist. These regions contain vast quantities of fresh water.
   a. AL 129-1
   b. Ice sheets
   c. AL 333
   d. AASHTO Soil Classification System

16. The _____ , usually abbreviated K for its German translation Kreide, is a geologic period and system from circa >145.5 >± 4 to >65.5 >± 0.3 million years ago . In the geologic timescale, the _____ follows on the Jurassic period and is followed by the Paleogene period. It is the youngest period of the Mesozoic era, and at 80 million years long, the longest period of the Phanerozoic eon. The end of the _____ defines the boundary between the Mesozoic and Cenozoic eras.
   a. Campanian
   b. Valanginian
   c. Hauterivian
   d. Cretaceous

17. The _____ in stratigraphy, Chronostratigraphy, paleontology and other natural sciences refers to the entirety of the layers of rock strata -- depositions laid down in volcanism or by weathering detritus (clays, sands etc.) including all its fossil content and the information it yields about the history of the Earth: its past climate, geography, geology and the evolution of life on its surface. According to the Law of Superposition (first proposed in the mid-seventeenth century by the Danish naturalist Nicolas Steno) sedimentary and volcanic rocklayers are deposited on top of each other.
   a. Geologic record
   b. Lichenometry
   c. Stage
   d. Paleomagnetism

18. The _____ is a geological epoch which began approximately 11‰700 years ago (10‰000 ^{14}C years ago). According to traditional geological thinking, the _____ continues to the present. The _____ is part of the Neogene and Quaternary periods.
   a. 1700 Cascadia earthquake
   b. Holocene
   c. Neoglaciation
   d. 1509 Istanbul earthquake

19. _____ is molten rock that is found beneath the surface of the Earth, and may also exist on other terrestrial planets. Besides molten rock, _____ may also contain suspended crystals and gas bubbles. _____ often collects in a _____ chamber inside a volcano. _____ is capable of intrusion into adjacent rocks, extrusion onto the surface as lava, and explosive ejection as tephra to form pyroclastic rock.
   a. Large igneous provinces
   b. Sedimentary rock
   c. Groundmass
   d. Magma

20. _____ is the slow creeping motion of Earth's rocky mantle in response to perpetual gravitationally unstable variations in its density. Material near the surface of the Earth, particularly oceanic lithosphere, cools down by conduction of heat into the oceans and atmosphere, then thermally contracts to become dense, and then sinks under its own weight at convergent plate boundaries. This subducted material sinks to some depth in the Earth's interior where it is prohibited, by inherent density stratification, from sinking further.
   a. Divergent boundary
   b. Plate tectonics
   c. Motagua Fault
   d. Mantle convection

21. _____ in the most general terms refers to the movement of molecules within fluids (i.e. liquids, gases and rheids.) _____ is one of the major modes of heat transfer and mass transfer. In fluids, convective heat and mass transfer take place through both diffusion - the random Brownian motion of individual particles in the fluid - and by advection, in which matter or heat is transported by the larger-scale motion of currents in the fluid.
   a. Convection
   b. Strong interaction
   c. Power
   d. Turbulent flow

22. In geology, _____ is the process that takes place at convergent boundaries by which one tectonic plate moves under another tectonic plate, sinking into the Earth's mantle, as the plates converge. A _____ zone is an area on Earth where two tectonic plates move towards one another and _____ occurs. Rates of _____ are typically measured in centimeters per year, with the average rate of convergence being approximately 2 to 8 centimeters per year (about the rate a fingernail grows.)
   a. Motagua Fault
   b. Subduction
   c. Mirovia
   d. Continental collision

23. The Ypresian is the first stage of the Eocene Epoch and usually corresponds to the _____ subepoch, though sometimes the Lutetian is included therein.

Chapter 19. Climate and Our Changing Planet

It spans the time between 55.8 >± 0.2 Ma and 48.6 >± 0.2 Ma (million years ago.) The stage is named after Ypres, Belgium.

a. AL 333
b. AL 129-1
c. AASHTO Soil Classification System
d. Early Eocene

24. The _____ epoch (55.8 >± 0.2 - 33.9 >± 0.1 Ma) is a major division of the geologic timescale and the second epoch of the Palaeogene period in the Cenozoic era. The _____ spans the time from the end of the Paleocene epoch to the beginning of the Oligocene epoch. The start of the _____ is marked by the emergence of the first modern mammals.

a. AL 333
b. AASHTO Soil Classification System
c. AL 129-1
d. Eocene

25. The _____ is the rigid outermost shell of a rocky planet.

In the Earth, the _____ includes the crust and the uppermost mantle, which constitute the hard and rigid outer layer of the planet. The _____ is underlain by the asthenosphere, the weaker, hotter, and deeper part of the upper mantle.

a. Continental crust
b. Subduction
c. Mantle convection
d. Lithosphere

26. _____ describes the large scale motions of Earth's lithosphere. The theory encompasses the older concepts of continental drift, developed during the first decades of the 20th century by Alfred Wegener, and seafloor spreading, understood during the 1960s.

The outermost part of the Earth's interior is made up of two layers: the lithosphere and the asthenosphere.

a. Continental crust
b. Nappe
c. Mantle convection
d. Plate tectonics

27. _____s is a field of study within geology concerned generally with the structures within the lithosphere of the Earth and particularly with the forces and movements that have operated in a region to create these structures.

_____s is concerned with the orogenies and _____ development of cratons and _____ terranes as well as the earthquake and volcanic belts which directly affect much of the global population. _____ studies are also important for understanding erosion patterns in geomorphology and as guides for the economic geologist searching for petroleum and metallic ores.

a. Cocos Plate
b. Rivera Plate
c. Tectonic
d. Fault trace

28. _____ is a field of study within geology concerned generally with the structures within the lithosphere of the Earth and particularly with the forces and movements that have operated in a region to create these structures.

_____ is concerned with the orogenies and tectonic development of cratons and tectonic terranes as well as the earthquake and volcanic belts which directly affect much of the global population. Tectonic studies are also important for understanding erosion patterns in geomorphology and as guides for the economic geologist searching for petroleum and metallic ores.

a. Cocos Plate
c. Rivera Plate
b. Fault trace
d. Tectonics

29. The _____ or Clovis comet hypothesis refers to the hypothesized large air burst or earth impact of an object or objects from outer space that initiated the Younger Dryas cold spell about 10,900 BP uncalibrated (12,900 BP calibrated.) The theory proposes that an air burst and/or earth impact with a rare swarm of carbonaceous chondrites or comets set vast areas of the North American continent on fire, causing the extinction of most of the large animals in North America and the demise of the North American Clovis culture at the end of the last glacial period. This swarm would have exploded above or even into the Laurentide Ice Sheet north of the Great Lakes.

a. 1700 Cascadia earthquake
c. 1703 Genroku earthquake
b. 1509 Istanbul earthquake
d. Younger Dryas impact event

Chapter 20. Earth Through Geologic Time

1. _____ is the movement of the Earth's continents relative to each other. The hypothesis that continents 'drift' was first put forward by Abraham Ortelius in 1596 and was fully developed by Alfred Wegener in 1912. However, it was not until the development of the theory of plate tectonics in the 1960s, that a sufficient geological explanation of that movement was found.
   a. Convergent boundary
   b. Nappe
   c. Continental collision
   d. Continental drift

2. _____, originally Gondwanaland, is the name given to a southern precursor-supercontinent and then as a remnant separated from Laurasia 180-200 million years ago during the breakup of the Pangaea supercontinent that existed about 500 to 200 Ma ago into two large segments. While the corresponding northern hemisphere continent Laurasia moved further north, the nearly equal in area _____ included most of the landmasses in today's southern hemisphere, including Antarctica, South America, Africa, Madagascar, Australia-New Guinea, and New Zealand, as well as Arabia and the Indian subcontinent, which have now moved into the Northern Hemisphere.
   a. Laurasia
   b. Gondwana
   c. 1700 Cascadia earthquake
   d. 1509 Istanbul earthquake

3. _____ was a supercontinent that most recently existed as a part of the split of the Pangaean supercontinent in the late Mesozoic era. It included most of the landmasses which make up today's continents of the northern hemisphere, chiefly Laurentia (the name given to the North American craton), Baltica, Siberia, Kazakhstania, and the North China and East China cratons.
   a. 1509 Istanbul earthquake
   b. Rodinia
   c. Laurasia
   d. 1700 Cascadia earthquake

4. _____ was the supercontinent that is theorized to have existed during the Paleozoic and Mesozoic eras about 250 million years ago, before the component continents were separated into their current configuration.

The name was first used by the German originator of the continental drift theory, Alfred Wegener, in the 1920 edition of his book The Origin of Continents and Oceans , in which a postulated supercontinent _____ played a key role.

The single enormous ocean which surrounded Pangaea is known as Panthalassa.

   a. 1700 Cascadia earthquake
   b. 1509 Istanbul earthquake
   c. 1703 Genroku earthquake
   d. Pangea

5. In geology, _____ is transported rock debris overlying the solid bedrock. The term is also sometimes refers to organic debris so-transported. In the largest sense, it refers to the material left behind by retreating continental glaciers.
   a. Geomechanics
   b. Metamorphic reaction
   c. Riegel
   d. Drift

6. _____ Paths support the idea of a super-continent. Geologists can determine the movement of continental plates by examining the orientation of magnetic minerals in rocks; when rocks are formed, they take on the magnetic properties of the Earth and indicate in which direction the poles lie relative to the rock. Because we know that the poles do not move more than a few degrees, magnetic anomalies in rocks can only be explained by the drifting of continents.
   a. AL 333
   b. AASHTO Soil Classification System
   c. Apparent polar wandering
   d. AL 129-1

Chapter 20. Earth Through Geologic Time

7. _____ are the preserved remains or traces of animals, plants, and other organisms from the remote past. The totality of _____, both discovered and undiscovered, and their placement in fossiliferous rock formations and sedimentary layers (strata) is known as the fossil record. The study of _____ across geological time, how they were formed, and the evolutionary relationships between taxa (phylogeny) are some of the most important functions of the science of paleontology.
   a. 1700 Cascadia earthquake
   b. 1509 Istanbul earthquake
   c. Fossils
   d. 1703 Genroku earthquake

8. _____ is the part of Earth's lithosphere that surfaces in the ocean basins. _____ is primarily composed of mafic rocks, or sima. It is thinner than continental crust, or sial, generally less than 10 kilometers thick, however it is denser, having a mean density of about 3.3 grams per cubic centimeter.
   a. AL 333
   b. AL 129-1
   c. AASHTO Soil Classification System
   d. Oceanic crust

9. _____ is the study of the record of the Earth's magnetic field preserved in various magnetic minerals through time. The study of _____ has demonstrated that the Earth's magnetic field varies substantially in both orientation and intensity through time. <
   a. Relative dating
   b. Chronozone
   c. Global Standard Stratigraphic Age
   d. Paleomagnetism

10. In materials science, _____ is a change in the shape or size of an object due to an applied force. This can be a result of tensile (pulling) forces, compressive (pushing) forces, shear, bending or torsion (twisting.) _____ is often described as strain.
   a. Submersion
   b. Stack
   c. Lingula
   d. Deformation

11. A _____ is a change in the orientation of Earth's magnetic field such that the positions of magnetic north and magnetic south become interchanged. These events often involve an extended decline in field strength followed by a rapid recovery after the new orientation has been established. These events occur on a scale of thousands of years or longer.
   a. 1509 Istanbul earthquake
   b. 1703 Genroku earthquake
   c. 1700 Cascadia earthquake
   d. Geomagnetic reversal

12. _____ is a technique used to date materials, usually based on a comparison between the observed abundance of a naturally occurring radioactive isotope and its decay products, using known decay rates. It is the principal source of information about the absolute age of rocks and other geological features, including the age of the Earth itself, and can be used to date a wide range of natural and man-made materials. Together with stratigraphic principles, _____ methods are used in geochronology to establish the geological time scale.
   a. Relative dating
   b. Radiometric dating
   c. Lichenometry
   d. Stage

13. _____ in the most general terms refers to the movement of molecules within fluids (i.e. liquids, gases and rheids.) _____ is one of the major modes of heat transfer and mass transfer. In fluids, convective heat and mass transfer take place through both diffusion - the random Brownian motion of individual particles in the fluid - and by advection, in which matter or heat is transported by the larger-scale motion of currents in the fluid.

Chapter 20. Earth Through Geologic Time

   a. Power
   c. Turbulent flow
   b. Strong interaction
   d. Convection

14. _____ is the slow creeping motion of Earth's rocky mantle in response to perpetual gravitationally unstable variations in its density. Material near the surface of the Earth, particularly oceanic lithosphere, cools down by conduction of heat into the oceans and atmosphere, then thermally contracts to become dense, and then sinks under its own weight at convergent plate boundaries. This subducted material sinks to some depth in the Earth's interior where it is prohibited, by inherent density stratification, from sinking further.
   a. Divergent boundary
   c. Plate tectonics
   b. Motagua Fault
   d. Mantle convection

15. An _____ is a section of the Earth's oceanic crust and the underlying upper mantle that has been uplifted or emplaced to be exposed within continental crustal rocks. Ophio is Greek for 'snake', lite means 'stone' from the Greek lithos.

The term _____ was originally used by Alexandre Brongniart for an assemblage of green rocks (serpentine, diabase) in the Alps; Steinmann (1927) later modified its use to include serpentine, pillow lava, and chert ('Steinmann's trinity'), again based on occurrences in the Alps.

   a. AL 129-1
   c. AL 333
   b. Ophiolite
   d. AASHTO Soil Classification System

16. The lithosphere is broken up into what are called _____. In the case of Earth, there are eight major and many minor plates The lithospheric plates ride on the asthenosphere. These plates move in relation to one another at one of three types of plate boundaries: convergent, or collisional boundaries; divergent boundaries, also called spreading centers; and transform boundaries.
   a. Nappe
   c. Supercontinent cycle
   b. Continental drift
   d. Tectonic plates

17. In geology, the term '_____' refers to structures or minerals from a parent rock that did not undergo metamorphosis when the surrounding rock did, or to rock that survived a destructive geologic process.
   a. Relict
   c. 1703 Genroku earthquake
   b. 1509 Istanbul earthquake
   d. 1700 Cascadia earthquake

18. _____ is a common extrusive volcanic rock. It is usually grey to black and fine-grained due to rapid cooling of lava at the surface of a planet. It may be porphyritic containing larger crystals in a fine matrix, or vesicular, or frothy scoria.
   a. 1509 Istanbul earthquake
   c. 1700 Cascadia earthquake
   b. 1703 Genroku earthquake
   d. Basalt

19. _____ is a rock that forms by the metamorphism of basalt and rocks with similar composition at high pressures and low temperatures, approximately corresponding to a depth of 15 to 30 kilometers and 200 to ~500 degrees Celsius. The blue color of the rock comes from the presence of the mineral glaucophane.

They are typically found within orogenic belts as terranes of lithology in faulted contact with greenschist or rarely eclogite facies rocks.

Chapter 20. Earth Through Geologic Time

a. Porphyroblast
c. Geothermobarometry
b. Blueschist
d. Metamorphic facies

20. _____ refers to a large group of dark, coarse-grained, intrusive igneous rocks chemically equivalent to basalt. The rocks are plutonic, formed when molten magma is trapped beneath the Earth's surface and cools into a crystalline mass.

The vast majority of the Earth's surface is underlain by _____ within the oceanic crust, produced by basalt magmatism at mid-ocean ridges.

a. 1700 Cascadia earthquake
c. 1509 Istanbul earthquake
b. 1703 Genroku earthquake
d. Gabbro

21. A _____ is a dense, coarse-grained igneous rock, consisting mostly of the minerals olivine and pyroxene. _____ is ultramafic, as the rock contains less than 45% silica. It is high in magnesium, reflecting the high proportions of magnesium-rich olivine, with appreciable iron.

_____ is the dominant rock of the upper part of the Earth's mantle. The compositions of _____ nodules found in certain basalts and diamond pipes (kimberlites) are of special interest, because they provide samples of the Earth's Mantle roots of continents brought up from depths from about 30 km or so to depths at least as great as about 200 km.

a. 1509 Istanbul earthquake
c. Peridotite
b. 1703 Genroku earthquake
d. 1700 Cascadia earthquake

22. In geology, _____ is the process that takes place at convergent boundaries by which one tectonic plate moves under another tectonic plate, sinking into the Earth's mantle, as the plates converge. A _____ zone is an area on Earth where two tectonic plates move towards one another and _____ occurs. Rates of _____ are typically measured in centimeters per year, with the average rate of convergence being approximately 2 to 8 centimeters per year (about the rate a fingernail grows.)
a. Mirovia
c. Continental collision
b. Motagua Fault
d. Subduction

23. _____ are geologic features, submarine basins associated with island arcs and subduction zones. They are found at some convergent plate boundaries, presently concentrated in the Western Pacific ocean. Most of them result from tensional forces caused by oceanic trench rollback and the collapse of the edge of the continent.
a. Back-arc basins
c. 1700 Cascadia earthquake
b. 1703 Genroku earthquake
d. 1509 Istanbul earthquake

24. In geology, a _____ is a landmass comprising more than one continental core, or craton. The assembly of cratons and accreted terranes that form Eurasia qualifies as a _____ today.

Most commonly, paleogeographers employ the term _____ to refer to a single landmass consisting of all the modern continents.

Chapter 20. Earth Through Geologic Time

a. Supercontinent
c. 1700 Cascadia earthquake
b. 1703 Genroku earthquake
d. 1509 Istanbul earthquake

25. The general term '_____' or, more precisely, 'glacial age' denotes a geological period of long-term reduction in the temperature of the Earth's surface and atmosphere, resulting in an expansion of continental ice sheets, polar ice sheets and alpine glaciers. Within a long-term _____, individual pulses of extra cold climate are termed 'glaciations'. Glaciologically, _____ implies the presence of extensive ice sheets in the northern and southern hemispheres; by this definition we are still in an _____

a. Ice Age
c. AASHTO Soil Classification System
b. AL 333
d. AL 129-1

26. _____, like all craton land, was created as continents moved about the surface of the Earth, bumping into other continents and drifting away.

Many times in its past, _____ has been a separate continent as it is now in the form of North America. During other times in its past, _____ has been part of a supercontinent.

a. South China
c. North China craton
b. Congo craton
d. Laurentia

27. In geology, _____ is the name of a supercontinent, a continent which contained most or all of Earth's landmass. According to plate tectonic reconstructions, _____ existed between 1100 and 750 million years ago, in the Neoproterozoic era.

In contrast with Pangaea, the last supercontinent about 300 million years ago, little is known yet about the exact configuration and geodynamic history of _____.

a. 1509 Istanbul earthquake
c. 1700 Cascadia earthquake
b. Rodinia
d. Laurasia

28. _____ refers to hypotheses regarding paleoclimatic global-scale glaciation, claiming that the Earth's surface was nearly or entirely frozen at some points in its past. The occurrence of _____ remains controversial. Proponents claim it best explains sedimentary deposits generally regarded as of glacial origin at tropical latitudes and other enigmatic features of the geological record.

a. Drumlin field
c. Wolstonian Stage
b. Quaternary glaciation
d. Snowball Earth

29. The _____ -- also called the Laurentian Plateau, or Bouclier Canadien -- is a massive geological shield covered by a thin layer of soil that forms the nucleus of the North American or Laurentia craton. It has a deep, common, joined bedrock region in eastern and central Canada and stretches North from the Great Lakes to the Arctic Ocean, covering over half of Canada; it also extends south into the northern reaches of the United States. Population is scarce, and industrial development is minimal, although the region has a large hydroelectric power potential.

a. Yilgarn Craton
c. Quaternary
b. Gawler craton
d. Canadian Shield

Chapter 20. Earth Through Geologic Time

30. The _____ is the zone of the ocean floor that separates the thin oceanic crust from thick continental crust. _____s constitute about 28% of the oceanic area.

The transition from continental to oceanic crust commonly occurs within the outer part of the margin, called continental rise.

   a. Continental margin
   b. Swash
   c. 1509 Istanbul earthquake
   d. Cuspate forelands

31. A _____ is generally a large area of exposed Precambrian crystalline igneous and high-grade metamorphic rocks that form tectonically stable areas. In all cases, the age of these rocks is greater than 570 million years and sometimes dates back 2 to 3.5 billion years. They have been little affected by tectonic events following the end of the Precambrian Era, and are relatively flat regions where mountain building, faulting, and other tectonic processes are greatly diminished compared with the activity that occurs at the margins of the _____s and the boundaries between tectonic plates.
   a. 1700 Cascadia earthquake
   b. Shield
   c. 1703 Genroku earthquake
   d. 1509 Istanbul earthquake

32. A _____ is an old and stable part of the continental crust that has survived the merging and splitting of continents and supercontinents for at least 500 million years. Some are over two billion years old. They are generally found in the interiors of continents and are characteristically composed of ancient crystalline basement crust of lightweight felsic igneous rock such as granite.
   a. Sebakwe proto-craton
   b. Wyoming craton
   c. Superior craton
   d. Craton

33. _____ refers to natural mountain building, and may be studied as a tectonic structural event, (b) as a geographical event, and (c) a chronological event. Orogenic events (a) cause distinctive structural phenomena and related tectonic activity, (b) affect certain regions of rocks and crust, and (c) happen within a specific period of time.
   a. Alice Springs Orogeny
   b. Antler orogeny
   c. Orogeny
   d. Orogenesis

34. In geology, a _____ is a continental area covered by relatively flat or gently tilted, mainly sedimentary strata, which overlie a basement of consolidated igneous or metamorphic rocks of an earlier deformation. They as well as, shields and the basement rocks together constitute cratons.

It is also common practice to use the term _____ as a very general term for a sequence of shallow water carbonate _____.

   a. Combe
   b. Texture
   c. Platform
   d. Compaction

35. In geology, a _____ is a place where the Earth's crust and lithosphere are being pulled apart and is an example of extensional tectonics.

Chapter 20. Earth Through Geologic Time

Typical _____ features are a central linear downdropped fault segment, called a graben, with parallel normal faulting and _____-flank uplifts on either side forming a _____ valley, where the _____ remains above sea level. The axis of the _____ area commonly contains volcanic rocks and active volcanism is a part of many, but not all active _____ systems.

    a. 1509 Istanbul earthquake   b. Rift
    c. 1700 Cascadia earthquake   d. 1703 Genroku earthquake

36. A _____ is a linear-shaped lowland between highlands or mountain ranges created by the action of a geologic rift or fault. This action is manifest as crustal extension, a spreading apart of the surface which is subsequently further deepened by the forces of erosion. When the tensional forces are strong enough to cause the plate to split apart it will do so such that a center block will drop down relative to its flanking blocks.
    a. 1700 Cascadia earthquake   b. 1509 Istanbul earthquake
    c. Rift Valley   d. 1703 Genroku earthquake

37. A _____ is the point where the boundaries of three tectonic plates meet. At the _____ a boundary will be one of 3 types - a ridge, trench or transform fault and _____s can be described according to the types of plate margin that meet at them. Of the many possible types of _____ only a few are stable through time.
    a. 1700 Cascadia earthquake   b. 1703 Genroku earthquake
    c. 1509 Istanbul earthquake   d. Triple junction

38. _____ is the branch of classical mechanics that describes the motion of objects without consideration of the causes leading to the motion.

_____ is not to be confused with another branch of classical mechanics: analytical dynamics (the study of the relationship between the motion of objects and its causes), sometimes subdivided into kinetics (the study of the relation between external forces and motion) and statics (the study of the relations in a system at equilibrium.) _____ also differs from dynamics as used in modern-day physics to describe time-evolution of a system.

    a. Strain rate   b. Kinematics
    c. 1509 Istanbul earthquake   d. 1700 Cascadia earthquake

39. A _____ is a chain of volcanic islands or mountains formed by plate tectonics as an oceanic tectonic plate subducts under another tectonic plate and produces magma. There are two types of these: oceanic arcs (commonly called island arcs, a type of archipelago) and continental arcs. In the former, oceanic crust subducts beneath other oceanic crust on an adjacent plate, while in the latter case the oceanic crust subducts beneath continental crust. In some situations, a single subduction zone may show both aspects along its length, as part of a plate subducts beneath a continent and part beneath adjacent oceanic crust.
    a. 1700 Cascadia earthquake   b. 1703 Genroku earthquake
    c. 1509 Istanbul earthquake   d. Volcanic arc

40. _____ is a phenomenon of the plate tectonics of Earth that occurs at convergent boundaries. _____ is a variation on the fundamental process of subduction, whereby the subduction zone is destroyed, mountains produced, and two continents sutured together. _____ is known only from this planet and is an interesting example of how our different crusts, oceanic and continental, behave during subduction.

a. Copperbelt Province
b. Supercontinent cycle
c. Mirovia
d. Continental collision

41. In geology, a _____ or _____ line is a planar fracture in rock in which the rock on one side of the fracture has moved with respect to the rock on the other side. Large _____s within the Earth's crust are the result of differential or shear motion and active _____ zones are the causal locations of most earthquakes. Earthquakes are caused by energy release during rapid slippage along a _____.
  a. Cleavage
  b. Drainage system
  c. Fault
  d. Compaction

42. The _____ is a continental transform fault that runs a length of roughly 800 miles (1,300 km) through California in the United States. The fault's motion is right-lateral strike-slip (horizontal motion.) It forms the tectonic boundary between the Pacific Plate and the North American Plate.
  a. 1700 Cascadia earthquake
  b. 1703 Genroku earthquake
  c. San Andreas Fault
  d. 1509 Istanbul earthquake

43. A _____ in geology is a fragment of crustal material formed on one tectonic plate and accreted -- 'sutured' -- to crust lying on another plate. The crustal block or fragment preserves its own distinctive geologic history, which is different from that of the surrounding areas (hence the term 'exotic' _____). The suture zone between a _____ and the crust it attaches to is usually identifiable as a fault.
  a. 1700 Cascadia earthquake
  b. 1703 Genroku earthquake
  c. 1509 Istanbul earthquake
  d. Terrane

44. A _____ or transform boundary is a fault which runs along the boundary of a tectonic plate. The relative motion of such plates is horizontal in either sinistral or dextral direction. Typically, some vertical motion may also exist, but the principal vectors in a _____ are oriented horizontally.
  a. Transform fault
  b. Structural geology
  c. Michoud fault
  d. Molasse basin

45. _____ describes the large scale motions of Earth's lithosphere. The theory encompasses the older concepts of continental drift, developed during the first decades of the 20th century by Alfred Wegener, and seafloor spreading, understood during the 1960s.

The outermost part of the Earth's interior is made up of two layers: the lithosphere and the asthenosphere.

  a. Nappe
  b. Plate tectonics
  c. Mantle convection
  d. Continental crust

46. _____s is a field of study within geology concerned generally with the structures within the lithosphere of the Earth and particularly with the forces and movements that have operated in a region to create these structures.

_____s is concerned with the orogenies and _____ development of cratons and _____ terranes as well as the earthquake and volcanic belts which directly affect much of the global population. _____ studies are also important for understanding erosion patterns in geomorphology and as guides for the economic geologist searching for petroleum and metallic ores.

a. Cocos Plate
b. Tectonic
c. Rivera Plate
d. Fault trace

47. _____ is a field of study within geology concerned generally with the structures within the lithosphere of the Earth and particularly with the forces and movements that have operated in a region to create these structures.

_____ is concerned with the orogenies and tectonic development of cratons and tectonic terranes as well as the earthquake and volcanic belts which directly affect much of the global population. Tectonic studies are also important for understanding erosion patterns in geomorphology and as guides for the economic geologist searching for petroleum and metallic ores.

a. Rivera Plate
b. Fault trace
c. Tectonics
d. Cocos Plate

48. _____ is the process by which the removal of material, through means of erosion and weathering, leads to a reduction of elevation and relief in landforms and landscapes. Exogenic processes, including the action of water, ice, and wind, predominantly involve _____. Denudation can involve the removal of both solid particles and dissolved material.

a. Palustrine
b. Mesa
c. Denudation
d. 1509 Istanbul earthquake

Chapter 21. Resources of Minerals and Energy

1. _____ is a gas consisting primarily of methane. It is found associated with fossil fuels, in coal beds, as methane clathrates, and is created by methanogenic organisms in marshes, bogs, and landfills. It is an important fuel source, a major feedstock for fertilizers, and a potent greenhouse gas.
   - a. 1700 Cascadia earthquake
   - b. 1703 Genroku earthquake
   - c. 1509 Istanbul earthquake
   - d. Natural gas

2. _____ is a water mass that forms in the North Atlantic Ocean. It is largely formed in the Labrador Sea and in the Greenland Sea by the sinking of highly saline, dense overflow water from the Greenland Sea. The watermass can be traced around the southern end of Greenland and then, at a depth of 2000-4000 meters, down the coast of Canada and the United States where it turns slightly east.
   - a. North Atlantic Deep Water
   - b. 1700 Cascadia earthquake
   - c. 1703 Genroku earthquake
   - d. 1509 Istanbul earthquake

3. In geology, a _____ deposit or _____ is an accumulation of valuable minerals formed by deposition of dense mineral phases in a trap site. Types of _____ deposits include alluvium, eluvium, beach _____ s, and paleoplacers.

   Typical locations for alluvial _____ deposits are on the inside bends of rivers and creeks, in natural hollows, at the break of slope on a stream, the base of an escarpment, waterfall or other barrier, within sand dunes, beach profiles or in gravel beds.

   - a. 1509 Istanbul earthquake
   - b. 1700 Cascadia earthquake
   - c. Placer
   - d. 1703 Genroku earthquake

4. The _____ of any physical feature such as a hill, stream, roof, railroad, or road refers to the amount of inclination of that surface where zero indicates level (with respect to gravity) and larger numbers indicate higher degrees of 'tilt'. Often slope is calculated as a ratio of 'rise over run' in which run is the horizontal distance and rise is the vertical distance.

   There are several systems for expressing slope:

   1. as an angle of inclination from the horizontal of a right triangle. (This is the angle >α opposite the 'rise' side of the triangle.)
   2. as a percentage (also known as the _____), the formula for which is [x] > which could also be expressed as the tangent of the angle of inclination times 100. In the U.S., the _____ is the most commonly used unit for communicating slopes in transportation, surveying, construction, and civil engineering.
   3. as a per mille figure, the formula for which is [x] > which could also be expressed as the tangent of the angle of inclination times 1000. This is commonly used in Europe to denote the incline of a railway.
   4. as a ratio of one part rise per so many parts run. For example, a slope that has a rise of 5 feet for every 100 feet of run would have a slope ratio of 1 in 20.

   Any one of these expressions may be used interchangeably to express the characteristics of a slope. _____ is usually expressed as a percentage, but this may easily be converted to the angle >α from horizontal since that carries the same information.

Chapter 21. Resources of Minerals and Energy

    a. Heavy metal
    c. Diamond Head
    b. Grade
    d. Compaction

5. An _____ is a type of rock that contains minerals such as gemstones and metals that can be extracted through mining and refined for use. Samples of _____ in the form of exceptionally beautiful crystals, exotic layering visible when sectioned or polished or metallic presentations such as large nuggets or crystalline formations of metals such as gold or copper may command a value far beyond their value as mere _____ or raw metal for subsequent reduction to utilitarian purposes.

The grade or concentration of an _____ mineral, or metal, as well as its form of occurrence, will directly affect the costs associated with mining the _____.

    a. Ore genesis
    c. Iron ores
    b. AASHTO Soil Classification System
    d. Ore

6. _____ circulation in its most general sense is the circulation of hot water; 'hydros' in the Greek meaning water and 'thermos' meaning heat. _____ circulation occurs most often in the vicinity of sources of heat within the Earth's crust. This generally occurs near volcanic activity, but can occur in the deep crust related to the intrusion of granite, or as the result of orogeny or metamorphism.
    a. Seafloor spreading
    c. Transgression
    b. Headward erosion
    d. Hydrothermal

7. A _____ is a fissure in a planet's surface from which geothermally heated water issues. they are commonly found near volcanically active places, areas where tectonic plates are moving apart, ocean basins, and hotspots.

They are locally very common because the earth is both geologically active and has large amounts of water on its surface and within its crust. Common land types include hot springs, fumaroles and geysers. The most famous _____ system on land is probably within Yellowstone National Park in the United States.

    a. 1700 Cascadia earthquake
    c. Hydrothermal vent
    b. 1703 Genroku earthquake
    d. 1509 Istanbul earthquake

8. _____ is one of the three main rock types (the others being igneous and metamorphic rock.) _____ is formed by deposition and consolidation of mineral and organic material and from precipitation of minerals from solution. The processes that form _____ occur at the surface of the Earth and within bodies of water.
    a. Sedimentary rock
    c. Felsic
    b. Serpentinite
    d. Large igneous provinces

9. _____ are water-soluble mineral sediments that result from the evaporation of bodies of surficial water. _____ are considered sedimentary rocks.

Although all water bodies on the surface and in aquifers contain dissolved salts, the water must evaporate into the atmosphere for the minerals to precipitate.

Chapter 21. Resources of Minerals and Energy

a. AL 129-1
b. AL 333
c. AASHTO Soil Classification System
d. Evaporites

10. In geology and related fields, a _____ is a layer of rock or soil with internally consistent characteristics that distinguishes it from contiguous layers. Each layer is generally one of a number of parallel layers that lie one upon another, laid down by natural forces. They may extend over hundreds of thousands of square kilometers of the Earth's surface.
   a. 1509 Istanbul earthquake
   b. 1703 Genroku earthquake
   c. Stratum
   d. 1700 Cascadia earthquake

11. _____ is the most important aluminium ore. It consists largely of the minerals gibbsite $Al(OH)_3$, boehmite >γ-AlO(OH), and diaspore >α-AlO(OH), together with the iron oxides goethite and hematite, the clay mineral kaolinite and small amounts of anatase TiO_2. It was named after the village Les Baux in southern France, where it was first discovered in 1821 by the geologist Pierre Berthier.
   a. 1700 Cascadia earthquake
   b. 1509 Istanbul earthquake
   c. 1703 Genroku earthquake
   d. Bauxite

12. _____ are the preserved remains or traces of animals, plants, and other organisms from the remote past. The totality of _____, both discovered and undiscovered, and their placement in fossiliferous rock formations and sedimentary layers (strata) is known as the fossil record. The study of _____ across geological time, how they were formed, and the evolutionary relationships between taxa (phylogeny) are some of the most important functions of the science of paleontology.
   a. 1700 Cascadia earthquake
   b. 1703 Genroku earthquake
   c. 1509 Istanbul earthquake
   d. Fossils

13. _____ is a surface formation in hot and wet tropical areas which is enriched in iron and aluminium and develops by intensive and long lasting weathering of the underlying parent rock. Nearly all kinds of rocks can be deeply decomposed by the action of high rainfall and elevated temperatures. The percolating rain water causes dissolution of primary rock minerals and decrease of easily soluble elements as sodium, potassium, calcium, magnesium and silicon.
   a. Soil horizon
   b. Pedogenesis
   c. Slickenside
   d. Laterite

14. _____ is a hard, compact variety of mineral coal that has a high lustre. It has the highest carbon count and contains the fewest impurities of all coals, despite its lower calorific content.

_____ is the highest of the metamorphic rank, in which the carbon content is between 92% and 98%.

a. AL 333
b. AASHTO Soil Classification System
c. AL 129-1
d. Anthracite

15. _____ is a relatively soft coal containing a tarlike substance called bitumen. It is of higher quality than lignite coal but of poorer quality than anthracite coal.

_____ is a sedimorphic rock formed by diagenetic and submetamorphic compression of peat bog material.

a. 1703 Genroku earthquake
b. 1509 Istanbul earthquake
c. 1700 Cascadia earthquake
d. Bituminous coal

16. _____ is a mixture of organic chemical compounds that make up a portion of the organic matter in sedimentary rocks. It is insoluble in normal organic solvents because of the huge molecular weight (upwards of 1,000 Daltons) of its component compounds. The soluble portion is known as bitumen.
   a. 1509 Istanbul earthquake
   b. 1703 Genroku earthquake
   c. 1700 Cascadia earthquake
   d. Kerogen

17. _____ is an organic-rich fine-grained sedimentary rock. It contains significant amounts of kerogen, a solid mixture of organic chemical compounds from which liquid hydrocarbons can be extracted. Deposits of _____ occur around the world, including major deposits in the United States of America. Estimates of global deposits range from 2.8 trillion to 3.3 trillion barrels >(450 >× 10^9 to 520 >× 10^9 m^3) of recoverable oil.
   a. AL 129-1
   b. AL 333
   c. AASHTO Soil Classification System
   d. Oil shale

18. Organic chemistry is the science concerned with all aspects of _____. Organic synthesis is the methodology of their preparation.

The name 'organic' is historical, dating back to the 19th century, when it was believed that _____ could only be synthesized in living organisms through vis vitalis - the 'life-force'.

   a. AL 333
   b. AL 129-1
   c. AASHTO Soil Classification System
   d. Organic compounds

19. _____ is an accumulation of partially decayed vegetation matter. _____ forms in wetlands or peatlands, variously called bogs, moors, muskegs, pocosins, mires, and _____ swamp forests. By volume there are about 4 trillion mÂÂ³ of _____ in the world covering a total of around 2% of global land mass (about 3 million km^2), containing about 8 billion terajoules of energy.
   a. 1703 Genroku earthquake
   b. 1700 Cascadia earthquake
   c. Peat
   d. 1509 Istanbul earthquake

20. _____ is a fine-grained sedimentary rock whose original constituents were clay minerals or muds. It is characterized by thin laminae breaking with an irregular curving fracture, often splintery and usually parallel to the often-indistinguishable bedding plane. This property is called fissility.
   a. Jasperoid
   b. Claystone
   c. Concretion
   d. Shale

21. _____ is a type of coal whose properties range from those of lignite to those of bituminous coal and are used primarily as fuel for steam-electric power generation.

_____s may be dull, dark brown to black, soft and crumbly at the lower end of the range, to bright jet-black, hard, and relatively strong at the upper end. They contain 15-30% inherent moisture by weight and are non-coking (undergo little swelling upon heating.)

Chapter 21. Resources of Minerals and Energy

a. 1703 Genroku earthquake
c. 1509 Istanbul earthquake
b. Sub-bituminous coal
d. 1700 Cascadia earthquake

22. _____ are the estimated quantities of crude oil that are claimed to be recoverable under existing economic and operating conditions.

The total estimated amount of oil in an oil reservoir, including both producible and non-producible oil, is called oil in place. However, because of reservoir characteristics and limitations in petroleum extraction technologies only a fraction of this oil can be brought to the surface, and it is only this producible fraction that is considered to be reserves.

a. AL 333
c. AASHTO Soil Classification System
b. AL 129-1
d. Oil reserves

23. _____ is a naturally occurring granular material composed of finely divided rock and mineral particles.

As the term is used by geologists, _____ particles range in diameter from 0.0625 (or $>^1\!/_{16}$ mm, or 62.5 micrometers) to 2 millimeters. An individual particle in this range size is termed a _____ grain.

a. 1700 Cascadia earthquake
c. Sand
b. 1703 Genroku earthquake
d. 1509 Istanbul earthquake

24. _____ is a process that converts carbonaceous materials, such as coal, petroleum, biofuel into carbon monoxide and hydrogen by reacting the raw material at high temperatures with a controlled amount of oxygen and/or steam. The resulting gas mixture is called synthesis gas or syngas and is itself a fuel. _____ is a method for extracting energy from many different types of organic materials.

a. 1703 Genroku earthquake
c. 1509 Istanbul earthquake
b. 1700 Cascadia earthquake
d. Gasification

25. In geology, _____ refers to heat sources within the planet. _____ is technically an adjective (e.g., _____ energy) but in U.S. English the word has attained frequent use as a noun.

The planet's internal heat was originally generated during its accretion, due to gravitational binding energy, and since then additional heat has continued to be generated by decay heat from the radioactive decay of elements.

a. Tarn
c. Geothermal
b. Grade
d. Cleavage

26. _____ is power extracted from heat stored in the earth. This geothermal energy originates from the original formation of the planet, from radioactive decay of minerals, and from solar energy absorbed at the surface. It has been used for space heating and bathing since ancient roman times, but is now better known for generating electricity.

a. Geothermal heat pump
c. Geothermal power
b. Geothermal desalination
d. Geothermal gradient

27. In physics, _____ is the rate at which work is performed or energy is transmitted, or the amount of energy required or expended for a given unit of time. As a rate of change of work done or the energy of a subsystem, _____ is:

$$P = \frac{W}{t}$$

where P is _____, W is work and t is time.

The average _____ (often simply called '_____' when the context makes it clear) is the average amount of work done or energy transferred per unit time.

    a. Potentiometric surface   b. Turbulent flow
    c. Power   d. Strong interaction

28. _____ describes the large scale motions of Earth's lithosphere. The theory encompasses the older concepts of continental drift, developed during the first decades of the 20th century by Alfred Wegener, and seafloor spreading, understood during the 1960s.

The outermost part of the Earth's interior is made up of two layers: the lithosphere and the asthenosphere.

    a. Nappe   b. Mantle convection
    c. Continental crust   d. Plate tectonics

29. _____s is a field of study within geology concerned generally with the structures within the lithosphere of the Earth and particularly with the forces and movements that have operated in a region to create these structures.

_____s is concerned with the orogenies and _____ development of cratons and _____ terranes as well as the earthquake and volcanic belts which directly affect much of the global population. _____ studies are also important for understanding erosion patterns in geomorphology and as guides for the economic geologist searching for petroleum and metallic ores.

    a. Rivera Plate   b. Fault trace
    c. Cocos Plate   d. Tectonic

30. _____ is a field of study within geology concerned generally with the structures within the lithosphere of the Earth and particularly with the forces and movements that have operated in a region to create these structures.

_____ is concerned with the orogenies and tectonic development of cratons and tectonic terranes as well as the earthquake and volcanic belts which directly affect much of the global population. Tectonic studies are also important for understanding erosion patterns in geomorphology and as guides for the economic geologist searching for petroleum and metallic ores.

    a. Fault trace   b. Cocos Plate
    c. Rivera Plate   d. Tectonics

Chapter 1

1. d	2. b	3. b	4. a	5. d	6. d	7. d	8. d	9. d	10. d
11. d	12. c	13. d	14. d	15. d	16. b	17. d	18. d	19. d	20. d
21. b	22. a	23. c	24. d	25. d	26. c	27. d	28. b	29. d	30. b
31. d	32. d	33. d	34. d	35. d	36. d	37. b	38. d	39. c	40. b
41. d	42. a	43. d	44. d	45. d	46. d	47. a	48. a	49. c	50. d
51. b	52. d								

Chapter 2

1. d	2. d	3. d	4. d	5. a	6. d	7. d	8. b	9. a	10. d
11. d	12. d	13. d	14. c	15. a	16. a	17. c	18. d	19. a	20. b
21. d	22. b	23. d	24. d	25. a	26. d	27. c	28. d	29. d	30. d
31. d	32. b	33. d	34. d	35. b	36. d	37. b	38. d	39. d	40. c
41. c	42. a	43. d	44. d	45. b	46. d	47. b	48. c	49. d	50. d
51. a	52. d								

Chapter 3

1. b	2. a	3. c	4. d	5. b	6. d	7. b	8. d	9. b	10. d
11. a	12. d	13. d	14. d	15. d	16. c	17. d	18. d	19. d	20. d
21. c	22. c	23. a	24. b	25. d	26. d	27. a	28. d	29. c	30. d
31. d	32. d	33. d	34. c	35. d	36. d	37. b	38. a	39. b	40. b
41. d	42. d	43. d	44. b	45. c					

Chapter 4

1. d	2. c	3. b	4. c	5. d	6. d	7. b	8. b	9. c	10. d
11. d	12. c	13. b	14. b	15. b	16. d	17. d	18. c	19. d	20. a
21. c	22. d	23. d	24. d	25. b	26. c	27. b	28. a	29. d	30. d
31. d	32. d	33. b	34. d	35. a	36. d	37. c	38. a	39. d	40. d
41. c	42. d	43. c	44. d	45. d	46. d	47. a	48. c		

Chapter 5

1. a	2. b	3. b	4. c	5. d	6. b	7. b	8. a	9. c	10. d
11. d	12. d	13. b	14. d	15. a	16. d	17. c	18. d	19. c	20. b
21. d	22. a	23. d	24. d	25. a	26. d	27. a	28. b	29. a	30. d
31. b	32. d	33. d	34. d	35. d	36. a	37. d	38. c	39. d	40. a

Chapter 6

1. c	2. d	3. d	4. d	5. b	6. d	7. d	8. d	9. d	10. d
11. c	12. d	13. d	14. a	15. a	16. a	17. d	18. a	19. a	20. d
21. c	22. d	23. b	24. d	25. d	26. c	27. d	28. b	29. b	30. b
31. d	32. b	33. d	34. d	35. d	36. d	37. b			

ANSWER KEY

Chapter 7

1. d	2. b	3. c	4. a	5. d	6. c	7. d	8. d	9. d	10. b
11. b	12. a	13. a	14. d	15. a	16. d	17. d	18. d	19. c	20. d
21. d	22. d	23. d	24. d	25. a	26. d	27. d	28. d	29. d	30. d
31. c	32. c	33. b	34. b	35. a	36. c	37. d	38. b	39. b	40. d
41. b	42. c	43. a	44. a	45. d	46. d	47. d	48. c	49. a	50. c
51. b	52. d	53. a	54. b	55. a	56. d	57. d	58. a	59. b	60. b
61. d	62. b	63. d							

Chapter 8

1. d	2. d	3. a	4. d	5. d	6. d	7. d	8. c	9. d	10. c
11. d	12. d	13. d	14. c	15. b	16. c	17. c	18. a	19. c	20. b
21. a	22. b	23. a	24. d	25. d	26. d	27. b	28. d	29. d	30. d
31. b	32. b	33. b	34. a	35. d	36. d	37. b	38. d	39. d	40. d
41. c	42. c	43. a	44. d	45. b					

Chapter 9

1. d	2. c	3. d	4. d	5. d	6. d	7. d	8. d	9. b	10. d
11. a	12. d	13. d	14. d	15. d	16. b	17. c	18. b	19. d	20. b
21. d	22. d	23. d	24. c	25. b	26. c	27. a	28. a	29. a	30. d
31. d									

Chapter 10

1. d	2. c	3. b	4. c	5. d	6. d	7. d	8. d	9. d	10. d
11. d	12. c	13. d	14. b	15. d	16. d	17. d	18. d	19. a	20. c
21. d	22. b	23. c	24. a	25. c	26. a	27. c	28. b	29. a	30. d
31. d	32. d	33. d	34. c	35. b	36. b	37. d			

Chapter 11

1. d	2. b	3. d	4. b	5. d	6. d	7. d	8. b	9. d	10. a
11. d	12. d	13. d	14. a	15. a	16. a	17. a	18. d	19. d	20. d
21. d	22. d	23. a	24. d	25. c	26. d	27. c	28. d	29. a	30. c
31. b	32. d	33. d	34. a						

Chapter 12

1. a	2. d	3. c	4. d	5. c	6. b	7. c	8. d	9. d	10. a
11. d	12. b	13. c	14. c	15. b	16. d	17. b	18. d	19. b	20. d

Chapter 13

1. d	2. d	3. d	4. b	5. d	6. d	7. b	8. d	9. d	10. a
11. d	12. d	13. d	14. d	15. a	16. d	17. a	18. d	19. d	20. d
21. d	22. d	23. d	24. b						

Chapter 14
1. a	2. a	3. b	4. d	5. d	6. d	7. d	8. c	9. a	10. a
11. d	12. d	13. a	14. d	15. d	16. a	17. d	18. d	19. d	20. d
21. d	22. c	23. a	24. c	25. d	26. d	27. b	28. d	29. c	30. d
31. d	32. d	33. b	34. d	35. d	36. d	37. b	38. d		

Chapter 15
1. d	2. b	3. d	4. b	5. a	6. d	7. d	8. d	9. b	10. d
11. d	12. c	13. d	14. c	15. d	16. c	17. a	18. b	19. d	20. c
21. b	22. d	23. d	24. b	25. c	26. d	27. d	28. d	29. a	30. d
31. c									

Chapter 16
1. a	2. d	3. d	4. d	5. d	6. d	7. a	8. d	9. d	10. d
11. b	12. b	13. b	14. a	15. b	16. a	17. d	18. c	19. d	20. d
21. d	22. a	23. b	24. c	25. c	26. d	27. d	28. d	29. d	30. d
31. b	32. c	33. d	34. a	35. d	36. d	37. b	38. a		

Chapter 17
1. a	2. b	3. d	4. d	5. c	6. d	7. b	8. d	9. d	10. a
11. d	12. d	13. d	14. b	15. b	16. d	17. d	18. d	19. d	20. c
21. a	22. d	23. d	24. c	25. a	26. d	27. d	28. d	29. d	30. b
31. d	32. b	33. d	34. d	35. c	36. a	37. d	38. d	39. b	40. c
41. c									

Chapter 18
1. d	2. a	3. d	4. b	5. c	6. d	7. d	8. a	9. d	10. c
11. b	12. d	13. b	14. b	15. d	16. d	17. d	18. d	19. d	20. b
21. c	22. a	23. b	24. c	25. b	26. d	27. c	28. b	29. a	30. d
31. d	32. b	33. d	34. c	35. d	36. a	37. c	38. d	39. c	40. d

Chapter 19
1. d	2. d	3. d	4. d	5. a	6. d	7. d	8. d	9. a	10. d
11. c	12. b	13. d	14. d	15. b	16. d	17. a	18. b	19. d	20. d
21. a	22. b	23. d	24. d	25. d	26. d	27. c	28. d	29. d	

Chapter 20
1. d	2. b	3. c	4. d	5. d	6. c	7. c	8. d	9. d	10. d
11. d	12. b	13. d	14. d	15. b	16. d	17. a	18. d	19. b	20. d
21. c	22. d	23. a	24. a	25. a	26. d	27. b	28. d	29. d	30. a
31. b	32. d	33. c	34. c	35. b	36. c	37. d	38. b	39. d	40. d
41. c	42. c	43. d	44. a	45. b	46. b	47. c	48. c		

ANSWER KEY

Chapter 21

1. d	2. a	3. c	4. b	5. d	6. d	7. c	8. a	9. d	10. c
11. d	12. d	13. d	14. d	15. d	16. d	17. d	18. d	19. c	20. d
21. b	22. d	23. c	24. d	25. c	26. c	27. c	28. d	29. d	30. d

www.ingramcontent.com/pod-product-compliance
Lightning Source LLC
Chambersburg PA
CBHW082204230426
43672CB00015B/2893